International Aid and Sustainable Development in North Korea

This book examines international aid in North Korea, in particular the ongoing policy of withholding aid, through the lens of the impact on the general population to present an argument for sustainable development.

Focusing on the human rights of North Koreans and presenting a case for the use of aid as a provision for social change, it explores an alternative narrative to the existing long-drawn-out rhetoric of 'denuclearisation-first'. The book's scope includes evaluations of the causes of international sanctions and their impact, the Kim regime's mitigation of sanctions through marketisation and a digital economy as well as barriers to aid monitoring and the reason for the absence of any mass anti-regime movement. It also posits that North Korea is a fragile state but cloaked by the image of a strong regime.

The book succinctly demonstrates that the key to unlocking the potential of North Korea's 'cloaked society' does not lie in sanctions, but is to be found in engagement with development aid. As such it will appeal to students of Korean Studies, Development Studies, Asian Politics and International Relations.

Sojin Lim is Reader in Asia Pacific Studies (with special reference to Korea), Course Leader for both MA North Korean Studies and MA Asia Pacific Studies, and Co-Director of the International Institute of Korean Studies at the University of Central Lancashire, UK. She is the author of articles and book chapters on sustainable development and political economy. Her recent publications include *Politics, International Relations and Diplomacy on the Korean Peninsula* (2024). She frequently discusses changes in the Korean Peninsula in media interviews.

Routledge Research on Korea

The Research on Korea series surveys key topics in the study of North and South Korea (both on the peninsula, and in the diaspora). It is a prestigious series that is multidisciplinary, covering the social sciences and arts and humanities. The series seeks to publish best new research from both senior and junior scholars.

Series Editors: Niki Alsford and Sojin Lim, University of Central Lancashire, UK.

1. South Korean Popular Culture in the Global Context
Beyond the Fandom
Edited by Sojin Lim

2. The North Korean Army
History, Structure, Daily Life
Fyodor Tertitskiy

3. Korea and the Global Society
Edited by Yonson Ahn

4. International Aid and Sustainable Development in North Korea
A Country Left Behind with Cloaked Society
Sojin Lim

5. Politics, International Relations and Diplomacy on the Korean Peninsula
Edited by Sojin Lim

International Aid and Sustainable Development in North Korea

A Country Left Behind with Cloaked Society

Sojin Lim

Routledge
Taylor & Francis Group
LONDON AND NEW YORK

First published 2023
by Routledge
4 Park Square, Milton Park, Abingdon, Oxon OX14 4RN

and by Routledge

605 Third Avenue, New York, NY 10158

Routledge is an imprint of the Taylor & Francis Group, an informa business

This work was supported by Core University Programme for Korean Studies through the Ministry of Education of the Republic of Korea and Korean Studies Promotion Service of the Academy of Korean Studies (AKS-2020-OLU-20200045).

British Library Cataloguing-in-Publication Data
A catalogue record for this book is available from the British Library

ISBN: 978-1-032-48689-5 (hbk)
ISBN: 978-1-032-48690-1 (pbk)
ISBN: 978-1-003-39028-2 (ebk)

DOI: 10.4324/9781003390282

Typeset in Times New Roman
by Deanta Global Publishing Services, Chennai, India

The Open Access version of this book was funded by University of Central Lancashire.

To my family, NA, and TA

Contents

Figures

Tables

Boxes

1 Introduction

In 2021, the Democratic People's Republic of Korea (known as DPRK, hereinafter North Korea) submitted its Voluntary National Review (VNR) to the United Nations (UN), charting the country's progress and challenges in implementing the Sustainable Development Goals (SDGs) and setting out its needs for continuing progress towards achieving the SDGs. The SDGs are the global development goals, which all UN members are expected to achieve by 2030 as the successor of the Millennium Development Goals (MDGs). In the case of the MDGs, United Nations Development Programme (UNDP) country offices led the monitoring of implementation in developing countries between 2000 and 2015. In contrast, under the sustainable development paradigm, all UN member countries have been encouraged to submit their own SDG implementation progress reports in the form of VNRs to the UN High-Level Political Forum since 2016. The VNR exercise can be a practical means for developing countries to build their institutional capacity for accountability, as the process has been designed to form part of the SDG follow-up and review architecture to promote international accountability.

Completed with the support of the United Nations Economic and Social Commission for Asia and the Pacific (UN ESCAP), the 63-page North Korean VNR clearly shows the will of the North Korean government to comply with the sustainable development agenda. As with most other developing countries, the government has identified national statistical capacity and financial capacity among the challenges it faces in achieving the SDGs. However, the report also contends that the international sanctions against the country are the reason for it not being on track to making progress in SDG implementation, while emphasising North Korean–style socialism, which still takes a non-conventional approach to national development by placing a huge focus, for example, on military development rather than on promoting social mobility through market expansion (see DPRK, 2021).

The fact that North Korea participated in this international accountability regime by submitting its VNR in difficult times could be a positive sign. However, it is unclear how Pyongyang will be able to show further progress, given that the country has not received a sufficient amount of development aid—except humanitarian aid in some instances—since 2006 when the first multilateral sanctions were imposed on it. North Korea is a very rare country in that it is isolated from the rest of the world due not only to the current international sanctions regime against it but also to its own political choice. Amid the COVID-19 pandemic, this isolation has

DOI: 10.4324/9781003390282-1

increased, with Pyongyang closing all its borders in January 2020. As of April 2022, the country remains completely locked down and locked out from the outside world. While current self-shielding of the country can end soon, the UN multilateral sanctions will contribute to the isolation of North Korea.

On many occasions, the international development community has asserted that the SDGs cannot be achieved without international support, especially in fragile countries. On top of it, the SDGs are based on the core value of 'leave no one behind'. However, paradoxically, it has been evident that ordinary North Koreans are left behind from this global value. They have been adversely affected by the multilateral sanctions which have been ineffective. Over the past 15 years, the sanctions have not affected the Kim regime as intended. It is worth noting that 'regime change' has not been explicitly mentioned as the main purpose of the sanctions against North Korea. Rather, the focus has been on dismantling Pyongyang's nuclear capabilities. In any case, it does not seem that any change can be attributed to the sanctions. Moreover, recent scholarship on sanctions on North Korea makes the ineffectiveness of the sanctions regime against it clear and evident, while showing sanctions to be an unethical approach due to their human costs (see, for example, Korea Peace Now, 2019; Smith, 2020).

This book thus asks the question as to whether we should continue to leave ordinary North Koreans behind in hardship just because the Kim regime persists in pursuing nuclear development. It further considers whether there are any alternative narratives that can help us escape the existing, long-drawn-out rhetoric of the security–development nexus and 'denuclearisation-first' and focus on the human rights of North Koreans and opportunities for social change. Considering the Universal Declaration of Human Rights, ordinary North Koreans equally deserve our attention. However, the realist paradigm of international relations, with its focus on security, does not seem to be willing to give up the denuclearisation-first rhetoric. Gaining nuclear status seems to be even more critical as a survival strategy—the only survival strategy—for Pyongyang. The Russian invasion of Ukraine in 2022 seems to have provided Kim Jong-un with even more reason to keep his nuclear tactic. Looking at what happened earlier to Muammar Gaddafi in Libya and Saddam Hussein in Iraq (Lim, 2019), and at what is now happening in nuclear-free Ukraine, could give the North Korean government the necessary excuse to emphasise its need to become a nuclear powerhouse in order to prevent external attacks against the country. In this account, the denuclearisation-first strategy, along with sanctions, would not succeed in bringing about North Korean engagement, but rather make the current status quo more difficult to resolve. Therefore, the book aims to offer alternative narratives that can contribute to the search for solutions to the lingering rhetoric of denuclearisation-first.

Going beyond arguments about the development–security nexus, the study intends to focus our attention on people and society. The subject of people and their well-being in North Korea has not been as fascinating for either researchers or ordinary people around the world, when thinking or talking about that country. For example, international media tends to mostly give attention to nuclear issues and missile tests or to the Kim family, especially in relation to the security dynamics in and around the Pacific region, with a particular focus on the United States (US). Within academia, while many of the existing research projects can be found in international relations and security studies, there is fast-growing interest in societal changes in North Korea, but this has a heavy focus on marketisation. Some attention has also been given in the scholarly literature on North Korea, albeit to a lesser extent, to human rights violations by the regime and the human rights of North Korean defectors. However, due to the current sanctions regime which greatly limits opportunities for international aid provision, less research has been done on the international aid regime and North Korea, except in the context of issues of denuclearisation, the effectiveness of sanctions, and economic development. Development aid has been seen as just a side story. Its potential to contribute to actual change in North Korea has not been considered. However, this book argues that development aid offers an alternative that can help us break through the seemingly stalemated denuclearisation–sanctions narrative, especially as it can bring to the foreground the concerns of ordinary people in North Korea who have remained hidden in mainstream accounts. The main premise of the research presented in this book is to be found in discussion on the ethics of sanctions. Echoing some of the existing research findings, it is a moral failure of the sanctions regime against North Korea that the sanctions hurt a majority of the civilian population rather than a target group in society or the regime.

With this in mind, following this introduction—Chapter 1—Chapter 2 analyses why and how international sanctions have been imposed against North Korea. It also considers the efficacy and effectiveness of the sanctions. Before examining the case of North Korea, the chapter first engages with the existing literature on sanctions regimes to provide a better understanding of the purposes and mechanisms of sanctions, including what makes sanctions effective and what can hinder the achievement of their aims. Then, following a review of the development of North Korea's nuclear programme, the chapter assesses the evolution of UN sanctions against Pyongyang. This includes a look at the most recent developments in the North Korean sanctions regime. Finally, the chapter discusses whether sanctions have brought about the intended changes in North Korea between 2006 and early 2022. In so doing and taking into account recent developments which have not yet been included in the published literature, Chapter 2 provides support for the argument that sanctions have not been successful against North Korea; rather, they have caused human suffering and have thus been a moral failure.

Chapter 3 investigates why and how the North Korean regime could have become resilient and remained resilient to international sanctions over such a long period of time. Starting with a discussion on the North Korean market's transition to a hybrid economy, the chapter introduces a new middle-class group in North Korean society, mostly represented by *donju*—individuals who gained financial power during the marketisation period. The chapter further discusses how the mobile communication revolution and digital economy have contributed to bringing about change in society as well as to sanctions evasion. In so doing, the chapter argues that North Korea has become resilient to international sanctions due to 'abnormal' marketisation that benefitted both the regime and the country's middle class as well as unofficial trade with China. There is path dependency in the sanctions evasion activities. The regime has long violated bilateral US sanctions, imposed on it since the Korean War, with the help of its allies, China and Russia, to its benefit. The experience has helped the North Korean government be creative in the current context. Continuing illicit trade with China and some other countries has also helped Pyongyang evade international sanctions. While the chapter looks at how the parallel existence of a market economy and a socialist planned economy has benefitted the power structure, it also echoes established research findings on changes in society, such as those focused on information influx and cultural changes. However, this account gives rise to two sets of questions. First, why have the people of North Korea not rebelled against government repression as they have learned—from foreign popular culture and foreign products—that the regime's policy towards them is not right and that they could be better off with more freedom, but have instead become agents of resilience against international sanctions? Second, why has there been no mass movement despite the level of small-scale resentments among people against the government's regulatory efforts to take power back from the market? Related to that, how has the North Korean authority managed the balance among state, market, and society?

In responding to these questions, Chapter 4 explains that such collective actions have not been mobilised in North Korea because the country lacks a culture of civil society. To that end, the chapter first examines the definition of civil society and the pattern of civil society engagement in Central and Eastern European (CEE) transition countries. It then applies this conceptualisation of civil society and navigates the dynamics of state, market, and society in North Korea to examine the environment for civil society there. The chapter argues that an alliance between street-level bureaucrats and *donju* has become a new layer that covers or cloaks the bottom levels of society. That is to say, bandwagoning with political elites by newly created economic elites has resulted in what the chapter defines as North Korea's 'cloaked society'. In addition, mass surveillance, including through mobile technology, makes it impossible for people to organise a civil movement. In this regard, the chapter suggests that development aid could become an agent for creating an enabling environment for civil society capacity building and for institutional capacity development that can provide a civil society–friendly environment.

Chapter 5 begins then by briefly analysing how international aid can support civil society capacity building for changes to occur, looking at the case of CEE countries, before examining various international aid mechanisms to distinguish between the different roles of development aid and humanitarian aid. This is followed by an examination of how international aid has been provided to North Korea. The discussion also considers what has been missing in the provision of this aid. The analysis is organised by donor, with a view to providing alternative narratives of how to provide aid to North Korea. The North Korean aid regime—given the tendency to treat it as a side story in the existing literature—has mostly been described in chronological terms in the existing literature. However, this chapter revisits aid flows to North Korea with a more focused analytical lens, asking how aid has arrived in the country, what effects it has had, and what has been missing in practice. In doing so, the chapter finds that international aid to North Korea has not adequately addressed capacity building issues as donors have not only focused mainly on humanitarian aid and not much on development aid, but have also not considered the country's situation to be fragile. As the research shows, North Korea is a fragile state in terms of the state's service delivery capacity and its capacity to communicate with society; therefore, aid to the country needs to be reconsidered within the context of fragility and provided in a tailored way that is suitable to its fragile context.

Chapter 6 expands on this argument by exploring the definition of fragile states and showing that North Korea is a fragile state in terms of its ability to function for its people. The chapter argues that the country's fragility has been rejected by existing studies in the fields of international relations and international security due to its stereotyped image of a strong regime that has not only survived under international sanctions but also advanced its military capability. However, when the situation in North Korea is viewed from the perspectives of society, state functions, human rights, and so on, it is clearly a fragile state. Therefore, we need to provide aid to North Korea within the international development cooperation framework for dysfunctional states by redesigning and customising our approach to aid.

In conclusion, Chapter 7 returns to the question as to why and how we should and would not leave the people of North Korea behind in global cooperation. That we should not leave North Koreans behind is clear, but the question of 'how' we do this poses an ethical conundrum. One way in which we could assist is by supporting capacity building processes that can help bring about changes in a society where the state has not been successful within the context of the people-to-people-based development aid regime. Altogether, the book—as the concluding chapter summaries highlight—emphasises the importance of local community and societal capacity building in a fragile context. The state–market–society relationship does not work as it should in North Korea. The prevalent corruption involving the North Korean state and market and the politics of fear embedded in society make it difficult to create an enabling environment for civil society. Sanctions do not help this situation, and as this book shows, they have also limited the potential for positive change in North Korean society.

The research in this book relies on primary and secondary data, although no fieldwork or interviews were conducted. Most fieldwork in the existing literature on North Korea is conducted in South Korea, the United Kingdom, US, China, or in other countries where researchers can carry out interviews with North Korea experts or North Korean defectors. Even in ordinary circumstances, and not only during the COVID-19 pandemic and lockdown, conducting fieldwork in North Korea is an unlikely prospect as the North Korean government does not allow any research trips. 'Tours' are the only available means to visit North Korea. Also, data released by the North Korean government is heavily manipulated and propaganda based, and thus, most of the data from inside North Korea comes either from officials in embassies and international organisations, staff in non-governmental organisations, or foreign educators, mostly at the university level, in the country.

However, their experiences are also very limited as they are not allowed to travel freely within North Korea, while their contact with locals is controlled. Some aid workers have had opportunities to visit local communities, but their experiences have been mostly at the observation level as they have either faced language barriers or engaged with locals who have told the aid workers what they have been told to say by the government. In rare cases, information can be collected from North Korean traders or foreign workers in North Korea who have better access to mobile phones, but they are not representative of the entire population of North Korea.

Therefore, most narratives about North Korea rely mainly on defector testimonials and surveys. In this sense, survey results and interview testimonials as secondary data were retrieved from existing research on North Korea and varied media (both South and North Korean sources, as well as international sources), while other kinds of original data were collected from government sources, official datasets of international organisations, and the like (both in Korean and in English). Media news as well as webinar or online discussions and presentations during the period of COVID-19 international travel bans were also used to collect the most up-to-date information.

In conventional wisdom, research on North Korea is considered to be very limited due to the lack of in-country fieldwork and in-country access to data, thus the field of study is limited in size. However, there is a tremendous amount of research dealing with North Korea. For example, a search for peer-reviewed journal articles using ‘North Korea’ or ‘DPRK’ as a keyword shows more than 100 publications on average every year in English while the number has increased in recent years, and the number becomes a lot larger in the case of publications in Korean. Around 15 book publications in English can be found each year on average, and again, searching for book publications in Korean yields a bigger result. Over 4,000 books in Korean have been published on subjects related to North Korea to date. The number further increases with the inclusion of additional keywords like ‘Kim Jong-un’, ‘defectors’, or ‘nuclear’. And countless research reports on North Korea are published by varied institutes and organisations—both in English and in Korean. While data collection remains a challenge, it does not seem to have discouraged researchers from studying North Korea.

Here, the validity of defector interviews and surveys has been questioned due to sample biases, monetary and publicity incentives, researcher–interviewee power relations, and language issues, which are typical problems in the field (Song and Denney, 2019). Among researchers who study North Korea, the so-called ‘70-70 bias’ is a well-known issue in the data retrieved from North Korean defector interviews and surveys. It refers to the fact that 70 per cent of the defectors are women and 70 per cent of the defectors are from the northern region of North Korea which shares a border with China. Even though a survey was conducted based on a wider range of sample demographics from most of the region in North Korea, the sample size is very small (for example, see the survey size of Cha and DuMond, 2016). Thus, what we hear from defectors is from a segment of the entire population. Another issue with the data relates to memory, except in cases in which the interviews or surveys have been conducted immediately with those who have just come out of North Korea. The problem is that retrospective memory tends to become compromised or to deteriorate into fading memory and repeating narratives to which defectors are exposed. Some memories can even degenerate over time. Consequently, in light of these concerns, researchers have had to look for ways to maximise the validity of the data and, to that end, have employed methods such as mixed approaches, data triangulation, and focus group interviews (Song and Denney, 2019; Tan, 2019). Researchers studying North Korea have thus become not only methodologically sophisticated but also highly 'innovative, data-driven, and theory-led' (Song, 2021: 220).

Yet, there is one final issue that has still not been thoroughly considered by scholars, but which this research has paid attention to: the discrepancies in information from among different *songbun* classes in North Korea (*songbun* is discussed in detail in Chapters 3 and 4). Groups from different *songbun* tend not to communicate with each other in North Korea, making the use of triangulation and mixed methods even more critical. In addition, given the limited number of defectors and the availability of interviews with them, most interviews and surveys have become embedded in the various perspectives of the existing research. With no defectors coming over the border from North Korea with more up-to-date information due to the COVID-19 border closure for more than two years, as of April 2022, no new interviews were available for inclusion in this book. While no interviews or surveys could be conducted for the purposes of this research—with the data collection period overlapping with COVID-19 travel bans—the existing dataset of defector interviews and surveys was sufficient for most of the analysis. Where such data was not sufficient, up-to-date information was available through online expert discussions or presentations, which have recently become a new norm during the pandemic. In this way, data was triangulated using media information, government documents, and expert discussions.

An example serves here to illustrate the data challenges in the study of North Korea and to underscore the importance of the use of triangulation in this research. This book cites one of the high-ranked members of the political elite in North Korea—former first minister at the North Korean embassy in London—but, at the same time, has been careful to distinguish between the factual data and narratives that he has produced from his own memory on the one hand, and those that he has gleaned from other existing defector narratives following his own defection on the other hand. In other words, his dialogue exchanges with the North Korean government and with other governments on aid from his time as a diplomat have been used but also triangulated with other data sources. Having said that, as discussed in Chapter 4, diplomats like him have relatively few opportunities to know North Korean society, including recent changes in that society. He himself did not have sufficient time to observe changes in North Korean society, especially in different *songbun* in different regions beyond Pyongyang, as he spent most of his time abroad as a diplomat when changes, such as marketisation, were happening (see Tae, 2018). He had barely any opportunities to communicate with people from the bottom class of the *songbun* system. As defectors like him do not have experience of how people actually live and think across geographies and in remote places in North Korea, their reflections on North Korean society before their defection are very limited. Not only that but given that they are part of the political elite who are considered to be an authority, ordinary people do not share what they actually think with them, especially when it comes to criticising the government or the Kim regime. For the same reason, his inside sources of information too are likely to be those in high-ranking positions in North Korea, who enjoy their own spaces. Further, although he has mentioned having access to inside information from North Korea, it has not been confirmed how much of this information is valid and how much of it is representative and can be generalised. For example, there was a lot of speculation about Kim Jong-un's whereabouts in April 2020. He stated that he was sure Kim was in a serious condition based on information from a reliable source in North Korea. However, it turned out that his strong assertion was incorrect (for example, see Lee, 2020). Thus, defector testimonials or interview contents on societal changes have not been taken on in full but selectively used, based on triangulation with other data sources, in the research for this book.

Indeed, doing research on North Korea is a puzzle and a challenge. However, as with other existing research, the efforts made for data validation and accuracy were not an impossible endeavour for this study. As mentioned earlier, this research has employed both English and Korean written sources. The Korean sources were useful not only for triangulation but also for substantive content that may have been missed or lost in interpretation and translation of the original—in Korean—in the existing literature. Also, there were some disparities, for instance, in the names of North Korean missiles, time periods, aid data, and so on between English and Korean research publications. In such instances, further investigation was conducted using additional sources of data to narrow the gap. In addition, this research includes analyses of data written in Korean that has not yet been introduced widely into the scholarship in English, which could be a significant contribution of this book to the field. For example, information about the digital economy and mobile communication revolution in relation to *servicha*, *igwangib*, the banking system, or 8•3 deposits has barely been discussed in the existing research in English. While some research studies have used data written in the original Korean, they have mostly relied on archival material from North Korean media and South Korean newspapers, direct interviews with North Korean defectors, or existing research findings, but they are not always drawn as much on the substantial details about changes in North Korea included in existing materials in the original Korean.

Another key contribution of this book lies in its disciplinary approach. Within the growing complexity of interdisciplinarity, this research is not only located within the field of Korean studies as part of the discipline of area studies but also has a basis in the discipline of development studies. Both area studies and development studies share their multidisciplinary nature in common. On the one hand, this study can provide a better understanding of the Asia Pacific region using the case of North Korea with special attention to the prospects for society development in the country, in line with the research norm in area studies. On the other hand, it can also widen the engagement of development studies to include the case of North Korea, which has not yet been rigorously dealt with in that field, through its discussion of development aid policy and practice. Considering this dual aspect of the book, it will be of interest to those in area studies and development studies, as well as to policymakers and practitioners interested in alternatives to the existing security-focused narratives on North Korea.

Also, as mentioned earlier, there is a substantial body of research on North Korea dealing with security issues, denuclearisation, and international relations, and more recently, with issues such as human rights and economic development in the country. However, discussions on international development cooperation with North Korea are very rare, especially in the context of sustainable development, even though international aid once played a critical role in the country's development pathway. For example, in the post-Korean War period, Kim Il-sung relied heavily on the erstwhile Soviet Union and its allies in Eastern Europe, and China. When North Korea experienced famine in the 1990s, Kim Jong-il called for international assistance between 1995 and 2005. However, with the imposition of multilateral sanctions against the country, the international community has barely considered discussing aid and development with North Korea, even though this could be a potential means to break through the current deadlock in its engagement with Pyongyang. In that sense, this research intends to contribute not only to the field of area studies but also to the field of development studies by moving beyond the denuclearisation-then-development paradigm. For example, while most scholars positioned in the fields of international relations and international security reject the idea that North Korea is a fragile state, those located in the discipline of development studies have been clear in defining North Korea as a fragile state (see Chapter 6). Ultimately, this research can have an impact on debates among policymakers and academics alike, as well as members of the public, by challenging existing narratives on denuclearisation and stereotypes of marketisation-driven change in North Korea.

References

Cha, Victor and Marie DuMond (2016). Meager Rations, Banned Markets, and Growing Anger Toward Government. 3 October 2016, *Beyond Parallel – CSIS Korea Chair*. https://beyondparallel.csis.org/view-inside-north-korea-meager-rations-banned-markets-and-growing-anger-toward-govt/. Accessed: 15 March 2022.

DPRK (2021). *Voluntary National Review on the Implementation of the 2030 agenda for the Sustainable Development*. Prepared by the Government of the Democratic People's Republic of Korea.

Korea Peace Now (2019). The Human Costs and Gendered Impact of Sanctions on North Korea. https://koreapeacenow.org/wp-content/uploads/2019/10/human-costs-and-gendered-impact-of-sanctions-on-north-korea.pdf. Accessed: 4 June 2021.

Lee, Ji-young (2020). Kim Jong-un Not Able to Walk or Died with 99 Percent Certainty, by Tae Yong-ho and Ji Sung-ho who Defected from North Korea, Turned Out False. 2 May 2020, *The JoongAng* [이지영, "김정은 못걸어", "99% 사망", 머쓱해진 北출신태영호, 지성호] 중앙일보, 2020년 5월 2일자]. https://www.joongang.co.kr/article/23767697. Accessed: 4 June 2021.

Lim, Sojin (2019). North Korea: What Latest Defection Tells Us about Hopes for peace on Peninsula. 8 January 2019, *The Conversation*. https://theconversation.com/north-korea-what-latest-defection-tells-us-about-hopes-for-peace-on-peninsula-109447. Accessed: 4 June 2021.

Smith, Hazel (2020). The Ethics of United Nations Sanctions on North Korea: Effectiveness, Necessity and Proportionality. *Critical Asian Studies*, 52(2): 182–203.

Song, Jay (2021). North Korea as a Method: A Critical Review. *Journal of Korean Studies*, 26(2): 205–228.

Song, Jay and Steven Denney (2019). Studying North Korea Through North Korean Migrants: Lessons From the Field. *Critical Asian Studies*, 51(3): 451–466.

Tae, Yong-ho (2018). *Testimonial of Former First Minister of the Embassy of the Democratic People's Republic of Korea in the United Kingdom, Tae Yong-ho*. Seoul: Giparang [태영호 (2018). 전 영국 주재 북한공사 태영호의 증언 : 3층 서기실의 암호. 서울, 기파랑].

Tan, Er-Win (2019). Source Triangulation as an Instrument of Research on North Korea. *North Korean Review*, 15(1): 34–50.

2 Sanctions and Unintended Consequences

It has become evident that most sanctions are not succeeding or have failed. Some sanctions may have been successful in signalling or stigmatising targets but not in changing or constraining their behaviour through coercion. For instance, Hufbauer et al. (2019)—one of the most well-known studies in sanctions research—examine 204 episodes of comprehensive trade sanctions imposed since 1914 and show how sanctions have not been widely effective. Only around 20–30 per cent of cases were successful or partially successful considering the purposes of sanctions. Published in 2019, Hufbauer et al.'s third and latest edition of their work is embedded in an original dataset of 103 cases since 1982 (the year that the first edition was published) and delineates the development of sanctions. The United Nations (UN) has also evidently noted that its own sanctions are not widely successful as only 10 per cent of them have achieved their goals (UN, 2022e: 4).

The North Korean case is not much different from most other sanctions cases in terms of efficiency and efficacy. Sanctions—both multilateral and bilateral—have been imposed on North Korea for more than a decade. The latest round even seems to be a case of moral failure as the sanctions affect the agricultural sector despite the 1977 Additional Protocol of the Geneva Convention clearly prohibiting any activities, including sanctions, that harm agricultural production, especially in peacetime (see Smith, 2020). With that in mind, this chapter first explores the concept of international sanctions and their impact. This chapter does not intend to suggest its own definition of sanctions, but rather to introduce various definitions and understandings of sanctions from existing studies as well as international organisations and governments. The chapter then discusses why and how sanctions have been imposed on North Korea. This discussion is followed by an analysis of the effectiveness of these sanctions by navigating existing arguments on the matter.

Understanding International Sanctions Regimes

Sanctions can be either multilateral or bilateral. Arguably, sanctions imposed by international organisations (multilateral or institutional) are the only legitimate measures, while unilateral sanctions by individual states (bilateral) are not because they tend to be at each state's own discretion. Accordingly, it is more appropriate to call unilateral sanctions 'countermeasures' rather than sanctions. Nevertheless, it seems that the term 'sanctions' is used in practice without strictly applying the

DOI: 10.4324/9781003390282-2

distinction between unilateral and multilateral approaches. The term 'sanctions' is also used interchangeably with trade or arms 'embargoes' and 'restrictions'. At the same time, sanctions have been defined slightly differently by various organisations, countries, and scholars (see Table 2.1). As Table 2.1 shows, most sanctions can be understood in the form of 'economic' sanctions. This is because they are 'less-costly and more convenient', and thus, can be 'tailored to specific circumstances', compared to military actions, according to former UN Secretary-General Kofi Annan (see Honda, 2021: 18). Here, economic sanctions and financial sanctions are used without a clear distinction being made between them, even though financial sanctions are a subset of economic sanctions (Yoshimura, 2021). Therefore, this research too does not make a strict distinction but uses the term 'sanctions' in general. Likewise, sanctions can be understood to have varied purposes (see Table 2.2). However, in general, they can be grouped into three main pillars based on their goals: to change the behaviour of the target country or to bring about regime change; to constrain the behaviour of the target; and to signal the target.

Sanctions measures can be comprehensive or targeted. The latter are known as smart sanctions and include arms embargoes, freezing of assets and bank accounts, and placing travel restrictions on individuals or firms with links to the target country. Smart sanctions were developed in response to the observed adverse humanitarian consequences of UN sanctions in the 1990s, which led the world body to impose more targeted sanctions, rather than comprehensive sanctions, from the mid-1990s onwards (Honda, 2021: 18). The difference between comprehensive sanctions and targeted sanctions (smart sanctions) is shown in Table 2.3.

As seen in Table 2.1, multilateral organisations emphasise that sanctions are not punitive; however, others clearly see sanctions as coercive. Even though sanctions influence a target country's economy, sanctions cannot be considered to have been successful if they have not led to political changes (Gray and Lee, 2021). While those who impose sanctions aim to change the policy or behaviour of a target state, the sanctions burden is more likely to fall on the general population rather than on the regime or target elites of the state, even though, for instance, the UN sanctions statement clearly indicates no intention to harm civilians.

One of the main reasons for the ineffectiveness of sanctions could be that the sanctions 'may simply be inadequate for the task' or that there is a lack of cooperation from other countries (Hufbauer et al., 2019: 7). In the case of multilateral sanctions, ineffectiveness is more likely to be due to the fact that not all member states abide by what was agreed. For example, in order for UN sanctions to be imposed, a specific resolution with details of the proposed measures needs to be drafted by a member state or group of member states. The draft then needs to be submitted to and adopted by the UN Security Council (UNSC) with at least nine affirmative votes, including all five permanent members of the UNSC (Article 27 (2) (3) of the UN Charter). Adopted resolutions are required to be implemented in domestic legislation by UN member states, and they are not legally binding until they are implemented nationally (soft law).

Table 2.1 Examples of Sanctions Definitions

UN	Sanctions measures encompass a broad range of enforcement options that do not involve the use of armed force. Contrary to the assumption that sanctions are punitive, many regimes are designed to support governments and regions working towards peaceful transition.
EU	Restrictive measures (sanctions) are an essential tool in the EU's common foreign and security policy, through which the EU can intervene where necessary to prevent conflict or respond to emerging or current crises. In spite of their colloquial name 'sanctions', EU restrictive measures are not punitive.
US	Sanctions are economic and trade enforcement against targeted foreign countries and regimes, terrorists, international narcotics traffickers, those engaged in activities related to the proliferation of weapons of mass destruction, and other threats to the national security, foreign policy, or economy of the United States.
UK	Financial sanctions can limit the provision of certain financial services or restrict access to financial markets, funds, and economic resources, to achieve a specific foreign policy or national security objective.
Abrahamian	Sanctions are an expression of coercive power, employed when one state (or states) wishes to influence the behaviour of a state or punish it for behaviours deemed unacceptable.
Anguelov	Economic sanctions refer to restrictions on trade and international financial assistance.
Carbaugh and Ghosh	Economic sanctions are commercial and financial punishments applied by one or more countries against a targeted country or important organisations or individuals within the target country.
Hakimdavar	Sanctions refer to an unarmed means of economic coercion for persuading a nation to change its behaviour or to penalise that nation for violating international law, and the deliberate, government-inspired withdrawal or threat of withdrawal, of customary trade or financial relations. Economic sanctions are a method of moving a state's political positions forward without war. Sanctions can be understood as a coercive measure regardless of whether the party applying sanctions is armed or not (military or economic means). Sanctions can also be in the form of moral condemnation or censure.
Hufbauer et al.	Economic sanctions are the deliberate, government-inspired withdrawal, or threat of withdrawal, of customary trade or financial relations.
Nephew	Sanctions are defined as the constellation of laws, authorities, and obligations laid out in a piece of legislation, government decree, UN resolution, or similar document that restrict or prohibit what is normally permissible conduct and against which performance will be assessed and compliance judged.
Portela	Sanctions can be defined as measures imposed in reaction to illegal or politically undesirable acts geared towards exercising pressure in pursuance of the ultimate aim of producing a change in the political behaviour of another actor.

Source: Author's own compilation based on Abrahamian, 2018: 138; Anguelov, 2015: 3; Carbaugh and Ghosh, 2019: 132; European Commission, 2022b; Hakimdavar, 2014: 20; HM Treasury, 2020: 8; Hufbauer et al. 2019: 3; Nephew, 2018: 8; Portela, 2011: 6; UN, 2022a; US Department of the Treasury, 2022.

Table 2.2 Examples of Sanctions Objectives

UN	To support peaceful transitions, deter non-constitutional changes, constrain terrorism, protect human rights, and promote non-proliferation.
EU	To bring about a change in policy or activity by targeting non-EU countries, as well as entities and individuals, responsible for the malign behaviour at stake.
US	To accomplish US foreign policy and national security goals.
UK	To coerce a regime or individuals within a regime into changing their behaviour, to constrain a target by denying them access to key resources needed to continue their offending behaviour, to signal disapproval, stigmatising and potentially isolating a regime or individual or as a way of sending broader political messages nationally or internationally, and/or to protect the value of assets that have been misappropriated from a country until these assets can be repatriated.
Anguelov	To compel the target country to change its policies or government, or to demonstrate sanctions-originator's opposition to the target country's politics in regard to specific domestic constituents, its citizens at large, other potential targets, and the international community.
Carbaugh and Ghosh	To impose sufficient economic hardship on a target government so that it adheres to internationally agreed upon goals such as the protection of human rights, reduction in nuclear proliferation, preservation of global security, and combating international terrorism.
Hakimdavar	To enforce the state's decision to comply with the restrictions of the treaty, even if the cost of compliance to the state supersedes the cost of non-compliance.
Hufbauer et al.	To encompass changes the sender state explicitly or implicitly seeks in the target state's political behaviour.
Nephew	To create hardship (or to be blunt, pain) that is sufficiently onerous that the sanctions target changes its behaviour.
Yoshimura	To achieve collective security.

Source: Author's own compilation based on Anguelov, 2015: 4; Carbaugh and Ghosh, 2019: 132; Hakimdavar, 2014: 20; HM Treasury, 2020: 8; Hufbauer et al. 2019: 3; Nephew, 2018: 9; UN, 2022a; US Department of the Treasury, 2022; Yoshimura, 2021: 1.

Another reason that sanctions are ineffective can be found in the 'loopholes' that tend to limit the sanctions' capacity to achieve their purposes. Sanctions loopholes refer to the gaps between the requirement to take immediate actions and the actual time to implement the required actions in accordance with the legislation and legal processes of the sender countries (Yoshimura, 2021). For instance, when the United Kingdom (UK) decided to impose sanctions on Russia for its invasion of Ukraine in 2022, it was not easy to immediately implement the decision at the business level, as British companies trading with Russian companies could not just stop working with them at once due to existing business contracts. The UK Department for Transport confirmed that Russian oil and gas could still be provided to the UK amid sanctions on Russia as vessels registered with other countries but carrying

Table 2.3 Examples of Sanctions Measures

UN	• Comprehensive economic and trade sanctions • Targeted measures (arms embargoes, travel bans, and financial or commodity restrictions)
EU	• Economic measures such as restrictions on imports and exports • Targeted measures (arms embargoes, restrictions on admission, travel bans, asset freezes)
US	• Comprehensive economic sanctions (trade restrictions) • Selective sanctions (blocking of assets)
UK	• Directions to cease all business • Restrictions on a wide variety of financial markets and services • Targeted asset freezes
Carbaugh and Ghosh	• Comprehensive package of trade sanctions (bans placed on imposing-country exports to the target country, import restrictions, quotas being placed on the target country's goods) • Targeted sanctions (travel bans and financial sanctions such as a freeze on foreign bank accounts of particular individuals or companies)

Source: Author's own compilation based on Carbaugh and Ghosh, 2019: 132; European Commission, 2022a:1; HM Treasury, 2020: 9–10; UN, 2022a; US Department of the Treasury, 2022.

oil from Russia would not be stopped, given that the sanctions only disallowed all ships owned, operated, chartered, or registered in Russia or by Russian individuals (Reuters, 2022).

Also, as Hakimdavar (2014: 25) explains, sanctions are not effective 'in [a] multipolar world because extensive intercontinental trade counteracts them in a globalised environment'. In the case of a country like Russia, which is one of the world's biggest energy providers, with international trade involving multiple overseas business partners, it is literally impossible to apply full sanctions against it. There are countries that could become alternative markets for Russia, which would diminish the effect of the sanctions imposed by like-minded countries. For example, it was reported that India was importing Russian oil and could begin to replace European countries as an oil export market for Russia amid the European sanctions in 2022 (Menon, 2022). Also, sanctions negatively affect the senders' economies if the target country has active international trade. The immediate increase in international gas prices resulting from the 2022 energy ban by North Atlantic Treaty Organization countries against Russia due to its war in Ukraine is a good example.

When it comes to successful cases of sanctions, it is more likely that they have been either only partially successful or successful due to other attributing factors coinciding with the sanctions. For example, the case of Myanmar (previously Burma) between 1996 and 2011 is known as a case of a successful bilateral economic sanctions regime. However, political reform in Myanmar in 2011 was possible not only due to sanctions, but more so because there were power structure changes in the military regime, a culture of pro-democracy, a desire to balance external influence from the bottom up, and a culture of civil society that supported the change. It was not evident that Myanmar's military leaders were negatively affected by the sanctions. Rather, the sanctions in Myanmar resulted in greater hardship for its citizens by worsening the economic, educational, and health systems. They also increased the country's industrial sector's unbalanced dependence on China (Lim, 2021). As Jeffrey Sachs, a former special adviser to UN Secretary-General Kofi Annan, once argued, imposing sanctions 'may weaken the regime, but it weakens the people, and it weakens civil society' (Radio Free Asia, 2004). At the same time, regardless of whether they have been successful or not, in many cases, sanctions tend to cause unexpected adverse consequences by affecting the standard of living of the people in target countries. The UN once admitted that the adverse humanitarian effect of sanctions had been observed as early as the 1990s (Honda, 2021).

It seems that the North Korean case is not an exception in terms of unintended human suffering due to sanctions. Bilateral sanctions against North Korea have been active since the post-Korean War period and UN multilateral sanctions since 2006. However, the North Korean regime has not seemed to show behavioural change, but rather has survived, while the adverse effect on ordinary people's lives has been significant. The following sections explore why and how sanctions have been imposed on North Korea and navigate whether they have been effective. The discussion covers the period from the end of Japanese colonialism in the Korean peninsula, in 1945, until March 2022.

Why Sanctions Have Been Imposed on North Korea: Development of the Nuclear Programme

The original reason Kim Il-sung was interested in nuclear technology was to export uranium so that the country could build its foreign currency reserves. This interest coincided with the Union of Soviet Socialist Republics' (USSR) desperate need for uranium for its atomic bomb project and its concern about the possible use of the uranium deposits in North Korea by China. As a result, the USSR and North Korea began joint investigations into the possibility of extracting uranium ore in late 1945 (Kim and Baek, 2017; Szalontai and Radchenko, 2006). However, when the Korean War broke out in 1950, and United States (US) President Harry Truman threatened Kim Il-sung with the possibility of an American atomic bomb attack on North Korea, it became a legitimate reason for Pyongyang to arm itself with nuclear weapons. Fearing the nuclear threat from the US to North Korea, Kim Il-sung established the Atomic Energy Research Institute in 1955 and signed a nuclear research agreement with the USSR in 1956, which allowed North Korean scientists and technicians to be trained at the Dubna Nuclear Research Institute in the Soviet Union. Since then, North Korea's nuclear programme has played a role as a survival method against possible nuclear threats from the US.

While North Korea continuously tried to obtain more aid from the USSR for the development of its nuclear programme, and later a nuclear power plant, the Soviets never fully provided this kind of support to Pyongyang (Clemens Jr., 2016), due to their strategic position between North Korea and China and towards Asian countries in the region (Ha, 1982). Accordingly, North Korea used the conflict between the Soviet Union and China to develop its nuclear programme. Following the Sino–Soviet break-up in the 1960s, the USSR provided training programmes to North Korea to keep Pyongyang on its side against China, while China also trained the North Koreans by signing a nuclear cooperation agreement with Pyongyang (Cho, 2018; Clemens Jr., 2016). With Soviet support, North Korea successfully established its nuclear research centre at Yongbyon in 1964 (Cho, 2018). China ceased its nuclear training programme in 1967 as the relationship between North Korea and the Soviet Union developed, and North Korea asked for further assistance from other countries in Eastern Europe for its nuclear programme development (Chapter 6 provides details about aid support from those countries to North Korea).

Pyongyang continued to push towards developing nuclear capability not only due to the US deployment of nuclear warheads in South Korea in 1958 but also due to South Korean President Park Jung-hee's announcement of the development of nuclear weapons by South Korea in 1975 (Kim and Baek, 2017). In between, in 1968, the Soviet Union and the US, along with several other countries, created the Nuclear Non-Proliferation Treaty (NPT), but North Korea rejected signing the NPT and continued its efforts to develop a nuclear programme. Later in 1974, North Korea joined the International Atomic Energy Agency (IAEA), and in 1977, Pyongyang initially signed a safeguards agreement with the IAEA. Finally, in 1985, North Korea agreed to join the NPT to receive further assistance from the USSR, just a year before when it began to operate the 5 MWe reactor at its Yongbyon facility, which made it possible to build nuclear weapons in 1986. In other words, North Korea's success in extracting plutonium led to its own 'indigenous nuclear programme' (Clemens Jr., 2016: 97; Kim and Baek, 2017). With US President George H.W. Bush announcing the removal of tactical nuclear weapons from South Korea in 1991, North and South Korea agreed to the 'Joint Declaration on the Denuclearisation of the Korean Peninsula' in 1992. However, this mood did not last long.

First Nuclear Crisis

Upon the resumption of the South Korea–US joint military exercises, North Korea announced its intention to withdraw from the NPT in March 1993, which triggered the 'first nuclear crisis' on the Korean peninsula. However, this decision was revoked when North Korea and the US signed the 'Joint Statement of the United States of America and the Democratic People's Republic of Korea' in June 1993 (Kim, 2019). But then, Pyongyang declared that it would leave the IAEA in 1994 when the agency announced that it would stop its technical assistance to North Korea due to lack of compliance (Smith, 2015). Amid these developments, North Korea test-fired a medium-range ballistic missile (MRBM), Rodong-1, in May 1993.

The first nuclear crisis raised concern about possible war in the region, but the situation was dramatically resolved with the signing of the Agreed Framework, also known as the Geneva Agreement, following a meeting between former US President Jimmy Carter and Kim Il-sung in Pyongyang in 1994. The US and North Korea signed the Agreed Framework in Geneva in October 1994, aiming to 'resolve the overall nuclear issue on the Korean Peninsula' (UN, 1994). The Agreed Framework's purpose included the establishment of the Korean Peninsula Energy Development Organization (KEDO), which was designed to build two light-water reactors (LWR) of the Korean Standard Nuclear Power Plant model in North Korea, with joint funding from the US, Japan, South Korea, and the European Union (EU) (Cho, 2018). Not only did Pyongyang maintain its membership in the NPT, but it also allowed the IAEA to monitor freezing of its graphite-moderated reactors.

Second Nuclear Crisis

The 'second nuclear crisis' was observed between 2002 and 2003, not long after the first inter-Korean summit in June 2000. Presidents Kim Dae-jung and Kim Il-sung had met for the first South–North Korea Summit as part of the South Korean president's Sunshine Policy, at which they had announced a 'Joint Statement' (6.15 Joint Statement)[1]. As the US detected a resumption of the uranium enrichment programme in North Korea, US President George W. Bush condemned and named the country, along with Iraq and Iran, as an axis of evil in 2002. Kim Jong-il subsequently proclaimed the restarting of North Korea's nuclear programme at Yongbyon in the same year. Then, in the following year, he announced Pyongyang's withdrawal from the NPT. As a result, KEDO was abandoned, LWR construction was suspended, and as Chapter 6 details, all energy aid ceased. In the meantime, as a result of the crisis, the first Six-Party Talks involving the US, China, Russia, Japan, North Korea, and South Korea were convened in Beijing in 2003. From this time onwards, North Korea's stance of 'security first, disarmament later' began while the US maintained its principle of 'disarmament for trade and aid' (Clemens Jr., 2016: 218).

In 2005, North Korea declared that it possessed nuclear weapons and would no longer participate in the Six-Party Talks. This was the first time that North Korea officially revealed the success of its nuclear programme to the international community (Kim and Baek, 2017). However, in the same year, Pyongyang was back again at the negotiating table for the fourth round of the Six-Party Talks and the 'Joint Statement of the Fourth Round of the Six-Party Talks' was agreed in September 2005 (9.19 Joint Statement). In this statement, the US affirmed that it would not invade North Korea while North Korea affirmed that it would comply with the NPT and IAEA safeguards. The statement included the provision of LWR as a subject so that North Korea could use nuclear energy, but without a specific timeline. Also, the US gave assurance that it did not have any nuclear weapons in South Korea (Clemens Jr., 2016; Kim, 2019). However, one year later, North Korea test-fired seven ballistic missiles: six short-range ballistic missiles (SRBMs) and MRBMs; and a long-range Taepodong-2 missile. It is known that North Korea took this provocative action mainly because the US froze its bank account at the Banco Delta Asia (BDA) in Macao, which was used as a money laundering source by the regime. Following the US action, China also froze North Korea's BDA account in 2006. In response to the North Korean missile launches, the UNSC unanimously adopted resolution 1695 in July 2006, with some member countries also imposing financial restrictions and suspending aid implementation.

First Nuclear Test

In the face of this international pressure, North Korea conducted its first underground nuclear test in 2006, and the UNSC adopted resolution 1718 imposing further sanctions. After its first nuclear test, North Korea gained a certain amount of bargaining power in bilateral negotiations with the US. Accordingly, North Korean and US delegations met and agreed that Pyongyang would shut down its Yongbyon facilities while Washington would release the frozen BDA funds. Both sides acted as promised, and the so-called 'nukes for food' tactic began to be used. Then, in 2007, the sixth round of the Six-Party Talks was held, with the participants agreeing on the 'Joint Statement of the Sixth Round of the Six-Party Talks' in October 2007 (10.3 Joint Statement), which in a way continued earlier commitments made during the fourth round (9.19 Joint Statement). While US–North Korea relations developed, South–North Korea relations also became cooperative. The second South–North Korea Summit between Presidents Roh Moo-hyun and Kim Jong-il was held in October 2007 and a 'Joint Statement' (10.4 Joint Statement) was agreed on, which marked a continuation of the joint statement of the first summit (6.15 Joint Statement).

Second Nuclear Test

In 2009, North Korea test-fired a long-range Unha-2 missile prior to its second nuclear test. Unha is the new name for the Taepodong series (YNA, 2017). The UNSC agreed on a presidential statement, and North Korea announced its withdrawal from the Six-Party Talks in response to this statement. The Six-Party Talks have never resumed. UNSC resolution 1874 was adopted in 2009, after another presidential statement following North Korea's second nuclear test in 2009. North Korea did not officially announce the reason for the second nuclear test; however, it is believed that it was related to the start of US President Barack Obama's first term in office in 2009. Then, in 2012, North Korea conducted a Unha-3 rocket test, which was called a 'satellite launch' but considered to be a long-range missile test. Consequently, UNSC resolution 2087 was adopted in 2013.

Third Nuclear Test

After the Unha-3 missile test, North Korea conducted its third nuclear test in 2013, and the UNSC adopted resolution 2094. In the time between the second and third nuclear tests, Kim Jong-il died in 2011, and Kim Jong-un became the new leader of North Korea. The nuclear programme under Kim Jong-il's initial 'military-first' government had given more weight to nuclear deterrence than to diplomacy in the absence of similarly strong civilian or political counterparts of this idea (Smith, 2015: 294).

Fourth Nuclear Test

In 2015, North Korea tested a submarine-launched ballistic missile (SLBM), Bukgeukseong-1, prior to its fourth nuclear test in January 2016 (YNA, 2017). After the fourth nuclear test, North Korea test-fired another long-range projectile in 2016. While Pyongyang insisted that it was a space launch vehicle—Gwangmyungseong-4—both Seoul and Washington condemned it as an intercontinental ballistic missile (ICBM) (Cho, 2016). Gwangmyungseong is the new name for the Unha series, which was called Taepodong prior to 2009. Taepodong, Unha, and Gwangmyungseong have been the names attached to North Korea's long-range missiles, while Bukgeukseong is the name of its SLBM series (YNA, 2017). Here, it is worth pointing out that another slightly different understanding of North Korean missile names exists. For instance, there is a view that the name 'Gwangmyungseong' was attached in parallel to both Taepodong and Unha in previous tests of these two missiles whenever the satellite launch vehicle was installed. In other words, Taepodong-1, when it was test-fired in 1998, already had a second name—Gwangmyunseong-1—as it was a satellite launch vehicle at the same time. Likewise, Taepodong-2, which was launched in 2009, was also named Gwangmyungseong-2 at the same time. In comparison, both Unha-3-1 and Unha-3-2, launched in 2012, were named Gwangmyungseong-3 as both the Unha-3 series missiles were installed with satellites (Cho, 2016). No matter what the names were, the fact remains that North Korea carried out its fourth nuclear test, with the Gwangmyungseong-4 missile in 2016, and in response, the UNSC passed resolution 2270.

Fifth Nuclear Test

The fifth nuclear test was carried out in 2016 after North Korea had requested that the US recognise the country as a nuclear state in the same year. As a result of the fifth nuclear test, UNSC resolution 2321 was adopted in November 2016. Before the fifth nuclear test, North Korea had test-fired an intermediate-range ballistic missile (IRBM), Hwasong-10. Other names for the Hwasong missile series are the Scud and Rodong series (YNA, 2017).

Sixth Nuclear Test

Just one year after its fifth nuclear test, North Korea conducted its sixth nuclear test in September 2017. It is known that the capacity was five to 20 times larger than the previous test (Byun, 2017). Between the nuclear tests, North Korea conducted a series of missile tests, which led to the adoption of UNSC resolution 2356 in June

2017. For example, while Japanese Prime Minister Shinzo Abe was visiting US President Donald Trump, North Korea launched a missile in February 2017. Then, following further North Korean provocation with two ICBM (Hwasong-14) launches in July 2017, the UNSC adopted resolution 2371 in August 2017. When North Korea carried out its sixth nuclear test in September 2017, UNSC resolution 2375 was passed in the same month, imposing the strongest ever sanctions against the Kim regime. However, Pyongyang did not stop its ballistic missile launches but continued, test-firing another ICBM, Hwasong-15, in November 2017, which resulted in UNSC resolution 2397. Four UNSC resolutions were passed within one year in 2017. A summary of North Korea's nuclear programme development and UN sanctions against it is provided in Table 2.4.

Amid continuing missile tests, when President Trump visited South Korea in November 2017, he asked South Korean President Moon Jae-in, 'Do you have to reunify?' (Rogin, 2017). The reason Trump asked this question is not clearly known. Some might suggest that the newly appointed US president, whose career path had not been one of a diplomat, mistakenly revealed the actual American position on the Korean peninsula—no unification but stalemate, with the peninsula as a buffer zone between the US and China. Or it could simply have been that President Trump did not understand the Korean peninsula well. Either way, his reckless question seemed to signal the indifference of US policymakers regarding the unification of the two Koreas. The US government began to consider conducting a pre-emptive 'bloody nose strike' on North Korea in early 2018, while Trump described Kim Jong-un as 'little rocket man'. However, the mood changed rapidly.

Intercontinental Ballistic Missile Moratorium

Following the Pyeongchang Winter Olympics in 2018, in which both North and South Korean athletes participated, and with Kim Yo-jong, Kim Jong-un's sister, coming to South Korea to attend the games, there was friendly engagement among the US, North Korea, and South Korea until December 2019. During this period, North Korea did not carry out any ICBM launches, with Kim Jong-un announcing a moratorium on nuclear and missile tests in April 2018. Not only were there handshake moments between Trump and Kim—in Singapore in 2018 and Hanoi in 2019—but Trump went so far as to say that 'we fell in love' while talking about the 'beautiful letters' that he had received from Kim in September 2018 (Jacobs, 2018). In 2018, Kim Jong-un shook hands with South Korean President Moon Jae-in in the demilitarised zone (DMZ) and crossed the border into South Korea, becoming the first North Korean leader to 'visit' South Korea even though the meeting only took place at the Peace House within the boundaries of the DMZ. Then, in September 2018, Kim greeted Moon in Pyongyang.

However, following Kim's visit to President Xi Jinping in China in January 2019, the Hanoi Summit between Trump and Kim, in February 2019, signalled the end of gesture politics as both the US and North Korea were unable to reach an agreement on denuclearisation vis-à-vis the lifting of sanctions. Kim then visited President Vladimir Putin in Russia in April 2019. Following two sets of

Table 2.4 Nuclear Programmes and UN Sanctions in North Korea

Year	*Main Events*	*Nuclear Programme Development*	*UN Sanctions*
Post-Independence	Reserve of foreign currency by trade	Building up interests in nuclear energy (uranium extraction)	—
Korean War and onwards	Security and deterrence against US nuclear attack Also, due to the possible nuclear development in South Korea under the Park regime	Nuclear programme development	—
1964	—	Establishment of Nuclear Research Centre at Yongbyon	—
1974	—	Entering into IAEA • IAEA safeguards agreement (1977)	—
1985	Russian assistance on nuclear facility as an exchange	Joining NPT	—
1986	Possible to equip nuclear weapons	Operating 5 MWe reactor at Yongbyon facility	
1992	US announcement on removal of nuclear weapons from South Korea (1991)	North–South Korea Joint Declaration on the Denuclearisation of the Korean Peninsula Signed further comprehensive safeguards agreement of IAEA	
1993–1994	Resuming South Korea–US joint military exercise	First nuclear crisis • Intention to withdraw from NPT (1993) • Medium-range missile Rodong-1 (1993) • Withdrawal from IAEA (1994)	UNSC Resolution 825 Joint Statement of US–North Korea (1993) Agreed Framework/Geneva Agreement, including KEDO provision (1994)

2000	Sunshine Policy	First South–North Summit (Presidents Kim Dae-jung and Kim Jong-il)	6.15 Joint Statement
2002–2003	Resuming uranium enrichment programme in North Korea US condemning North Korea as an axis of evil	Second nuclear crisis • Yongbyon nuclear facility resumption (2002) • Withdrawal from NPT (2003)	KEDO suspension, along with aid cessation (2003) Creation of Six-Party Talks (2003) Six rounds of Six-Party Talks between 2003 and 2007
2005	—	Official Declaration of Nuclear Programme Success Suspension of Six-Party Talks participation	9.19 Joint Statement of the Fourth Round of the Six-Party Talks
2006	Freezing BDA assets	Missile provocation: Seven ballistic missiles; six short- and medium-range missiles; and one long-range Taepodong-2 missile	UNSC Resolution 1695
	UNSC Resolution 1695	First Nuclear Test	UNSC Resolution 1718 US–North Korea negotiation on freezing Yongbyon and releasing BDA funds
2007	—	Sixth (final) Six-Party Talk	10.3 Joint Statement
	—	Second South–North Korea Summit (Presidents Roh Moo-hyun and Kim Jong-il)	10.4 Joint Statement
2009	Probably upon President Barack Obama's inauguration	Missile provocation: Long-range Unha-2 missile (former Taepodong series)	UNSC Presidential Statement
	UNSC Presidential Statement	Withdrawal from the Six-Party Talks	—
	Probably upon President Barack Obama's inauguration	Second Nuclear Test	UNSC Presidential Statement UNSC Resolution 1874

(*Continued*)

Table 2.4 Continued

Year	*Main Events*	*Nuclear Programme Development*	*UN Sanctions*
2012	—	Missile provocation: Long-range Unha-3 missile	UNSC Resolution 2087 (adopted in 2013)
2013	—	Third Nuclear Test	UNSC Resolution 2094
2015	—	Missile provocation: SLBM Bukgeukseong-1 missile	—
2016	—	Fourth Nuclear Test	UNSC Resolution 2270
	—	Missile provocation: Long-range Gwangmyungseong-4 missile (former Unha series)	
	—	Missile provocation: Intermediate-range Hwasong-10 missile	—
	Request to admit as nuclear state	Fifth Nuclear Test	UNSC Resolution 2321
2016–2017	—	Missile provocation: Multiple missiles since 9 September 2016	UNSC Resolution 2356
2017	—	Missile provocation: Two ICBM Hwasong-14	UNSC Resolution 2371
	—	Sixth Nuclear Test	UNSC Resolution 2375
	—	Missile provocation: ICBM Hwasong-14 and 15 missiles	UNSC Resolution 2397

Source: Author's own compilation.

projectile tests in May 2019, Kim Jong-un made another official visit to China in June 2019. It seemed that the dynamics in the region were returning to those of the pre-Pyeongchang Winter Olympic period. Then, suddenly, Kim Jong-un, Moon Jae-in, and Donald Trump held a meeting in the DMZ in June 2019, with Trump having suggested to Kim that they meet during the US president's visit to South Korea. However, it turned out that the meeting of the three leaders was just a photo opportunity as part of their gesture politics (Lim, 2020). With no tangible progress on reconciling between Washington's stance of 'complete, verifiable, irreversible denuclearisation (CVID)' and Pyongyang's request to lift sanctions, Kim Jong-un's North Korea returned to (the new) normal.

Next Nuclear Test

North Korea tested its missiles 14 times in 2019, six times in 2020, and eight times in 2021. Pyongyang closed the country's borders as a COVID-19 pandemic measure in January 2020, but it did not stop projectile tests. Only SRBMs were tested until September 2021, when testing of both IRBMs and ICBMs resumed. Since September 2021, rail-based missiles have also been launched. In January 2022, the IRBM Hwasong-12 was tested for the first time since 2017. UN Secretary-General António Guterres released a statement condemning North Korea for breaking its 2018 moratorium on long-range missile tests in February 2022 (UN, 2022c). At the UNSC, the US—joined by Council members, such as Albania, Brazil, France, Ireland, Norway, the United Arab Emirates, and the UK—submitted a joint statement criticising the North Korean breach of its own moratorium. However, the statement was not fully agreed upon as member states like China, Gabon, India, Kenya, Mexico, and Russia did not sign up to it. The Chinese ambassador to the UN emphasised the need for 'more attractive, more practical, and more flexible approaches, policies, and actions in accommodating concerns' regarding North Korea (Nichols, 2022). Meanwhile, the US strengthened its bilateral sanctions on Russian individuals and companies associated with North Korean procurement activities (Brunnstrom and Ahmann, 2022).

During the first quarter of 2022, the Kim regime conducted 12 missile tests. At the time of writing, the most recent was a test of an ICBM in the Hwasong series on 24 March 2022. While the UN concluded that the missile tested was Hwasong-17 based on the North Korean government's claim (for instance, see UN, 2022b), South Korean military authorities argued that it was the same kind of missile as in 2017, for example, Hwasong-15 (see YNA, 2022). Following the ICBM launch, there has been increasing concern about a possible seventh nuclear test in the near future. Following the March 2022 missile test, the UN Secretary-General released a statement strongly condemning the ICBM launch (UN, 2022d). While the UNSC did not impose further sanctions after this latest ICBM test by North Korea, it adopted resolution 2627 in 2022, extending the mandate of the existing Panel of Experts (PoE) created by previous resolutions in 2016 and 2017 until the end of April 2023. While the UNSC Sanctions Committee oversees the implementation of the imposed sanctions, the PoE investigates sanctions compliance against the relevant resolutions and publishes the results of its assessments. Since 2012, the PoE has published annual and midterm reports on the sanctions against North Korea. The most recent PoE report was the midterm report of the 1718 PoE, published in September 2021. With the adoption of resolution 2627, the PoE was expected to provide a midterm report by 3 August 2022 and two final reports by 3 February and 3 March 2023, as of April 2022 (UN, 2022b).

How Sanctions Have Been Imposed on North Korea: The Case of the United Nations

The UNSC started its sanctions regime in North Korea by imposing smart sanctions, but the measures have escalated into a more comprehensive sanctions regime, as North Korea has continued in its pursuit of becoming a nuclear state.

Response to the First Nuclear Crisis

The very first UNSC resolution directly addressing the nuclear issue was resolution 825 (see UN, 1993). It was adopted in 1993 as a result of North Korea's announcement of its intention to withdraw from the NPT—prompting the first nuclear crisis, as discussed earlier—and called for four actions to be taken: for North Korea to reconsider its withdrawal plan; for North Korea to honour its NPT obligations; for the IAEA to continue to consult with North Korea; and for all UN members to facilitate and to encourage North Korea to respond to the UNSC resolution. However, the resolution did not impose any sanctions. Then, there were no further UNSC resolutions until 2006, which means there was no UN response to the second nuclear crisis. As mentioned earlier, the KEDO project was suspended during this period and bilateral sanctions were imposed.

Response to the First Nuclear Test

In reaction to the first nuclear test, UNSC resolution 1695 was passed in July 2006. It called for seven actions, including sanctions. Paragraphs 3 and 4 of the resolution contained the main contents of the very first multilateral sanctions imposed on North Korea by the UN. North Korea was already subject to bilateral sanctions imposed by the US from the time of the Korean War. As seen in Box 2.1, resolution 1695 required member countries to prevent missile and missile-related trade with North Korea and the weapons of mass destruction (WMD) programme, including through financial transfers.

Box 2.1 UNSC Resolution 1695 (2006), Paragraphs 3–4

3. Requires all Member States, in accordance with their national legal authorities and legislation and consistent with international law, to exercise vigilance and prevent missile and missile-related items,

materials, goods and technology being transferred to DPRK's missile or WMD programmes.

4. Requires all Member States, in accordance with their national legal authorities and legislation and consistent with international law, to exercise vigilance and prevent the procurement of missiles or missile related-items, materials, goods and technology from the DPRK, and the transfer of any financial resources in relation to DPRK's missile or WMD programmes.

Source: UN, 2006a: 2

In October of the same year, UNSC resolution 1718 was adopted as a result of North Korea's first nuclear test. Whereas the previous two resolutions on the issue were two-page documents, this resolution was double those in length and much more detailed. Resolution 1718 outlined 16 actions, five of which were a direct demand for the imposition of sanctions against North Korea. As Box 2.2 shows, the sanctions imposed by resolution 1718 were 'smart sanctions' as they were targeted, for instance, against specific individuals with actions such as the freezing of assets to be taken against designated persons and entities. Also, bans on technical training, advice, services, or assistance related to the provision, manufacture, maintenance, or use of items were new actions included in paragraph 8 of the resolution, in addition to the sanctions on financial transactions (see Box 2.2). In other words, sanctions on official development assistance (ODA) were officially imposed on North Korea from 2006 onwards.

Box 2.2 UNSC Resolution 1718 (2006), Paragraphs 3–4 and 8–10

3. Demands that the DPRK immediately retract its announcement of withdrawal from the NPT.
4. Demands further that the DPRK return to the NPT and IAEA safeguards, and underlines the need for all States Parties to the NPT to continue to comply with their Treaty obligations.
8. Decides that:
   (a) All member States shall prevent the direct or indirect supply, sale or transfer to the DPRK, through their territories or by their nationals, or using their flag vessels or aircraft, and whether or not originating in their territories, of:
      (i) Any battle tanks, armoured combat vehicles, large calibre artillery systems, combat aircraft, attack helicopters, warships, missiles or missile systems as defined for the purpose of the UN Register on Conventional Arms, or related materiel including spare parts, or items as determined by the Security Council or the Committee established by paragraph 12 below (the Committee);

(ii) All items, materials, equipment, goods and technology as set out in the lists in documents S/2006/814 and S/2006/815, unless within 14 days of adoption of this resolution the Committee has amended or completed their provisions also taking into account the list in document S/2006/816, as well as other items, materials, equipment, goods and technology, determined by the Security Council or the Committee, which could contribute to DPRK's nuclear-related, ballistic missile-related or other WMD-related programmes;

(iii) Luxury goods;

(b) The DPRK shall cease the export of all items covered in subparagraphs (a)(i) and (a)(ii) above and that all Member States shall prohibit the procurement of such items from the DPRK by their nationals, or using their flagged vessels or aircraft, and whether or not originating in the territory of the DPRK;

(c) All Member States shall prevent any transfers to the DPRK by their nationals or from their territories, or from the DPRK by its nationals or from its territory, of technical training, advice, services or assistance related to the provision, manufacture, maintenance or use of the items in subparagraphs (a)(i) and (a)(ii) above;

(d) All member States shall, in accordance with their respective legal processes, freeze immediately the funds, other financial assets and economic resources which are on their territories at the date of the adoption of this resolution or at any time thereafter, that are owned or controlled, directly or indirectly, by the persons or entities designated by the Committee or by the Security Council as being engaged in or providing support for, including through other illicit means, DPRK's nuclear-related, other WMD-related and ballistic missile-related programmes, or by persons or entities acting on their behalf or at their direction, and ensure that any funds, financial assets or economic resources are prevented from being made available by their nationals or by any persons or entities within their territories, to or for the benefit of such persons or entities;

(e) All Member States shall take the necessary steps to prevent the entry into or transit through their territories of the persons designated by the Committee or by the Security Council as being responsible for, including through supporting or promoting, DPRK policies in relation to the DPRK's nuclear-related, ballistic missile-related and other WMD-related programmes, together with their family members, provided that nothing in this paragraph shall oblige a state to refuse its own nationals entry into its territory;

(f) In order to ensure compliance with the requirements of this paragraph, and thereby preventing illicit trafficking in nuclear, chemical or biological weapons, their means of delivery and related materials, all Member States are called upon to take, in accordance with their national authorities and legislation, and consistent with international law, cooperative action including through inspection of cargo to and from the DPRK, as necessary.

9. Decides that the provisions of paragraph 8(d) above do not apply to financial or other assets or resources that have been determined by relevant States:

   (a) To be necessary for basic expenses, including payment for foodstuffs, rent or mortgage, medicines and medical treatment, taxes, insurance premiums, and public utility charges, or exclusively for payment of reasonable professional fees and reimbursement of incurred expenses associated with the provision of legal services, or fees or service charges, in accordance with national laws, for routine holding or maintenance of frozen funds, other financial assets and economic resources, after notification by the relevant States to the Committee of the intention to authorize, where appropriate, access to such funds, other financial assets and economic resources and in the absence of a negative decision by the Committee within five working days of such notification;

   (b) To be necessary for extraordinary expenses, provided that such determination has been notified by the relevant States to the Committee and has been approved by the Committee; or

   (c) To be subject of a judicial, administrative or arbitral lien or judgement, in which case the funds, other financial assets and economic resources may be used to satisfy that lien or judgement provided that the lien or judgement was entered prior to the date of the present resolution, is not for the benefit of a person referred to in paragraph 8 (d) above or an individual or entity identified by the Security Council or the Committee, and has been notified by the relevant States to the Committee.

10. Decides that the measures imposed by paragraph 8(e) above shall not apply where the Committee determines on a case-by-case basis that such travel is justified on the grounds of humanitarian need, including religious obligations, or where the Committee concludes that an exemption would otherwise further the objectives of the present resolution.

Source: UN, 2006b: 2–4

Response to the Second Nuclear Test

UNSC resolution 1874 was adopted in 2009 when North Korea carried out its second nuclear test. In this resolution, a total of 33 actions to be taken were included, and many of the paragraphs related to sanctions aimed at expanding the scale of the existing sanctions, especially those that had been imposed in resolution 1718 (2006) (from para. 8 onwards) (see Box 2.2). For instance, paragraphs 9 and 10 of resolution 1874 expanded the original range of sanctions to 'all arms and related materiel as well as to financial transactions, technical training, advice, services, or assistance related to the provision, manufacture, maintenance, or use of such arms or materiel' (see Box 2.3). The range of arms covered by the sanctions was expanded from ballistic missile related and other WMD related to 'all' except for small arms and light weapons and their related materiel (see Box 2.3).

Box 2.3 UNSC Resolution 1874 (2009), Paragraphs 9–10

9. Decides that the measures in paragraph 8(b) of resolution 1718 (2006) shall also apply to all arms and related materiel, as well as to financial transactions, technical training, advice, services or assistance related to the provision, manufacture, maintenance or use of such arms or materiel.
10. Decides that the measures in paragraph 8(a) of resolution 1718 (2006) shall also apply to all arms and related materiel, as well as to financial transactions, technical training, advice, services or assistance related to the provision, manufacture, maintenance or use of such arms, except for small arms and light weapons and their related materiel, and calls upon States to exercise vigilance over the direct or indirect supply, sale or transfer to the DPRK of small arms or light weapons, and further decides that States shall notify the Committee at least five days prior to selling, supplying or transferring small arms or light weapons to the DPRK.

Source: UN, 2009: 2

Response to the Third Nuclear Test

In 2012, North Korea launched a long-range ballistic missile, breaching resolutions 1718 (2006) and 1874 (2009). Following the missile test, the UNSC passed a new resolution—resolution 2087—in 2013. In this resolution, the UNSC member countries did not provide for new or expanded sanctions, but rather reaffirmed resolutions 1718 (2006) and 1874 (2009), as in paragraph 4 (see UN, 2013a: para. 5). Also, this resolution provided the actual names of sanctioned individuals and entities by applying paragraphs 8(d) and 8(e) of resolution 1718 (2006) (Box 2.2) to the list of individuals and entities in annexes I (travel ban/ asset freeze) and II (asset freeze) (see UN, 2013a: para. 5). The travel ban applied to four individuals—Paek Chang-Ho, Chang Myong-Chin, Ra Ky'ong-su, and Kim Kwang-il—who were listed with descriptions and/or identifiers, including alternative spellings of their names as they might appear on different documents (see UN, 2013a: 4). Meanwhile, six entities were targeted for an asset freeze. They included the Korean Committee for Space Technology, Bank of East Land, Korea Kumryong Trading Corporation, Tosong Technology Trading Corporation, Korea Ryonha Machinery Joint Venture Corporation, and Leader (Hong Kong) International, each of which was similarly listed with a description, location, and other existing spellings of its name (see UN, 2013a: 5–6).

Then, as North Korea conducted its third nuclear missile test, UNSC resolution 2094 was passed, in 2013, condemning the test in the 'strongest terms' (UN, 2013b: 2). While this resolution reaffirmed the previous three resolutions—resolutions 1718 (2006), 1874 (2009), and 2087 (2013)—it added another three individuals to the list of those already targeted, making them subject not only to a travel ban but also to an asset freeze, in its annex I. The three individuals were Yo'n Cho'ng Nam, Ko Cho'o'l-Chae, and Mun Cho'ng-Ch'o'l (see UN, 2013b: 7). UNSC resolution 2087 (2013) had only targeted entities, not individuals, with an asset freeze, as mentioned earlier. Also, two more entities were made subject to an asset freeze in annex II, namely the Second Academy of Natural Sciences and Korea Complex Equipment Import Corporation (see UN, 2013b: 3). Resolution 2094, in annex III, further specified new items, materials, equipment, goods, and technology which were to be subject to the measures in paragraphs 8(a) and 8(b) of resolution 1718 (2006) (see UN, 2013b: 4). This list was divided into three categories: nuclear items; missile items; and chemical weapons list. Also, a list of luxury items was provided for the first time. Previously, luxury items had just been mentioned as 'luxury goods' in paragraph 8 of resolution 1718 (2006) and had simply been referred to in resolutions 1874 (2009) and 2087 (2013), without a specific definition. This list of luxury goods, included in annex IV, specified jewellery and transportation items, such as yachts, luxury automobiles, and racing cars (see UN, 2013b: 9–10).

Response to the Fourth Nuclear Test

After North Korea conducted its fourth nuclear test, UNSC resolution 2270 was adopted in 2016. This resolution reaffirmed existing resolutions with a heavy focus on paragraph 8 of resolution 1718 (2006). In addition, resolution 2270 banned North Korea from exporting natural resources such as coal and iron for the first time (see UN, 2016a: para. 29). The resolution further placed 16 individuals on the travel ban and asset freeze list while adding 12 entities to the asset freeze list. These lists were a lot longer than in previous resolutions. Also, Ocean Maritime Management (OMM) vessels were newly specified in annex III of this resolution and made subject to the asset freeze as economic resources and assets controlled or operated by OMM, through reference to paragraph 8(d) of resolution 1718 (2006) (see UN, 2016a: 6). A total of 31 OMM vessels were listed in the annex (see UN, 2016a: 17). The luxury goods list was re-categorised into luxury watches, transportation items, items of lead crystal, and recreational sports equipment, and the transportation items were redefined as aquatic recreational vehicles and snowmobiles this time (see UN, 2016a: 18).

Response to the Fifth Nuclear Test

UNSC resolution 2321 (2016) against the fifth North Korean nuclear test was adopted in November 2016. This resolution imposed the maximum measures to date in 2016, with extensively expanded, enhanced, replaced, and newly sanctioned items. The newly added sanctions measures included, for example, scientific and technical cooperation, except for activities that did 'not' contribute to North Korea's proliferation sensitive nuclear activities or ballistic missile–related programmes and except for medical exchanges (see UN, 2016b: para. 11), entry into or transit through UN member states by North Koreans involved in programmes or activities prohibited by existing resolutions (see UN, 2016b: para. 15), new helicopters and vessels (see UN, 2016b: para. 30), and North Korean workers overseas (see UN, 2016b: para. 34). Further, paragraph 26 of resolution 2321 (2016) noted the replacement of paragraph 29 of resolution 2270 (2016) dealing with the coal and iron ban. Box 2.4 compares the two paragraphs.

Box 2.4 Replacement of UNSC Resolution 2270 (2016) by UNSC Resolution 2321 (2016)

UNSC Resolution 2270 (2016) paragraph 29

29. Decides that the DPRK shall not supply, sell or transfer, directly or indirectly, from its territory or by its nationals or using its flag vessels or aircraft, coal, iron, and iron ore, and that all States shall prohibit the procurement of such material from the DPRK by their nationals, or using their flag vessels or aircraft, and whether or not originating in the territory of the DPRK, and decides that this provision shall not apply with respect to:
    (a) Coal that the procuring State confirms on the basis of credible information has originated outside the DPRK and was transported through the DPRK solely for export from the Port of Rajin (Rason), provided that the State notifies the Committee in advance and such transactions are unrelated to generating revenue for the DPRK's nuclear or ballistic missile programs or other activities prohibited by resolutions 1718 (2006), 1874 (2009), 2087 (2013), 2094 (2013) or this resolution; and,
    (b) Transactions that are determined to be exclusively for livelihood purposes and unrelated to generating revenue for the DPRK's nuclear or ballistic missile programs or other activities prohibited

by resolutions 1718 (2006), 1874 (2009), 2087 (2013), 2094 (2013) or this resolution.

UNSC Resolution 2321 (2016) paragraph 26

26. Decides that paragraph 29 of resolution 2270 (2016) shall be replaced by the following:
'Decides that the DPRK shall not supply, sell or transfer, directly or indirectly, from its territory or by its nationals or using its flag vessels or aircraft, coal, iron, and iron ore, and that all States shall prohibit the procurement of such material from the DPRK by their nationals, or using their flag vessels or aircraft, and whether or not originating in the territory of the DPRK, and decides that this provision shall not apply with respect to:
(a) Coal that the procuring State confirms on the basis of credible information has originated outside the DPRK and was transported through the DPRK solely for export from the Port of Rajin (Rason), provided that the State notifies the Committee in advance and such transactions are unrelated to generating revenue for the DPRK's nuclear or ballistic missile programmes or other activities prohibited by resolutions 1718 (2006), 1874 (2009), 2087 (2013), 2094 (2013) or this resolution;
(b) Total exports to all Member States of coal originating in the DPRK that in the aggregate do not exceed 53,495,894 US dollars or 1,000,866 metric tons, whichever is lower, between the date of adoption of this resolution and 31 December 2016, and total exports to all Member States of coal originating in the DPRK that in the aggregate do not exceed 400,870,018 US dollars or 7,500,000 metric tons per year, whichever is lower, beginning 1 January 2017, provided that the procurements (i) involve no individuals or entities that are associated with the DPRK's nuclear or ballistic missile programmes or other activities prohibited by resolutions 1718 (2006), 1874 (2009), 2087 (2013), 2094 (2013), 2270 (2016) or this resolution, including designated individuals or entities, or individuals or entities acting on their behalf or at their direction, or entities owned or controlled by them, directly or indirectly, or individuals or entities assisting in the evasion of sanctions, and (ii) are exclusively for livelihood purposes of DPRK nationals and unrelated to generating revenue for the DPRK's nuclear or ballistic missile programmes or other activities prohibited by resolutions 1718 (2006), 1874 (2009), 2087 (2013), 2094 (2013), 2270 (2016) or this resolution, and decides that each Member State that procures coal from the DPRK shall notify the Committee of the aggregate

amount of the volume of such procurement for each month no later than 30 days after the conclusion of that month on the form in annex V to this resolution, directs the Committee to make publicly available on its website the volume of procurement of coal from the DPRK reported by Member States and value calculated by the Committee Secretary, as well as the amount reported for each month and with the number of States that reported for each month, directs the Committee to update this information on a real-time basis as it receives notifications, calls upon all States that import coal from the DPRK to periodically review this website to ensure that they do not exceed the mandatory aggregate annual limit, directs the Committee Secretary to notify all Member States when an aggregate value or volume of coal procurements from the DPRK of 75 per cent of the aggregate yearly amount has been reached, also directs the Committee Secretary to notify all Member States when an aggregate value or volume of coal procurements from the DPRK of 90 per cent of the aggregate yearly amount has been reached, further directs the Committee Secretary to notify all Member States when an aggregate value or volume of coal procurements from the DPRK of 95 per cent of the aggregate yearly amount has been reached and to inform them that they must immediately cease procuring coal from the DPRK for the year, and requests the Secretary-General to make the necessary arrangements to this effect and provide additional resources in this regard; and

(c) Transactions in iron and iron ore that are determined to be exclusively for livelihood purposes and unrelated to generating revenue for the DPRK's nuclear or ballistic missile programmes or other activities prohibited by resolutions 1718 (2006), 1874 (2009), 2087 (2013), 2094 (2013), 2270 (2016) or this resolution'.

Source: UN, 2016a: 7; and UN, 2016b: 5–6

Not only the addition of new sanctions measures but also the replacement of the paragraph dealing with coal and ban are clear examples of the extent to which resolution 2321 (2016) enhanced and expanded the existing sanctions regime against North Korea. On the one hand, compared to previous resolutions, this resolution designated a slightly smaller number of sanctions targets in annexes I and II, which included 11 individuals and 10 entities, respectively (see UN, 2016b: 11–14). Also, annex IV on luxury goods was simpler, listing rugs and tapestries, and tableware of porcelain or bone china (see UN, 2016b: 16). This does not mean that the sanctions applied only to these newly designated items, but rather that these items were added to the existing lists in previous resolutions. On the other hand, resolution 2321 (2016) brought in new sub-titles in annex III on 'items, materials, equipment, goods, and technology' which were now divided into nuclear- and/or missile-usable items, and chemical/biological weapons-usable items (see UN, 2016b: 15).

Response to the Sixth Nuclear Test

In 2017, four UNSC resolutions were adopted against North Korea. First, the UNSC member states agreed on resolution 2356 (2017) in June 2017 as North Korea continued to violate existing resolutions, including conducting ballistic missile tests. This resolution recalled all existing relevant resolutions and especially emphasised paragraph 8 of resolution 1718 (2006) (see UN, 2017a: 1–2). 14 individuals were added in annex I (travel ban and asset freeze), while four new entities were listed in annex II (asset freeze) (see UN, 2017a: 4–6). This resolution did not include a luxury items list.

Second, UNSC resolution 2371 (2017) was passed in August 2017, following the two ICBM launches in July 2017 by North Korea. This resolution reaffirmed previous resolutions and, in paragraph 16, specifically demanded North Korea's full compliance with the Vienna Convention (see UN, 2017b: 4). Also, the resolution replaced paragraph 26 of resolution 2321 (2016) with its paragraph 8 as shown in Box 2.5. As seen in Box 2.4, this paragraph, which banned the export of resources such as coal and iron, had previously been replaced once already when paragraph 29 of resolution 2270 (2016) had been substituted with paragraph 26 of resolution 2321 (2016). It was again revised by this resolution. Further, resolution 2371 (2017) added nine individuals to the travel ban and asset freeze list while providing a 'list update for aliases' of Jang Bom Su and Jon Myong Guk (see UN, 2017b: 7–8). Even though no list of luxury items was attached to it, the resolution placed four more entities on the asset freeze list (see UN, 2017b: 9).

Box 2.5 Replacement of UNSC Resolution 2321 (2016) by UNSC Resolution 2371 (2017)

UNSC Resolution 2321 (2016) paragraph 26

26. Decides that the DPRK shall not supply, sell or transfer, directly or indirectly, from its territory or by its nationals or using its flag vessels or aircraft, coal, iron, and iron ore, and that all States shall prohibit the procurement of such material from the DPRK by their nationals, or using their flag vessels or aircraft, and whether or not originating in the territory of the DPRK, and decides that this provision shall not apply with respect to:
  (a) Coal that the procuring State confirms on the basis of credible information has originated outside the DPRK and was transported

through the DPRK solely for export from the Port of Rajin (Rason), provided that the State notifies the Committee in advance and such transactions are unrelated to generating revenue for the DPRK's nuclear or ballistic missile programmes or other activities prohibited by resolutions 1718 (2006), 1874 (2009), 2087 (2013), 2094 (2013) or this resolution;

(b) Total exports to all Member States of coal originating in the DPRK that in the aggregate do not exceed 53,495,894 US dollars or 1,000,866 metric tons, whichever is lower, between the date of adoption of this resolution and 31 December 2016, and total exports to all Member States of coal originating in the DPRK that in the aggregate do not exceed 400,870,018 US dollars or 7,500,000 metric tons per year, whichever is lower, beginning 1 January 2017, provided that the procurements (i) involve no individuals or entities that are associated with the DPRK's nuclear or ballistic missile programmes or other activities prohibited by resolutions 1718 (2006), 1874 (2009), 2087 (2013), 2094 (2013), 2270 (2016) or this resolution, including designated individuals or entities, or individuals or entities acting on their behalf or at their direction, or entities owned or controlled by them, directly or indirectly, or individuals or entities assisting in the evasion of sanctions, and (ii) are exclusively for livelihood purposes of DPRK nationals and unrelated to generating revenue for the DPRK's nuclear or ballistic missile programmes or other activities prohibited by resolutions 1718 (2006), 1874 (2009), 2087 (2013), 2094 (2013), 2270 (2016) or this resolution, and decides that each Member State that procures coal from the DPRK shall notify the Committee of the aggregate amount of the volume of such procurement for each month no later than 30 days after the conclusion of that month on the form in annex V to this resolution, directs the Committee to make publicly available on its website the volume of procurement of coal from the DPRK reported by Member States and value calculated by the Committee Secretary, as well as the amount reported for each month and with the number of States that reported for each month, directs the Committee to update this information on a real-time basis as it receives notifications, calls upon all States that import coal from the DPRK to periodically review this website to ensure that they do not exceed the mandatory aggregate annual limit, directs the Committee Secretary to notify all Member States when an aggregate value or volume of coal procurements from the DPRK of 75 per cent of the aggregate yearly amount has been reached, also directs the Committee Secretary to notify all Member States when an aggregate value or volume of coal procurements from the DPRK of 90 per cent of the aggregate yearly amount has been reached, further directs the Committee Secretary to notify all Member States when an aggregate value or volume of coal procurements from the DPRK of 95 per cent of the aggregate yearly amount has been reached and to inform them that they must immediately cease procuring coal from the DPRK for the year, and requests the Secretary-General to make the necessary arrangements to this effect and provide additional resources in this regard; and

(c) Transactions in iron and iron ore that are determined to be exclusively for livelihood purposes and unrelated to generating revenue for the DPRK's nuclear or ballistic missile programmes or other activities prohibited by resolutions 1718 (2006), 1874 (2009), 2087 (2013), 2094 (2013), 2270 (2016) or this resolution.

UNSC Resolution 2371 (2017) paragraph 8

8. Decides that paragraph 26 of resolution 2321 (2016) shall be replaced by the following:
'Decides that the DPRK shall not supply, sell or transfer, directly or indirectly, from its territory or by its nationals or using its flag vessels or aircraft, coal, iron, and iron ore, and that all States shall prohibit the procurement of such material from the DPRK by their nationals, or using their flag vessels or aircraft, and whether or not originating in the territory of the DPRK, decides that for sales and transactions of iron and iron ore for which written contracts have been finalized prior to the adoption of this resolution, all States may allow those shipments to be imported into their territories up to 30 days from the date of adoption of this resolution with notification provided to the Committee containing details on those imports by no later than 45 days after the date of adoption of this resolution, and decides further that this provision shall not apply with respect to coal that the exporting State confirms on the basis of credible information has originated outside the DPRK and was transported through the DPRK solely for export from the Port of Rajin (Rason), provided that the exporting State notifies the Committee in advance and such transactions involving coal originating outside of the DPRK are unrelated to generating revenue for the DPRK's nuclear or ballistic missile programs or other activities prohibited by resolutions 1718 (2006), 1874 (2009), 2087 (2013), 2094 (2013), 2270 (2016), 2321 (2016), 2356 (2017), or this resolution'.

Source: UN, 2016b: 5–6; UN, 2017b: 3–4

Third, in September 2017, UNSC resolution 2375 (2017) was adopted against North Korea's sixth nuclear test. It did not list luxury items and added only one individual to the travel ban and asset freeze list, along with three entities on the asset freeze list (see UN, 2017c: 8–9). However, this resolution is known to be the maximum measures under UN sanctions as it not only enhanced and expanded the existing sanctions imposed by previous resolutions but also included new sanctions on items such as ship-to-ship transfers (see UN, 2017c: para. 11), refined petroleum products (see UN, 2017c: para. 14), crude oil (see UN, 2017c: para. 15), textiles (see UN, 2017c: para. 16), and work authorisation for North Korean nationals (see UN, 2017c: para. 16), as well as a financial ban on all joint ventures or cooperative entities with North Korea (see UN, 2017c: para. 17). According to the South Korean Ministry of Foreign Affairs, these new sanctions would reduce 55 per cent of the refined petroleum products and 30 per cent of the crude oil going into North Korea (Back, 2017). Also, with resolution 2375 (2017) prohibiting work permits for North Koreans and banning textile exports from North Korea, it was anticipated that Pyongyang would have decreased foreign currency revenue (Back, 2017).

Finally, UNSC resolution 2397 (2017) was passed in December 2017 against another ballistic missile test. This resolution was more comprehensive than resolution 2375 (2017) in banning all commodities and products from North Korea. It banned North Korean exports of food and agricultural products, machinery, electrical equipment, earth and stone, wood, and vessels (see UN, 2017d: para. 6) and North Korean imports of all industrial machinery, transportation vehicles, and iron, steel, and other metals (see UN, 2017d: para. 7), and required UN member states to repatriate North Korean workers (see UN, 2017d: para. 8) and strengthen inspections of cargo vessels suspected of carrying illicit cargo to or from North Korea (see UN, 2017d: para. 9). Again, although the resolution did not specify luxury items, it included a travel ban and asset freeze list with 16 new individuals and made one new entity subject to an asset freeze (see UN, 2017d: 8–11).

Ineffective Sanctions Regime Against North Korea

Despite the UN having become aware of the adverse impact of sanctions in the 1990s, it seems that the same old rhetoric still repeats in the international arena. While not succeeding in restraining the Kim regime's policy or behaviour, the current sanctions regime has imposed greater burdens on ordinary and vulnerable North Koreans. The 2021 PoE report reaffirmed that the humanitarian situation in North Korea was deteriorating, while emphasising that the UN sanctions were not intended to have adverse humanitarian consequences for the civilian population of the DPRK or to affect negatively or restrict those activities, including economic activities and cooperation, food aid and humanitarian assistance, that were not prohibited by Council resolutions and also stressed that it was the country's primary responsibility and need to fully provide for the livelihood needs of its people (UN, 2021: 51). Yet, it is the sanctions that have directly and indirectly caused hardship for the civilians of North Korea.

As discussed at the beginning of this chapter, it is evident that sanctions do not work, and the case of North Korea confirms the theory that sanctions are ineffective due to the lack of cooperation among countries: not only has the sanctions regime been unsuccessful in bringing about behavioural or policy change in the target country but it has also failed to receive the full support of other countries. Given the lack of support from China and Russia, the UN's institutional sanctions on North Korea have been busted. In 2018, the US ambassador to the UN, Nikki Haley, accused Russia of violating sanctions on North Korea as well as censoring the PoE's reports (Borger, 2018). In early 2022, both China and Russia even called for an easing of the sanctions on North Korea at the UNSC (Independent, 2022). Bilateral sanctions imposed by the US have not been effective either due to North Korea's increasing dependency on China (Gray and Lee, 2021). It is a well-known fact that North Korea heavily relies on illegal trade with China. Both China and Russia have provided North Korea with an escape from the economic burden of sanctions by providing aid throughout. Not only these two main allies of Pyongyang, but also other countries such as Macao, Singapore, Cambodia, Cuba, and Uganda have been sanctions havens for North Korea (Cho, 2018: 163).

The North Korean economy has survived the long-term sanctions regime, but between 2017 and 2019, the country's economic growth rate signalled some negative effects (Song, 2020). However, it cannot be validated as to whether the situation would have led to a change in the regime's behaviour, as there is more appealing evidence that the COVID-19 border closure, which forbids illegal trade between North Korea and China, has since affected the North Korean economy more seriously than the sanctions. Based on the evidence of sanctions evasion, it seems more likely that the North Korean regime would have again survived the impact of the 2016–2017 sanctions. Not only China but also some other African countries have supported activities disallowed under the sanctions (Grzelczyk, 2018; Young, 2021), and as the PoE's report also stated, 'increasing illicit imports will mean that the Democratic People's Republic of Korea is still likely to exceed the cap in 2021' (UN, 2021: 13).

In addition, it has become obvious that the Kim regime has established concrete methods of evading sanctions and secured funding sources for its nuclear programme. The 2022 PoE report confirmed that North Korea 'continued to develop its capability for production of nuclear fissile materials'. In the same report, it was pointed out that 'cyberattacks, particularly on cryptocurrency assets, remain an important revenue source', having yielded more than USD 50 million between 2020 and mid-2021 (BBC, 2022). Previously, the 2019 PoE report had examined how sophisticated cyberattacks were conducted and cyber activity was utilised by the North Korean authority as a way of evading sanctions and bringing in significant income. Paragraphs 109 through 115 of the report provided an intensive analysis of North Korean cyberattacks (see UN, 2019).

It is known that North Korea used to produce counterfeit banknotes, mostly US dollars in the 2000s and Chinese yuan (or renminbi) in the late 2010s. However, recently, the mode of acquiring physical foreign currency has changed to cryptocurrency theft. North Korea had already begun building its cyber capabilities in the 1990s, but its cyber activities have not yet to be restricted by sanctions, except those imposed by the US from 2020. North Korea's recent technological evolvement can be found in its bitcoin hacking system (Park, 2022: 5–9). As has been observed, following marketisation, North Korea's so-called emerging digital economy has been associated with the regime's development of technology for its armament programme. In other words, under current sanctions, the North Korean regime has focused on its capacity to develop sanctions evasion methods and has also become a de facto nuclear state but has abandoned its people in an economic system of self-survival due to the lack of state capacity to deal with the survival needs of both the regime and the people. State capacity has been developed in an inappropriate and skewed manner and may have thus made the regime stronger while weakening society. In this, the next chapter investigates how North Korea has been able to survive under economic sanctions, and how and why its economic system could become resilient.

Note

1 The expression '6.15' is taken from the date of the summit as Koreans tend to use month-day rather than day-month date system.

References

Abrahamian, Andray (2018). *North Korea and Myanmar*. North Carolina: McFarland and Company.

Anguelov, Nikolay (2015). *Economic Sanctions Vs Soft Power: Lessons From North Korea, Myanmar, and the Middle East*. New York: Palgrave MacMillan.

Back, Yong Jin (2017). UNSC Adoption of Resolution 2375 against North Korea. 12 September 2017, *Ministry of Foreign Affairs of South Korea Press Release* [백용진 (2017). 유엔 안보리 대북제재 결의 2375호 채택. 외교부 보도자료, 2017년 9월 12일자]. https://www.mofa.go.kr/www/brd/m_3976/view.do?seq=366621&srchFr=&srchTo=&srchWord=&srchTp=&multi_itm_seq=0&itm_seq_1=0&itm_seq_2=0&company_cd=&company_nm=&page=8. Accessed: 5 June 2021.

BBC (2022). North Korea: Missile Programme Funded Through Stolen Crypto, Un Report Says. 2 February 2022, *BBC News*. https://www.bbc.co.uk/news/world-asia-60281129. Accessed: 15 March 2022.

Borger, Julian (2018). US Accuses Russia of Covering Up North Korea Sanctions Violations. 17 September 2018, *The Guardian*. https://www.theguardian.com/world/2018/sep/17/us-russia-north-korea-sanctions-violations-nikki-haley. Accessed: 15 March 2022.

Brunnstrom, David and Tim Ahmann (2022). US Targets Russians in New North Korea Sanctions After Missile Launches. 11 March 2022, *Reuters*. https://www.reuters.com/world/china/us-imposes-new-north-korea-related-sanctions-after-missile-launches-2022-03-11/. Accessed: 15 March 2022.

Byun, Chang Ku (2017). South Korea's Perception and Counter-Strategies Toward the North Korea's Sixth Nuclear Test. *Unification Strategy*, 17(4): 111–135 [변창구 (2017). 북한의 제6차 핵실험에 대한 인식과 대응 – 현실주의적 관점에서. 통일전략, 17(4): 111–135.]

Carbaugh, Bob and Koushik Ghosh (2019). Economic Sanctions and North Korea. *The American Economist*, 64(1): 131–141.

Cho, Dong-sin (2018). *North Korea in 100 Questions*. Seoul: Sejong Books. Translated from Juliette Morillot and Dorian Malovic (2016). La Coree due Nord en 100 Questions. Paris: Editions Tallandier [조동신 (2018). 100가지 질문으로 본 북한. 서울, 세종서적(주)].

Cho, Kyung-Keun (2016). North Korea's 4th Nuclear Test and UN Security Council Resolution 2270 – A Factor Analysis. *Unification Strategy*, 16(2): 113–150 [조경근 (2016). 북한의 4차 핵실험과 유엔 대북 제재 결의안 2270호 - 요인 분석과 과제. 통일전략, 16(2): 113–150].

Clemens Jr., Walter C. (2016). *North Korea and the World: Human Rights, Arms Control, and Strategies for Negotiation*. Lexington, Kentucky: University Press of Kentucky.

European Commission (2022a). *Frequently Asked Questions: Restrictive Measures (Sanctions)*. Brussels: European Commission.

European Commission (2022b). *Restrictive Measures (Sanctions)*. https://ec.europa.eu/info/business-economy-euro/banking-and-finance/international-relations/restrictive-measures-sanctions_en. Accessed: 22 February 2022.

Gray, Kevin and Jong-Woon Lee (2021). *North Korea and the Geopolitics of Development*. Cambridge: Cambridge University Press.

Grzelczyk, Virginie (2018). *North Korea's New Diplomacy: Challenging Political Isolation in the 21st Century*. London: Palgrave.

Ha, Joseph M. (1982). Soviet Perceptions of North Korea. *Asian Perspectives*, 6(2): 105–131.

Hakimdavar, Golnoosh (2014). *A Strategic Understanding of UN Economic Sanctions; International Relations, Law, and Development*. Oxfordshire: Routledge.

HM Treasury (2020). *UK Financial Sanctions: General Guidance for Financial Sanctions Under the Sanctions and Anti-Money Laundering Act 2018*. London: Office of Financial Sanction Implementation.

Honda, Miki (2021). "Smart Sanctions" by the UN and Financial Sanctions. In: Yoshimura, Sachiko (ed.). *United Nations Financial Sanctions*. New York: Routledge, pp. 18–33.

Hufbauer, Gary Clyde, Jeffrey J. Schott, Kimberly Ann Elliott and Barbara Oegg (2019). *Economic Sanctions Reconsidered* (3rd edition). Washington D.C.: Peterson Institute for International Economics.

Independent (2022). *China, Russia Cool to US Aim for More N. Korea Sanctions*. 26 March 2022. https://www.independent.co.uk/news/china-ap-north-korea-russia-korea-b2044504.html. Accessed: 29 March 2022.

Jacobs, Ben (2018). Trump Professes Love for Kim and Hate for Kavanaugh Torment in Freewheeling Speech. 30 September 2018, *The Guardian*. https://www.theguardian.com/us-news/2018/sep/30/trump-love-kim-nasty-democrat-kavanaugh-west-virginia. Accessed: 25 March 2022.

Kim, Kyung-mook and Yeon-joo Baek (2017). A Study on North Koreas Patterns of Missile Launching and Nuclear Testing. *The Journal of Strategic Studies*, 24(3): 153–194 [김경묵, 백연주 (2017). 북한의 미사일 발사 및 핵실험 패턴에 관한 연구. 전략연구, 24(3): 153–194].

Kim, Young-Joon (2019). Theories and Practice of Nonaggression Pacts: The Case of US-DPRK. *Journal of Northeast Asian Studies*, 24(1): 25–42 [김영준 (2019). 미국의 대북 불가침 약속 사례에 대한 이론적 평가. 한국동북아논총, 24(1): 25–42].

Lankov, Andrei (2015). *The Real North Korea: Life and Politics in the Failed Stalinist Utopia*. New York: Oxford University Press.

Lim, Sojin (2020). Why North Korea and America's Theatre of Gesture Politics Is Now at and End. 15 May 2020, *The National Interest*. https://nationalinterest.org/blog/korea-watch/why-north-korea-and-americas-theater-gesture-politics-now-and-end-154941. Accessed: 25 March 2022.

Lim, Sojin (2021). *Development Cooperation in Post-Sanctions Myanmar and Its Implications for North Korea*. Presentation at the 30th Association for Korean Studies in Europe (AKSE) Conference. 30 October 2021, La Rochelle University, France (online).

Menon, Shruti (2022). Ukraine Crisis: Why India Is Buying More Russian Oil. 14 April 2022, *BBC News*. https://www.bbc.co.uk/news/world-asia-india-60783874. Accessed: 14 April 2022.

Nephew, Richard (2018). *The Art of Sanctions: A View From the Field*. New York: Columbia University Press.

Newsis (2019). North Korea's Another Short-Range Missile Launch in 17 Days, Which Was 10th Missile Test Within a Year. 10 September 2019, *DongA.com* [뉴시스 (2019). 北, 17일 만에 또 단거리 미사일 발사… 올해만 10번째. 동아닷컴, 2019년 9월 10일자]. https://www.donga.com/news/Politics/article/all/20190910/97362400/1. Accessed: 4 June 2021.

Nichols, Michelle (2022). Want North Korea Breakthrough? China Tells US to Show Flexibility. 5 February 2022, *Reuters*. https://www.reuters.com/world/china/want-north-korea-breakthrough-china-tells-us-show-flexibility-2022-02-04/. Accessed: 15 March 2022.

Park, June (2022). *Cyber-hacking as a Means of "Self-reliance": North Korea's Ransomware-Based Cyber-Hacking for Economic Gains in the Absence of Regulations on Cryptocurrencies in Global Finance*. Understanding North Korea Paper Series. Washington, D.C.: National Committee on North Korea, and Woodrow Wilson Center.

Portela, Clara (2011). *Impact of Sanctions and Isolation Measurement with North Korea, Burma/Myanmar, Iran and Zimbabwe as Case Studies*. Directorate-General for External Policies of the Union. Brussels: European Parliament.

Radio Free Asia (2004). Noted Economist Urges End to Burma Sanctions. 25 August 2004, *Radio Free Asia*. https://www.rfa.org/english/news/business/burma_sanctions-20040825.html. Accessed: 25 March 2022.

Reuters (2022). *Russia Can Still Send Oil and Gas to Britain Despite Port Ban*. 2 March 2022. https://www.reuters.com/business/energy/russia-can-still-send-oil-gas-britain-despite-port-ban-2022-03-02/. Accessed: 25 March 2022.

Rogin, Josh (2017). Trump Asks South Korea's President: 'Do You Have to Reunify?. 15 November 2017, *The Washington Post*. https://www.washingtonpost.com/news/josh-rogin/wp/2017/11/15/trump-asks-south-koreas-president-do-you-have-to-reunify/. Accessed: 25 March 2022.

Smith, Hazel (2015). *North Korea: Markets and Military Rule*. Cambridge: Cambridge University Press.

Smith, Hazel (2020). The Ethics of United Nations Sanctions on North Korea: Effectiveness, Necessity and Proportionality. *Critical Asian Studies*, 52(2): 182–203.

Song, Jaeguk (2020). *COVID-19 Import Decrease and Its Implications to North Korean Economy*. Seoul: Industrial Bank of Korea Economic Research Institute [송재국 (2020). COVID19 이후 수입 감소가 북한경제에 미치는 영향. 서울, IBK경제연구소].

Sriyai, Surachanee (2020). How Economic Sanctions Discourage the Prospect of Reunification of the Korean Peninsula (and What Might Help). *North Korean Review*, 16(1): 121–130.

Szalontai, Balazs and Sergey Radchenko (2006). *North Korea's Efforts to Acquire Nuclear Technology and Nuclear Weapons: Evidence From Russian and Hungarian Archives*. Cold War International History Project Working Paper No. 53. Washington, D.C.: Woodrow Wilson International Center for Scholars.

UN (1993). *Resolution 825 Adopted by the Security Council at its 3212th Meeting, on 11 May 1993.* S/RES/825 (1993). New York: United Nations.
UN (1994). Agreed Framework Between the United States of America and the Democratic People's Republic of Korea. 21 October 2014, *United Nations Peacemaker*. https://peacemaker.un.org/node/1129. Accessed: 25 March 2022.
UN (2006a). *Resolution 1695 Adopted by the Security Council at its 5490th Meeting, on 15 July 2006.* S/RES/1695 (2006). New York: United Nations.
UN (2006b). *Resolution 1718 Adopted by the Security Council at its 5551st Meeting, on 14 October 2006.* S/RES/1718 (2006). New York: United Nations.
UN (2009). *Resolution 1874 Adopted by the Security Council at its 6141st Meeting, on 12 June 2009.* S/RES/1874 (2009). New York: United Nations.
UN (2013a). *Resolution 2087 Adopted by the Security Council at its 6904th Meeting, on 22 January 2013.* S/RES/2087 (2013). New York: United Nations.
UN (2013b). *Resolution 2094 Adopted by the Security Council at its 6932nd Meeting, on 7 March 2013.* S/RES/2094 (2013). New York: United Nations.
UN (2016a). *Resolution 2270 Adopted by the Security Council at its 7638th Meeting, on 2 March 2016.* S/RES/2270 (2016). New York: United Nations.
UN (2016b). *Resolution 2321 Adopted by the Security Council at its 7821st Meeting, on 30 November 2016.* S/RES/2321 (2016). New York: United Nations.
UN (2017a). *Resolution 2356 Adopted by the Security Council at its 7958th Meeting, on 2 June 2017.* S/RES/2356 (2017). New York: United Nations.
UN (2017b). *Resolution 2371 Adopted by the Security Council at its 8019th Meeting, on 5 August 2017.* S/RES/2371 (2017). New York: United Nations.
UN (2017c). *Resolution 2375 Adopted by the Security Council at its 8042nd Meeting, on 11 September 2017.* S/RES/2375 (2017). New York: United Nations.
UN (2017d). *Resolution 2397 Adopted by the Security Council at its 8151st Meeting, on 22 December 2017.* S/RES/2397 (2017). New York: United Nations.
UN (2019). *Letter Dated 21 February 2019 From the Panel of Experts Established Pursuant to Resolution 1874 (2009) Addressed to the President of the Security Council.* S/2019/171. New York: United Nations.
UN (2021). *Letter Dated 3 September 2021 from the Panel of Experts Established Pursuant to Resolution 1874 (2009) Addressed to the Chair of the Security Council Committee Established Pursuant to Resolution 1718 (2006).* S/2021/777. New York: United Nations.
UN (2022a). *United Nations Security Council Sanctions.* https://www.un.org/securitycouncil/sanctions/information. Accessed: 22 February 2022.
UN (2022b). Security Council Extends Mandate of Expert Panel Overseeing Sanctions Against Democratic People's Republic of Korea Until 30 April 2023. 25 March 2022, *UN Meeting Coverage*. https://www.un.org/press/en/2022/sc14841.doc.htm. Accessed: 25 March 2022.
UN (2022c). Secretary-General Condemns Ballistic Missile Launch by Democratic People's Republic of Korea as Breach of 2018 Moratorium. 1 February 2022, *United Nations Press Release*. https://www.un.org/press/en/2022/sgsm21127.doc.htm. Accessed: 25 March 2022.
UN (2022d). Secretary-General Strongly Condemns Launch of Intercontinental-Range Ballistic Missile by Democratic People's Republic of Korea. 24 March 2022, *United Nations Press Release*. https://www.un.org/press/en/2022/sgsm21206.doc.htm. Accessed: 25 March 2022.

UN (2022e). *Subsidiary Organs of the United Nations Security Council*. New York: United Nations.

US Department of the Treasury (2022). *Office of Foreign Assets Control – Sanctions Programmes and Information*. https://home.treasury.gov/policy-issues/office-of-foreign-assets-control-sanctions-programs-and-information. Accessed: 22 February 2022.

Wertz, Daniel (2020). *Understanding US and International Sanctions on North Korea*. Washington, D.C.: The National Committee on North Korea.

YNA (2017). Real Names of North Korean Missile Series: Hwaseong, Bukgeukseong, and Gwangmyungseong. 14 February 2017, *Yonhap News TV* [북한 미사일 진짜 이름은 '화성 · 북극성 · 광명성'. 연합뉴스 TV, 2017년 2월 14일자]. https://www.yna.co.kr/view/MYH20170214000900038. Accessed: 4 June 2021.

YNA (2022). N. Korea Seems to Have Fired Hwasong-15 ICBM Last Week, S. Korea's Military Tells Lawmakers. 29 March 2022, *Yonhap News Agency*. https://en.yna.co.kr/view/AEN20220329008000325. Accessed: 29 March 2022.

Yoshimura, Sachiko (2021). UN Economic Sanctions and Financial Measures – Evolution and Challenges. In: Sachiko Yoshimura (ed.). *United Nations Financial Sanctions*. New York: Routledge, pp. 1–17.

Young, Benjamin R. (2021). *North Korea in Africa: Historical Solidarity, China's Role, and Sanctions Evasion*. Special Report, No. 490. Washington, D.C.: United States Institute of Peace.

3 Resilience through Marketisation and the Digital Economy

According to most of the existing literature, the North Korean economy has survived due to marketisation from below (for example, Cha and Collins, 2018; Hazel, 2015; Lim and Yoon, 2011; Yeo, 2021). This implies that marketisation has sustained the country's fragile economy by overcoming the great famine and sanctions. However, this chapter challenges this dominant view by revisiting the development of North Korea's economic structure since the famine in the 1990s. Based on an in-depth look at more recent developments while building on existing research on North Korean marketisation, the chapter argues that the resilience of North Korea's hybrid economy, comprising socialist and free market structures, has been supported not only by marketisation from below but also by information and communications technology (ICT) development and a digital economy driven from the top. Also, it gives weight to the argument that North Korean marketisation did not occur truly autonomously from below but was enabled by the regime's tolerance of and adaptation to marketisation. The chapter reframes this latter account by suggesting that an enabling environment for marketisation within North Korea's socialist economy was created due to dysfunctional state capacity. This chapter delves into marketisation and ICT as well as the digital economy to explain how the Kim regime has been resilient to the prolonged sanctions and has further managed to fund its nuclear programme.

From Socialist Economy to Hybrid Economy

The development of the economy of North Korea can be understood in two main phases: before and after the food crisis in the 1990s. The food crisis of the 1990s brought about massive changes in the North Korean economic system. Economic growth had been gradually decreasing since the 1960s. When the Soviet bloc and thus Soviet assistance and energy supply to North Korea collapsed in the late 1980s, food and basic goods rations provided through the government's public distribution system (PDS) began to decline. In the 1990s, natural disasters further hampered the country by harshening the environment for state production, and the government eventually lost its ability to cope with the circumstances.

Under the post-Soviet socialist economic system, the North Korean regime managed the planned economy based on three main structures: the PDS; planned production; and centralised trade. The PDS in particular played an important

DOI: 10.4324/9781003390282-3

role as it helped the Kim regime to control people, to suppress consumption, to impose ideology, and to discipline labour (Min, 2002: 54 & 63). But as the PDS was grounded to a halt, the whole economic system began to dissolve. The North Korean government could no longer sustain production and supply, and ordinary people had to find their own way to survive. Under the socialist planned economy, private production was not allowed in principle. However, due to the economic hardship and the demand for self-survival, individual plots for cultivation began to expand and restrictions on local markets were eased. The free market mechanism of supply and demand was activated through these local markets.

Before this period, local markets were isolated within each region. Products like rice and corn were not allowed to be traded in the markets as those were controlled by the government through the PDS. The North Korean authority did not allow a free market system and local markets thus remained very limited. However, as people began to engage in 'trade' with greater autonomy, the boundaries of the markets grew to make room for *jangmadang* (grey, informal, or blanket markets), which literally means 'ground markets' or 'outdoor markets' in Korean. When *jangmadang* were initially created, they were not officially approved by the authority. In this regard, a so-called shadow economy—a term used interchangeably with unofficial, informal, hidden, second, or parallel economy—came into being through *jangmadang*.

In other words, starting from a small size, the market system rapidly grew and expanded based on the platform provided by *jangmadang*. Earning currency became an important means of livelihood. As people took their earnings from market activities, they became more reliant on markets than on the state. So-called 8•3 workers increased in numbers as more people sought to make money in the markets. Workers at state-owned firms or factories could be excused from mandatory labour by paying an 8•3 deposit, which originated in the 8•3 Consumer Goods Production Campaign. On 3 August 1984 (the expression '8•3' is from this date as Koreans tend to use a month-day rather than a day-month date system), Kim Jong-il announced this campaign to satisfy the needs of the public for food products and necessities. As state-owned stores were unable to provide sufficient stocks of goods due to increasing economic difficulties, people were allowed to produce consumer goods by using waste, recycled materials, and extra resources from state-owned firms and to sell them at 8•3 stores, for which they had to obtain certificates from the authority. By submitting these certificates at state factories, they were waived from doing mandatory labour at the factories while being able to earn more than their wages through 8•3 activities (Kim, 2017; Kim, 2018; Lee, 2018; Lim and Yoon, 2011; Min, 2002). Based on the legacy of 8•3 workers from the 1980s, their 'modern equivalent' 8•3 production units have become shadowy private enterprises (Lim and Yoon, 2011: 89). Some began to buy goods from either 8•3 stores or these shadowy private enterprises to sell in local markets at higher prices. By doing so, local markets became connected and formed the larger space of *jangmadang*.

As this market resource allocation system became the norm for ordinary people, the government officially introduced 'general markets' as authorised marketplaces, adopting a free market system in the socialist economy as part of its 7•1 Policy of Economic Management Improvement Measures, also known as the July 2002 economic reform. Since 2003, about 3,000 general markets have been established by converting existing local markets and *jangmadang* (Lee, 2018: 207). The regime decided to distribute 'markets' rather than food and goods as a temporary way of filling the gap created by a failure of the planned economy (Min, 2002: 88 & 185). The authority collected tax from the general markets, and as a result, its own financial dependency on the markets increased too. The coexistence of formal general markets and informal *jangmadang* has since continued. In a survey carried out by Yeo (2020: 644), about 70 per cent of defector respondents reported participating in the informal economy and about 50 per cent in the official economy. About 4 million North Koreans seem to earn their income through markets, and their income from the informal economy is 80 times higher than from state-sanctioned jobs. The expansion of blanket markets from below—for instance, *jangmadang*—prompted the authority to institutionalise the free market system within the socialist economy, and eventually, marketisation was carried out from above through the 2002 July economic reform.

Even though the 2002 reform turned many *jangmadang* into legal marketplaces, illegitimate market activities as well as illegal *jangmadang* did not disappear. Illegal trade—sometimes unofficially allowed by the government to sustain the economy—and smuggling activities continue to be conducted, mostly through the border regions between North Korea and China. Both tangible and intangible foreign products disallowed by the regime, such as external information, are included in these illicit movements. At *jangmadang*, vendors sell CDs and DVDs with covers of North Korean animations; however, these CDs and DVDs only initially play original North Korean cultural content before showing smuggled South Korean content, such as K-pop, K-drama, or K-film (Kim-S, 2021). A survey of North Korean defectors revealed that 83 per cent of the respondents who were involved in market activities had been impacted by outside information and foreign products (Cha and Collins, 2018). People now learn about how 'happiness' can be the core value of life through the lyrics of K-pop and the contents of K-drama. They gain knowledge, and thus, awareness of the importance of equality, women's empowerment, and quality of life. In addition, they absorb the cultures of capitalism and democratic society through South Korean products (Anguelov, 2019). Not only have illegal materials become easier to smuggle due to the small size of DVDs, USBs, and SD cards compared to video and cassette tapes, but gadgets have also become more versatile. With increasing mobile phone use, some North Koreans now watch or listen to South Korean drama and music using mobile phones (Kim-S, 2021). Traders sell second-hand portable MP3 or DVD players and mobile phones from China, and Chinese tourists also 'dump' their old gadgets in North Korea, given the increasing wealth in China. The use of mobile phones is discussed in greater detail later in this chapter.

At the same time, *jangmadang* have served as a platform for information sharing and have become venues for clandestine gatherings (Zadeh-Cummings, 2017). North Koreans increasingly use doublespeak for forbidden expressions, while using vocabulary that they are supposed to use in the public sphere. Using such secret or coded language in the form of doublespeak tends to build trust among those involved in illegal activities—for example, smuggling foreign media. They share unacceptable behaviour—such as criticising the regime—or illegitimate activities. In this context, new social or trade networks and partnerships are created (Kim-S, 2021; Yeo, 2020 & 2021). The shadow economy has served as a mechanism to 'corrode the regime's power by diminishing its control over society, encouraging scepticism about collective ideologies, and providing networks and material that can be used for opposition to the state' (Dukalskis, 2016: 287). While domestic information is controlled and foreign information is reproduced by the government, *jangmadang* have contributed to facilitating the influx of original information from outside the country into North Korea. Not only are people gaining more knowledge about the outside world, but they have also realised the gap between the information that the government produces and the information that shows the reality of their lives. An ignorant public has tended to become enlightened. In this way, the information inflows through the markets have challenged the regime's legitimacy even though this is not yet sufficient to change the regime (Yeo, 2020).

The shadow economy has thus created a 'shadow culture' (Anguelov, 2019: 67). The information influx has now reached the scale of a cultural influx. For example, it is evident that South Korean culture in the form of make-up, hairstyles, fashion, and the manner of speaking has become prevalent in North Korean society. Since the mid-1990s, women in North Korea have become breadwinners, mostly working at *jangmadang*. With *jangmadang* and thus marketisation widespread, women with purchasing power gained through trading at the markets have become the subject of the fashion industry in North Korea. Kim and Park (2019) define this phenomenon as '*Jangmadang* Beauty', which satisfies women's desire to express themselves and has become an innovative change in society. In the process of marketisation in the 2000s, the gap between the rich and the poor widened, and due to the increasing import of K-wave and Chinese goods, a futuristic approach was established in society. As the effects of currency reform took hold in the 2010s, a wider gap was observed, and people were able to compare South Korean, North Korean, and Chinese goods in the cosmetics industry. The wedding industry has similarly developed through this process. Yet, as access to make-up and fashion requires purchasing power, this new phenomenon has not necessarily spread among the entire population but is limited to the rich class. In other words, the adoption of uniquely South Korean expressions is more pervasive among those who have the financial capacity to access foreign media.

Both the shadow economy and shadow culture have created a shadow class in society. This shadow class exists outside the official class system called *songbun*, which literally means 'ingredient' in Korean but is rooted in the expression *chulsin songbun*, meaning the family background of a person in Korean. Traditionally, there are three main social classes in North Korea based on family origin: core; wavering; and hostile. While the members of the party or the elites are positioned in the core class, ordinary residents mostly belong to the wavering or hostile class. Here, for ordinary citizens who do not belong to political elite groups, this class system is more commonly known to comprise of 'officials, upper common people, lower common people, and people at the bottom' (Kim, 2018: 160). The *songbun* system clearly divides North Korean society and discriminates against citizens from birth based on their classification. However, since the 2000s, market actors—those who have become moneylenders, currency traders, big merchants, or international traders—have appeared as new upper- and middle-class groups in the context of an economic power class. They are those who have a capitalist's mindset, especially among the young generation, and those who are called *donju* (individual entrepreneurs), which literally means the owners of money in Korean as they own cash assets. These financially equipped population—mostly represented by *donju*—tend to bribe officials and buy privileged status in society. In this context, as of 2009, about 28 per cent of the population belonged to the core class, 45 per cent to the wavering, and 27 per cent the hostile (UN, 2014: 78). Previously, it was reported that the core comprised about 26 per cent, wavering about 21 per cent, and hostile about 53 per cent of the people in the 1970s (Hong, Park, and Ham, 2000: 197).

In other words, their growing capital-based power has allowed 'lower-class North Koreans to use private wealth and personal connections to access the markers of social status' (Robertson, 2016), and marketisation has thus provided individuals with not only a means of self-survival but also a method of social mobility (Lee, 2018). Marketisation is gradually dismantling the existing class system by restructuring social hierarchy (Lee, 2014). *Donju* and some others who gained private wealth are the new social class that has benefited from marketisation, outside of the *songbun* system. The emergence of *donju* also resulted in more inequality in society (Gray and Lee, 2021). Also, as most *donju* tend to be women, the effect of gender empowerment has increased. It is reported that more than 90 per cent of market actors are women in their 40s and 50s (Lee, 2018: 209; Smith, 2015). Traditionally, North Korea is a typical patriarchal society, and women were expected to take more responsibility for providing food to sustain the family during the famine. Ironically, this created more opportunities for women to earn cash in the markets, and as a result, more women than men have become *donju*. However, it remains unclear how much of the North Korean population is comprised of *donju* (Lee, 2018), or new wealthy middle class. It is also incorrect to see the new private wealth population, including *donju*, being truly free from government control. Thus, without knowing the exact current class make-up of North Korea, existing research has provided us with a vague image of the new wealthy population and *donju*'s status in the North Korean class system. Figure 3.1 clarifies the changes in the *songbun* system during the marketisation period in North Korea.

Regardless, the *donju*'s role is not limited to the market sector. Given the *donju*'s financial capacity, they have contributed to the growth of state-owned enterprises (Lim and Yoon, 2011). Their power has grown stronger as they have replaced some parts of the national banking system. The North Korean financial architecture is controlled by the state. During the economic turmoil, the government monetary and financial systems became dysfunctional, and thus, people avoided depositing their savings in banks. The national budget had very low liquidity already in

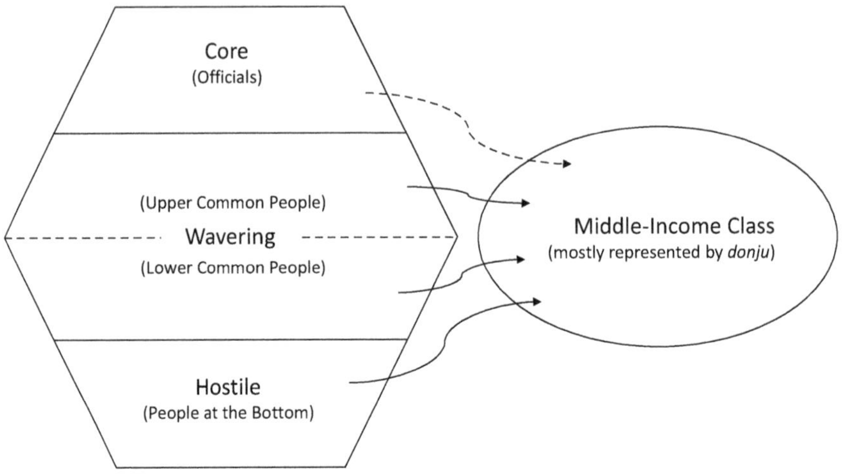

Figure 3.1 Changes in the *Songbun* System During Marketisation in North Korea.
Source: Author's own compilation.

the mid-1990s, and the monetary capacity remained with residents that became equivalent to a two-year national budget through marketisation, according to an internal document of the Chosun Labour Party as reported before the 7•1 measures in 2002 (Min, 2002: 111; Yang, 2020). Figure 3.2 shows the situation of the financial system of North Korea before and after the economic crisis in the 1990s.

Eventually, the official financial system became paralysed in a vicious cycle, as shown in Figure 3.3. While public banks ran out of liquidity, private finance—mostly provided by *donju*—filled the gap. Gradually, not only residents but also state-owned firms, trading companies, and cooperative farms began to borrow money from *donju* (Yang, 2020). In this way, *donju* have come to play a more important role in sustaining the finances of the regime and have thus gained a certain amount of power in the system as well as in society.

Against this backdrop, and to increase savings in central bank deposits for the proper working of the monetary circulation system, the government introduced a pre-paid card system for ordinary North Koreans in December 2010. By increasing liquidity in the national banking system, the government intended to increase its control over the market as well as the economy. A new card—named the Narae card—was issued by Chosun Trade Bank, with residents guided to deposit their money in the bank and pay with Narae card (Cho, 2011a). It is noteworthy that the North Korean card works more like a top-up card than a debit card. North Korean banks offer two kinds of accounts: accounts for payments and accounts for savings (Kim and Moon, 2021). It was reported that the North Korean authority forced foreigners, too, to use the Narae card by prohibiting them from exchanging cash and making them deposit foreign currency at the bank in order to collect this from them (Kim, 2015). Then, in 2015, Koryo Bank issued another card, called the

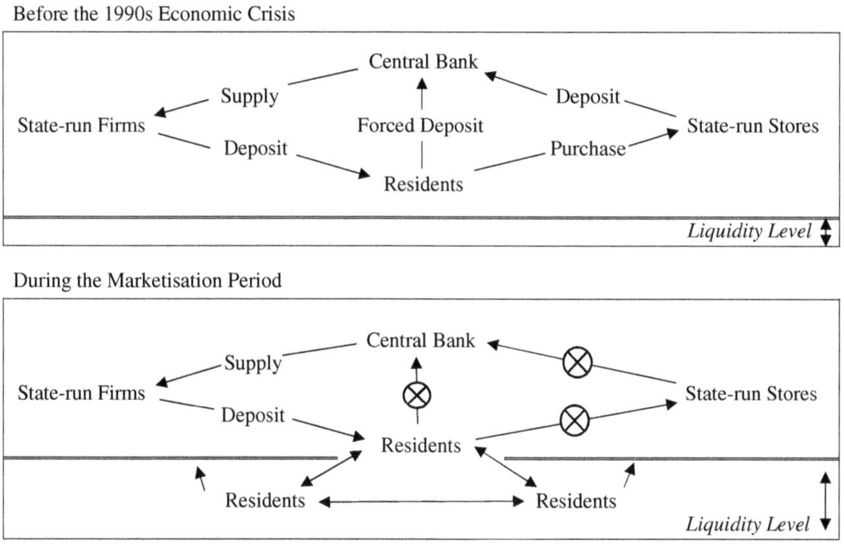

Figure 3.2 North Korean Monetary Cycle and Liquidity.

Source: Revised from Min, 2002: 114.

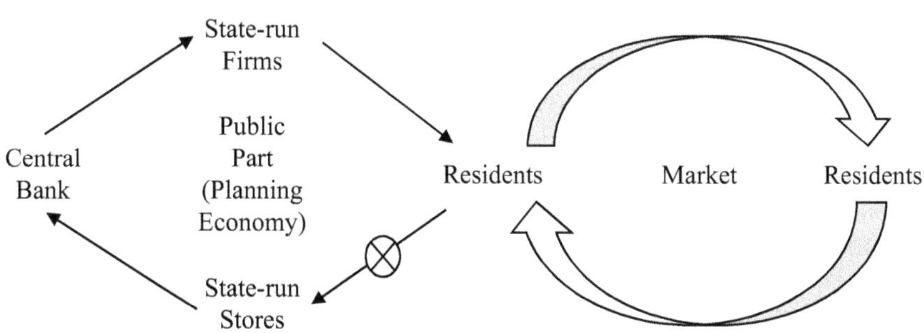

Figure 3.3 North Korean Finance Circulation During the Marketisation Period.

Source: Adapted from Yang, 2020.

Koryo card, which also worked as a 'debit card' (Cho, 2011b). While the Narae card allowed foreign currency deposits only, the Koryo card was available in the North Korean currency. By encouraging everyone, including foreign businesses and visitors, to use the cards, the government was attempting to collect cash at its banks. Following the introduction of the Narae and Koryo cards, other pre-paid cards were also issued, such as the Jeongsung card by Chosun Central Bank, the Geumgil card by Daesung Bank, and the Sunbong card by Golden Triangle Bank. Currently, more than 20 'debit cards' are known to be in use in North Korea. Among these, the use of the Sunbong card is limited to the Rason Special Economic Zone (Yim, 2015). North Korean pre-paid cards were initially available at mobile service centres and have since become available in stores and at cash dispenser machines.

Also, with the markets having expanded so fast, since 2005, the authority has tried to put a few new regulations in place to limit the expansion of the markets. For example, people younger than 40 years of age were prohibited from working as market vendors in 2005 (Lee, 2018). The regime announced the abolishment of general markets in 2008 (Min, 2002). Some *jangmadang* were closed. However, the Kim regime's anti-market measures as well as the 2009 currency reform were not successful, partially due to public discontent. Several occasions of unrest were reported (McNeill, 2010). In response, the state publicly executed Park Nam-ki, director of the Planning and Financial Department of the Central Committee of the Korean Workers' Party (KWP), in 2009 in Pyongyang, as a scapegoat, placing responsibility for the redenomination effort on him. Most existing research tends to interpret the attempted currency revaluation as Kim Jong-il trying to reassert the power of the command economy over the autonomy of marketisation (for example, see Cha and Collins, 2018). However, some scholars such as Min (2002) argue that the Kim regime's measures were never intended to entirely dismantle the market mechanism in North Korea, but more so to maximise the collection of revenue from people and to maintain control over the markets. As a matter of fact, North Koreans perceived it as a way to take away their saved seed money and to seize their assets.

In accordance with this, collusion between the authority and *donju* increased, as did the exclusion and monopoly of market activities. The *jangmadang* generation that grew up during the marketisation process with less of a socialist economic system is pro-money and less loyal to the regime. The concept of 'money is power' has been embedded in their minds. Famine as well as increasing involvement in *jangmadang* took people away from the government's ideological education. Students could not attend classes but had to go out onto the streets to look for food. Already in the late 1990s, students had reportedly begun avoiding classes and thinking that 'it is better to work in markets than going to school' (for instance, see Hong et al., 2000). Considering that the Arduous March began in the mid-1990s, the noticeable number of students who were already out of the state education system by the late 1990s confirms the severity of the situation. The number of *kotjebi*—the term used for those orphaned and made homeless during the famine—also increased in the 1990s. A surge of defections occurred during this period due to the economic hardship. For the *jangmadang* generation or millennials (those born between 1981 and 1996), daily survival became more critical than regime survival. They could not attend school and were thus excused from the state's ideology of education. Later, Gen(eration) Z (those born between 1997 and 2012) joined this trend. For Gen Z, media content from outside North Korea is savvier than the state's ideology (Kim-S, 2021). For both groups, 'money' is more important than their loyalty to the regime, and they have yielded a new generation of defectors who are looking for (economic) freedom (see also Chapter 4).

It has become clear that marketisation is irreversible. Accordingly, strong reforms to repress market activities have been abandoned. When Kim Jong-un succeeded Kim Jong-il in 2011, he implemented the 'economic management methods of our style' and proclaimed his *byungjin* policy, which means simultaneous economic and military development by embracing the market system within the economy. Later, in 2018, he changed his policy further towards economic development. Meanwhile, there have been noticeable advancements in communications technology and with regard to the internet in the North Korean economy under Kim Jong-un.

Mobile Communication Revolution and the Digital Economy

During the pre-Kim Jong-un period, mobile phones were used mostly by a very limited number of high-level officials and mostly *donju*. When Kim Jong-un came to power, he allowed greater use of mobile phones even though it was still seemingly limited. As a result, as of 2020, about 4.5 million people are known to own mobile phones in North Korea, while 6 million subscribers—about 20 per cent of the population—are registered with the provider *Koryolink*, implying that some have more than one mobile phone (Korea JoongAng Daily, 2020; Lee, 2018: 221). It seems that Kim has pushed advancements in ICT, including both the mobile network and the internet. For instance, although users as well as items are limited, online shopping is available on mobile phones. During the 8th Party Congress in January 2021, Kim Jong-un noted that 'the field should step up technical updating of its infrastructure and turn mobile communications into a next-generation one as early as possible by developing the relevant technology' and added that 'the telecommunications sector needs to upgrade its infrastructure' (Rodong Sinmun, 2021a). At the congress, Kim further emphasised 'Korean-style socialist construction'.

As mobile communication has become more popular along with marketisation, the so-called digital economy has added to the survival system, whereas *jangmadang* sustained individuals and helped them survive the Arduous March in the late 1990s. Here, there have been four main changes in North Korea's economy and society with the recent development of this digital economy. First, at the market level, mobile phones have become a crucial part of trade in North Korea. Using mobile phones in markets is now an important attributing factor to wider income generation for market actors. Mobile phones are used not only to make payments (Kim, 2020), but their use has also become a crucial tool to bargain over market price without requiring physical contact between buyers and sellers. As both buyers and sellers can negotiate the price of goods over mobile calls, this has increased business opportunities for actors, contributing to the culture of 'trust-based business' in society (Choi, 2021). Wholesalers (sellers) do not even need to physically go to marketplaces to sell their products because vendors (buyers) can place orders with them over the mobile phone. Upon receipt of goods, buyers pay for the products at local remittance houses called *igwanjib* and then the sellers confirm receipt of payment with the *igwanjib* over the mobile phone (Kim, 2014).

Second, by taking away the need for people to physically move around, mobile communication has contributed to the expansion of businesses to remote places. In terms of delivery of goods, when the order is placed, a supplier sends the product using a logistics system called *servicha* (Cha, 2018; Lee, 2018)—'servi' is from the English word 'service', while '*cha*' is Korean for 'car'.[1] In other words, the mobile communication revolution has led to the development of the service industry in North Korea by overcoming the immobility of people. With the unofficial easing of mobility restrictions, coinciding with mobile phone user expansion, mobility between regions has been activated. As mentioned, customers began to place orders for goods by mobile phones, with delivery happening between regions. Due to the poor train system, there has been a lack of long-distance logistics and supply chains in North Korea. Accordingly, some people, mostly *donju*, began buying or (illegally) renting lorries, vans, military vehicles, buses, motorbikes, and taxis from military camps, public businesses, or Chinese traders and replacing runner merchants. Petrol was illegally purchased from military camps or smuggled in from China or Russia. This *servicha* system had already come into being in the mid-1990s as a private logistics service system, and it initially operated within the region. However, with the increasing number of mobile phone users, the *bus-servicha* service was invented, and delivery services between cities began to expand from 2010 onwards. As *servicha* has become popular in North Korea, it has been almost impossible for the authority to stop the system, at least from 2014 onwards, and thus, *servicha* has been able to move across regions. Not only goods but also money is delivered by *servicha* (Cha, 2018; Han, 2017; Lee, 2018). Figure 3.4 shows how the *servicha* system works. The immobility barrier has been

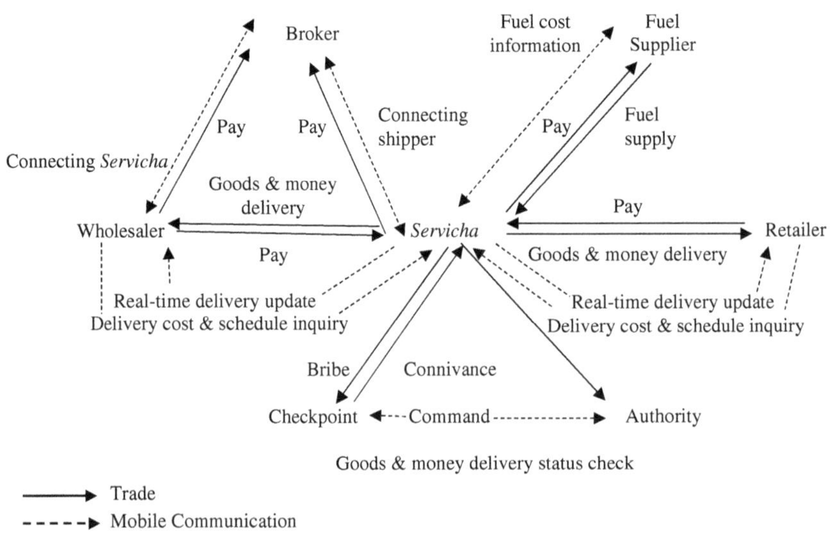

Figure 3.4 Servicha System in North Korea.

Source: Revised from Cha, 2018.

broken in North Korean society by the *servicha* system that has been accelerated by marketisation and mobile technology development.

Third, with the proliferation of mobile phone usage, there has been an increase in person-to-person contacts at the mobile phone charging service centres where people top-up mobile phone credits for pre-paid minutes (Kim-S, 2021). Therefore, the activity of using mobile phones serves the function of an information dissemination channel. At the same time, the mobile phone revolution has accelerated information and cultural influxes into North Korean society. As briefly mentioned earlier, North Koreans can access foreign media by inserting USBs or SD cards containing K-pop or K-drama into their mobile phones. An increasing number of North Korean youth carry South Korean contents in their mobile phones. In other words, ICT development accelerated by the Kim regime has resulted in more active information influx into society albeit this was not the intention of the regime. As a result, the government authority randomly searches mobile phones in order to control the influx of foreign information through mobile phone use. For instance, 20 university students in Chongjin were caught listening to and watching South Korean products with their mobile phones and were sent to a labour-training centre (Kim, 2014). Mobile phones have now become both a part of the surveillance system and a route for propaganda. More analysis of mobile technology as a surveillance system and propaganda platform is provided in Chapter 4.

Fourth and finally, at the family level, mobile phones have become a crucial part of remittances. Remittances are known as an important financial modality to sustain the family economy in most developing countries, and it seems that defectors' remittance activities affect the family economy in North Korea as well. The international average for commissions on remittances was 7.9 per cent in 2018, but the rate for sending remittances from South to North Korea, through brokers, was around 30 per cent (Lee, 2019: 248). More than 50 per cent of North Korean defectors in South Korea between 2013 and 2014—rising to around 60 per cent since 2015—had wired remittances to their families (about 36 per cent to parents, about 38 per cent to siblings, and about 11 per cent to sons or daughters), which was a record number by the time of the 2020 border closure (Lee, 2019: 222). Even though the cost of sending remittances is very high, defectors in South Korea send money to their remaining families in North Korea in order to contribute to the family economy, to maintain a connection with their families, and/or to maintain the social status of their families (Kim-K, 2021; Lee, 2019). While a defector family's *songbun* tends to be relatively stable, the remaining family members are no longer treated the same as before since they tend to be socially and/or politically punished due to their joint responsibility for the family member's defection. Thus, remittances sent to the remaining family members enable them to bribe the authority so that they can escape the punishment. Also, there are cases of family members becoming *donju* owing to the accumulation of financial capacity from remittances (Kim-K, 2021).

Once they begin to generate income, defectors arriving and living in South Korea transfer money to their family members in North Korea through brokers.

A defector wires funds from their South Korean bank account or from a South Korean broker's bank account to a Chinese broker's bank account in China. The broker then delivers cash from the bank to the *igwanjib* located in the region near where the recipient family lives. Sometimes, a *donju* plays the role of both broker and *igwanjib*. A recipient family member in North Korea collects money from the *igwanjib* (Kim-K, 2021; Kim-S, 2021). Before the availability of mobile phones, family members had to collect cash directly in the border region, with mobility not allowed in most cases. However, with the expansion of mobile phone accessibility, and thus, the emergence of *igwanjib*, sending remittances between defectors and remaining families has become a lot simpler and easier (Kim-K, 2021). Also, as the 'trust network' has built up with the conduct of business through mobile communications (see Lee, 2019), pre-collection of remittances through a broker or at an *igwanjib* has become available as *donju* (brokers or owners of *igwanjib*) have good levels of liquidity. For example, a North Korean can borrow money from a broker or *igwanjib*, and request remittance of the money to their defected family member in South Korea, with the broker and *igwanjib* then able to collect it (with commission) later. Since the COVID-19 border closure, the commission rate has gone up to 50 per cent as the risks have increased or the liquidity of brokers or *igwanjib* has decreased (Kim-K, 2021: 121–124 & 129), and this has become another threat to the North Korean economy to a certain extent.

In some cases, a method known as the 'mobile phone kiss' is used to confirm receipt of remittances. The broker from China meets the broker from North Korea in the China–North Korea border region, or even in North Korea itself. While the broker from China calls the defector sending the remittance in South Korea, the other broker from North Korea calls the family member receiving the remittance in North Korea. Upon doing so, the two brokers touch their mobile phones together—hence the expression 'mobile phone kiss'—so that the family members can speak to one another. Due to the need to avoid surveillance, this conversation tends not to last long, but it is long enough for the defector to share about their life in South Korea, and thus, more North Koreans with financial affordability of this practice learn of the gap between the two countries (Kim, 2014; Kim-S, 2021). Some previous recipients of remittances have since become senders of remittances, having defected from North to South Korea based on their experience of indirect income generation outside of North Korea (Lee, 2019). Not only that, but defector interviews also confirm that mobile phone communication plays a 'critically instrumental role' in the defection journey (for example, see Kang and Chib, 2018: 3546). Here, it is noteworthy that mobile phone use is not yet widely prevalent among ordinary North Korean citizens. As mentioned earlier, only about 20 per cent of the population is registered with the country's mobile provider. In many cases, bribery has become the norm to access mobile communication or to be excused by the authority upon getting caught in the illegitimate activity (Kim-K, 2021). Nevertheless, it is evident that the use of mobile phones has recently increased and become a critical part of life in North Korea for some, but not for the entire population.

ICT in North Korea has gradually advanced, not only for mobile phones but also for the country's intranet system called *Kwangmyong*. Before the so-called third-generation mobile phone system was launched in 2008, the nationwide intranet network was introduced in 2002 (Bruce, 2012). North Korea Tech[2] is a web-based platform, affiliated with the Stimson Center–run project 38 North,[3] which provides up-to-date information and analysis about North Korea's communications and internet technology. According to North Korea Tech, only high-level officials, aid workers, diplomats, and foreign tourists have limited access to the internet, while ordinary North Koreans are only allowed to access the intranet. There are some very limited occasions when university students are allowed to participate in online seminar series over the internet, but in most cases, students at major universities in North Korea tend to use the intranet for remote online learning as part of the North Korean distance education system (for example, see Williams, 2021a & 2021b). Since the COVID-19 lockdown when some of the foreign academics working in universities in Pyongyang had to leave the country, students have received their lectures through the internet while academics deliver their lectures online from other countries.

Amid COVID-19 national self-isolation, the government conducted its annual expo—the National Exhibition of Information Technology (IT) Successes—online (Williams, 2022). In 2020, 'national development strategies for the digital economy', along with the introduction of 3D printing, the possible adoption of artificial intelligence technology, robotics, the Internet of Things, facial recognition systems, and e-commerce and e-payment, were discussed in North Korea (Park, 2020). A discussion of such issues suggests that IT development in North Korea is not much different from that taking place at the global level.[4] However, the actual users of such IT are highly limited to a privileged few, comprising about 5 per cent of the country's entire population (Bruce, 2012: 2). In other words, use of the internet as well as the intranet in North Korea is strictly limited to a very small share of the populace.

The regime's advancement of IT and its push towards a digital economy are aimed at gaining greater strategic control of the population, for instance, by using big data methods (Hayes, Bruce and Mardon, 2011). At the same time, as mentioned earlier, the regime is trying to promote an e-commerce and e-payment system. Seemingly, this is because the 'origin and destination of these online transactions can be difficult to trace' (Bartlett, 2020). The demand for science and technology development is also linked to the opportunities in cyberspace for further evasion of sanctions (Park, 2022). An increasing number of illegal cyber fundraising cases linked to North Korean cyberattacks have been observed. In 2018, it was reported that an estimated USD 15–200 million in bitcoin was created and sold, and turned into hard currency (Ward, 2018).

The problem here is not only the evasion of sanctions but also the regime's use of illicitly gained cybercurrency for weapons development. Also, the lack of enforceable laws against cybercrime has resulted in the North Korean regime having digital financial autonomy. Neither the hackers nor the regime is likely to be punished for their cybercrimes any time soon. For example, in a case that involved

North Korean hackers attempting to steal USD 1.3 billion in cryptocurrency, three North Korean officers known to be working in the Reconnaissance General Bureau, the North Korean military intelligence hacking group, were charged in a United States (US) court (The Guardian, 2021). However, only a US expert, Virgil Griffith, was actually sentenced to prison—for more than five years—for his alleged involvement in helping North Korea evade sanctions with cryptocurrency in April 2022 (BBC, 2022). It was only in 2022 that the Australian government announced a plan to introduce cyber security laws (see Fildes, 2022). The United Kingdom published its new foreign policy document in 2021, which mentions its aim to become a leader in global cyber regulation and its existing cyber security hub (see HM Government, 2021); however, it is unclear when and how global cyber regulation will begin to take effect. North Korea's ongoing transformation into a digital economy, along with its cyber activities, seems to have become a new challenge for the international community.

Marketisation Reconsidered

As seen, marketisation has brought about changes and greater autonomy in North Korean society. While aware that markets could become a potential threat to it, the regime could not crack down on the emerging system entirely. A few measures were imposed to balance and restrict the market power, but the regime also allowed the emergence of a dual system of official and unofficial economies because the shadow (or unofficial) economy sustained the country while the government could not perform its supposed function in the national economy. The digital economy with mobile phones then reinforced this existing self-survival system. At the same time, the development of ICT has made the regime stronger militarily as a new mode of sanctions evasion in the form of internet hacking and illicit cybercurrency has evolved to fund the regime's nuclear programme development. In other words, sanctions evasion methods have transformed from the physical to the virtual.

It is hard to find evidence in existing studies of any significant impact that sanctions have had on the North Korean economy, except for increasing sacrifices at the citizen level. North Korea already had a dysfunctional state economy in the 1980s, even before multilateral sanctions were imposed. Past heavy reliance on the Soviets hampered the state's planned production and distribution system for its people when the Soviet Union collapsed, with natural disasters worsening economic conditions in the 1990s. In any case, North Korea's trade was not highly dependent on international markets, and it did not receive any significant amount of official development assistance (ODA) or development aid support from others. Thus, considering that the people of North Korea had not been the beneficiaries of massive ODA or dynamic international trade relations, sanctions have not had much impact on the North Korean economy. Economic hardship and self-survival already prevailed and had long been the norm in people's lives.

In this context, some would argue that a greater information influx would be more effective than sanctions in bringing about regime change in the case of North Korea. The digital economy has not only favoured the regime but has also contributed to societal changes to some extent. With the development of ICT and the digital economy with mobile phones, the gap between political information and external information has led to people changing within a shadow society. More mobile phones are allowed, and there is greater access to foreign information and culture. A culture of resistance at the individual level has been seeded against the government's restrictions and suppression in the course of the *jangmadang*'s survival. While the state tries to oppress citizens, the citizens too have become assertive in maintaining their self-survival system. But then why has there not been a massive uprising in North Korean society yet, as observed in other countries? With the recent COVID-19 lockdown, the government is believed to have imposed further restrictions on society as well as on markets. Once the economic and social systems are changed, they are irreversible. It would thus be reasonable to expect a stronger rebellious movement in North Korean society against the regime.

However, it is highly unlikely that we will see a popular uprising in North Korea in the near future. If we consider the Arab Spring, for example, and consider what we observed there and what is missing in the case of North Korea, we see that gaining more information may be necessary but not sufficient to give rise to activism. People should be able to creatively and freely share their opinions based on the information in the public sphere. During the Arab Spring in 2011, people utilised social media as a tool with their mobile phones. The use of social media, along with the use of mobile phones, made it possible for people to exchange ideas and opinions, leading to an online campaign by activists. More importantly, those who were empowered (as leaders who converted ideas and opinions into actions) were at the core of the movement (Goldin, 2013). In North Korea, we now know that there are a growing number of internet-savvy youth; however, they are not free to use hashtags or to criticise the government. Public frustration has been cloaked rather than widely or openly shared. The politics of fear still works. As mentioned earlier, while mobile communication has benefitted both the economy and society, IT development has also created a new generation of surveillance system. Moreover, the structure of society and relations between the authority and newly created rich groups have contributed to the unlikelihood of a strong societal movement for regime change in North Korea. In relation to this, the next chapter navigates civil society in North Korea and analyses how the conditions for (possible) collective action against the government are different for North Koreans and unlike those for people in other countries.

Notes

1 The creation of terms such as *servicha* can be considered a result of the cultural influx into North Korea from foreign countries. Combining English ('service') and Korean (*cha*, meaning car) is not common in North Korea. Many North Korean defectors arriving in South Korea tend to say that one of the most difficult adjustments for them is acclimatising to the adoption of foreign vocabulary into South Korean expressions. For instance, the word 'lift' (or 'elevator' in American English) is written as *sengganggi* in

the Korean alphabet (*Hangul*) in official South Korean documents, but South Koreans use the word 'elevator', as it sounds, in daily verbal conversations or unofficial writings. Ice-cream is called 'ice-cream', as it sounds, in South Korea and is also written as 'ice-cream' in *Hangul*. However, in North Korea, ice-cream is called *ureum-bosung-i*, meaning ice junk or paste. South Koreans do not use the expression *bosung-i* but *gomul* instead. Currently, the South Korean Ministry of Unification provides a comparison table for South and North Korean vocabularies and expressions on its website (https://unibook.unikorea.go.kr/data/dictionary). While the two Koreas share the same language, the development of certain vocabularies and expressions has varied since the Korean War.

2 https://www.northkoreatech.org/.

3 https://www.38north.org/.

4 In this context, for North Korea, 'access to the internet' can be more about expanding the regime's propaganda and the Kim family's cult of personality to wider audiences at the global level. Nowadays, it is not uncommon to find accounts with fake individual names that are run by, or include the participation of, the North Korean authority, not only on Twitter and Facebook but also on YouTube. For example, while there are quite a few Twitter accounts under the name and photo of either Kim Jong-un or Kim Yo-jong, the YouTube channel 'Echo of Truth', run by vlogger 'Un A', is quite popular as she presents clips in English and other languages, and has been one of the most known propaganda media backed by the North Korean government. In a Facebook group called 'North Korea Study Group', a member by the name of 'Kim So Ho' frequently posts information about and photos of ongoing activities in North Korea, mostly in North Korean syntaxes but sometimes in English, along with Korean texts. In this case, the name 'Kim So Ho' can be a fake, which is unlikely to be a real name of the person who posts messages in this group.

References

Anguelov, Nikolay (2019). Popular Culture in Transitional Societies: An Eastern European Perspective. In: Youna Kim (ed.). *South Korean Popular Culture and North Korea*. New York: Routledge, pp. 67–80.

Bartlett, Jason (2020). Exposing the Financial Footprints of North Korea's Hackers. 18 November 2020, *Center for a New American Security*. https://www.cnas.org/publications/reports/exposing-the-financial-footprints-of-north-koreas-hackers. Accessed: 15 March 2022.

BBC (2022). *US Cryptocurrency Expert Jailed for Helping North Korea Evade Sanctions*. 13 April 2022. https://www.bbc.co.uk/news/business-61090064 Accessed: 13 April 2022.

Bruce, Scott Thomas (2012). *A Double-Edged Sword: Information Technology in North Korea*. Asia Pacific Issues No. 105. Hawaii: East-West Center.

Cha, Sehyun (2018). Logistics Revolution With Servicha and Mobile Phones in North Korea. 2 June 2018, *The JoongAng* [차세현 (2018). 북한은 '서비차' 물류혁명 중, 휴대전화 주문, 어디든 배송. 중앙 Sunday, 2018년 6월 2일자] https://www.joongang.co.kr/article/22679034#home. Accessed: 15 March 2022.

Cha, Victor and Lisa Collins (2018). The Markets: Private Economy and Capitalism in North Korea? 26 August 2018, *Beyond Parallel – CSIS Korea Chair*. https://beyondparallel.csis.org/markets-private-economy-capitalism-north-korea/. Accessed: 15 March 2022.

Cho, Minjung (2011a). North Korean Check Card, NaRae. 18 March 2011, *Yonhap News* [IC칩 내장 북한 체크카드 '나래' 공개. 연합뉴스, 2011년 3월 18일자] https://www.yna.co.kr/view/AKR20110318090800014. Accessed: 15 March 2022.

Cho, Minjung (2011b). North Korean Card, Koryo. 14 October 2011, *Yonhap News* [北고려은행 전자결제카드 '고려' 발행. 연합뉴스, 2011년 10월 14일자] https://www.yna.co.kr/view/AKR20111014091800014. Accessed: 15 March 2022.

Choi, Sunkyung (2021). Mobile Phone Use and the 'Trust' Network of Market Activity in North Korea. *Review of North Korean Studies*, 24(1): 7–40 [최선경 (2021). 북한 주민의 휴대폰 사용과 시장 활동에서의 '신뢰' 네트워크. 현대북한연구, 24(1): 7-40].

Dukalskis, Alexander (2016). North Korea's Shadow Economy: A Force for Authoritarian Resilience or Corrosion? *Europe: Asia Studies*, 68(3): 487–507.

Fildes, Nic (2022). Australia to Pass Cyber Laws to Protect Critical Networks Against Foreign Attacks. 30 March 2022, *Financial Times*. https://www.ft.com/content/e552819e-e3ea-47a9-ad5e-bf826481fd33. Accessed: 1 April 2022.

Goldin, Ian (2013). *Divided Nations: Why Global Governance Is Failing, and What We Can Do About It*. Oxford: Oxford University Press.

Gray, Kevin and Jong-Woon Lee (2021). *North Korea and the Geopolitics of Development*. Cambridge: Cambridge University Press.

Han, Youngjin (2017). Servicha in North Korea. 9 January 2017, *RFA* [한영진 (2017). 북한의 서비차 서비버스를 아시나요? 자유아시아방송, 2017년 1월 9일자] https://www.rfa.org/korean/weekly_program/c27dac8c-d480c5b4bcf4b294-bd81d55c-bb3cac00/priceindex-01052017152045.html. Accessed: 15 March 2022.

Hayes, Peter, Scott Bruce and Dyana Mardon (2011). North Korea's Digital Transformation: Implications for North Korea Policy. 8 November 2011, *NAPSNet Policy Forum*. https://nautilus.org/napsnet/napsnet-policy-forum/north-koreas-digital-transformation-implications-for-noth-korea-policy. Accessed: 15 March 2022.

HM Government (2021). *Global Britain in a Competitive Age: The Integrated Review of Security, Defence, Development and Foreign Policy*.

Hong, Sunho, Joonyoung Park and Inhee Ham (2000). *Understanding North Korea and Korea Peninsula*. Seoul: Salim Publishing [홍순호, 박준영, 함인희 (2000). 북한 인식과 한반도. 서울, (주)살림출판사].

Kang, Juhee and Richard Ling Arul Chib (2018). The Flip: Mobile Communication of North Korean Migrant Women During Their Journey to South Korea. *International Journal of Communication*, 12: 3533–3552.

Kim, Byung-Yeon (2017). *Unveiling the North Korean Economy: Collapse and Transition*. Cambridge: Cambridge University Press.

Kim, Kyoung Ryeol (2021). Remittance Analysis of North Korean Defectors: The Actor-Network Theory. *Review of North Korean Studies*, 24(3): 107–142 [김경렬 (2021). 북한이탈주민의 송금 분석 : 행위자-연결망 이론(ANT)을 중심으로. 현대북한연구, 12: 107-142].

Kim, Kyungyoon (2020). Mobile Payment System Developed in North Korea. 21 October 2020, *Yonhap News* [김경윤 (2020). 북한에도 'ㅇㅇ페이' 등장하나, 휴대폰 통한 결제시스템 개발. 연합뉴스, 2020년 10월 21일자] https://www.yna.co.kr/view/AKR20201021053300504. Accessed: 15 March 2022.

Kim, Minjung and Sungmin Moon (2021). *North Korean Financial System During Kim Jong-un's Period*. BOK Economy Study 2021-6. Seoul: Bank of Korea. [김민정, 문성민 (2021). 김정은 시대 북한의 금융제도 변화 – 북한 문헌 분석을 중심으로. BOK 경제연구 제2021-6호. 서울, 한국은행].

Kim, Seok Hyang (2018). *Story by North Korean Defectors About North Korea*. Seoul: Konrad Adenauer Stftung [김석향 (2018). 북한이탈주민이 들려주는 북녘 땅 고향 이야기. 서울, 콘라드 아데나워 재단].

Kim, Seok Hyang and Minju Park (2019). *"Women in North Chosun", Expressing Hidden Desire Through Jangmadang Beauty*. Seoul: Sunin [김석향, 박민주 (2019). "북조선 여성", 장마당 뷰티로 잠자던 욕망을 분출하다!. 서울, 도서출판 선인].

Kim, Suk-Young (2021). *Millennial North Korea: New Media Technologies and Living Creatively with Surveillance*. Presentation at the 12th Critical Issues Form, Center for Korean Studies at the University of Hawaii. 31 March 2021, Webinar.

Kim, Yonho (2014). *Cell Phones in North Korea: Has North Korea Entered the Telecommunications Revolution?* Washington, D.C.: US Korea Institute at SAIS and Voice of America.

Kim, Yongman (2015). North Korea Forces Foreigners to Use Pre-Paid Card System. 5 June 2015, *Yonhap News* [김영만 (2015). 북한, 외국인들에 카드결제 강요하며 폭리 챙겨. 연합뉴스, 2015년 6월 5일자] https://www.yna.co.kr/view/AKR20150605041900014. Accessed: 15 March 2022.

Korea JoongAng Daily (2020). *18 Percent of North Koreans Now Thought to Own Mobile Phones.* 11 August 2020. https://koreajoongangdaily.joins.com/2020/08/11/business/tech/North-Korea-smartphone/20200811180400430.html. Accessed: 15 March 2022.

Lee, Haejung (2018). Market Individualisation in North Korea and Its Implications. In: Ewha Womans University North Korea Research Group (ed.). *Kim Jong Un's Regime: What Has Changed and What Hasn't*. Seoul: Hanul Academy, pp. 203–227 [이해정 (2018). 이화여대 북한연구회 (엮음), '김정은 체제 : 변한것과 변하지 않는 것' 중 제7장, 북한의 사경제화 현황과 시사점.서울, 한울 아카데미].

Lee, Ji Yeon (2019). Performativity of North Korean Migrants' Family Remittances and Governmentality in the South-North Korean Division. *Economy and Society*, 12: 221–254 [이지연 (2019). 탈북민의 북한 가족 송금의 수행성과 분단 통치성. 경제와 사회, 12: 221–254].

Lim, Jae-Cheon and In Joo Yoon (2011). Institutional Entrepreneurs in North Korea: Emerging Shadowy Private Enterprises Under Dire Economic Conditions. *North Korean Review*, 7(2): 82–93.

Lee, Woo-young (2014). The Process of Social Change in North Korea. In: Jong-Woo Han and Tae-Hern Jung (eds.). *Understanding North Korea: Indigenous Perspectives*. New York: Lexington Books, pp. 131–146.

McNeill, David (2010). North Korean Blamed for Currency Crash is Executed. 19 March 2010, *Independent*. https://www.independent.co.uk/news/world/asia/north-korean-blamed-for-currency-crash-is-executed-1923810.html. Accessed: 15 March 2022.

Min, Young-ki (2002). *Money and Market in North Korea: Supreme Leader, Money, Market*. Seoul: Hanul Academy [민영기 (2002). 북한의 화폐와 시장 : 수령, 돈, 시장. 서울, 한울 아카데미].

Park, Jae-hyuk (2020). North Korea Seeks Digital Transformation in 2020. 5 January 2020, *The Korea Times*. https://www.koreatimes.co.kr/www/nation/2021/06/103_281423.html. Accessed: 15 March 2022.

Park, June (2022). *Cyber-Hacking as a Means of "Self-reliance": North Korea's Rensomware-Based Cyber-hacking for Economic Gains in the Absence of Regulations on Cryptocurrencies in Global Finance*. Understanding North Korea Paper Series. Washington, D.C.: National Committee on North Korea, and Woodrow Wilson Center.

Robertson, Phil (2016). North Korea's Caste System: The Trouble With Songbun. 30 June 2016, *Foreign Affairs*. https://www.foreignaffairs.com/articles/north-korea/2016-06-30/north-koreas-caste-system. Accessed: 15 March 2022.

Rodong Sinmun (2021a). *Great Programme for Struggle Leading Korean-style Socialist Construction to Fresh Victory on Report Made by Supreme Leader Kim Jong Un at Eighth Congress of WPK*. 10 January 2021. http://www.rodong.rep.kp/en/index.php?strPageID=SF01_02_01&newsID=2021-01-10-0004. Accessed: 15 March 2022.

Smith, Hazel (2015). *North Korea: Markets and Military Rule*. Cambridge: Cambridge University Press.

The Guardian (2021). *US Charges Three North Korean Hackers Over USD 1.3 bn Cryptocurrency Attacks*. 17 February 2021. https://www.theguardian.com/technology/2021/feb/17/north-korea-hack-cryptocurrency-us-charges. Accessed: 15 March 2022.

UN (2014). *Report of the Detailed Findings of the Commission of Inquiry on Human Rights in the Democratic People's Republic of Korea*. A/HRC/25/CRP.1. Human Rights Council.

Ward, Alex (2018). How North Korea Uses Bitcoin to Get Around US Sanctions. 28 February 2018, *Vox*. https://www.vox.com/world/2018/2/28/17055762/north-korea-sanctions-bitcoin-nuclear-weapons. Accessed: 15 March 2022.

Williams, Martyn (2021a). North Korean University Links With Foreign Lecturers for Live Internet Seminars. 14 May 2021, *North Korea Tech*. https://www.northkoreatech.org/2021/05/14/north-korean-university-links-with-foreign-lecturers-for-live-internet-seminars/. Accessed: 15 March 2022.

Williams, Martyn (2021b). Smartcard Login for Distance Education. 21 July 2021, *North Korea Tech*. https://www.northkoreatech.org/2021/07/01/smartcard-login-for-distance-education/. Accessed: 15 March 2022.

Williams, Martyn (2022). North Korea's Online IT Exhibitions. 12 January 2022, *North Korea Tech*. https://www.northkoreatech.org/2022/01/12/north-koreas-online-it-exhibitions/. Accessed: 15 March 2022.

Yang, Moon-Soo (2020). *Assessing North Korea's Financial 'Reform' Measures: Mobilising Domestic Financial Resources amid Sanctions*. GW Institute for Korean Studies North Korea Economic Forum Special Public Webinar. 17 December 2020, Webinar.

Yeo, Andrew (2020). Assessing Domestic Change and Continuity in North Korea. *Asian Studies Review*, 44(4): 641–651.

Yeo, Andrew (2021). *State, Society, and Markets in North Korea*. Cambridge: Cambridge University Press.

Yim, Eunjin (2015). North Korean Golden Triangle Bank Issued Pre-Paid Card, Sunbong. 12 August 2015, *Yonhap News* [임은진 (2015). 북한 황금의삼각주은행, 선불카드 '선봉' 발행. 연합뉴스, 2015년 8월 12일자] https://www.yna.co.kr/view/AKR20150812159500014. Accessed: 15 March 2022.

Zadeh-Cummings, Nananin (2017). Illusion of Independence: North Korea's "Civil Organizations" and NGOs. 12 October 2017, *NK News*. https://www.nknews.org/2017/10/illusion-of-independence-north-koreas-civil-organisations-and-ngos. Accessed: 15 March 2022.

4 Street-Level Bureaucrats and Cloaked Society

It is not uncommon to think of North Korea as a country without civil society due to the regime's strong repressive strategy against its people. One could argue that the absence of civil society in North Korea is mostly due to the prevailing legacy of Confucianism in North Korean society at large. Like other East Asian societies, North Korean society is governed by Confucian values, and the thinking goes that ordinary people are thus hesitant to challenge the state (Cotton, 1991; Park, 2009). However, this latter account needs to be reassessed in view of the case of, for example, South Korea. Confucian values are embedded in South Korean society as well, yet civil society movements have occurred throughout the democratisation process there. Thus, civil society's absence in North Korea is not down to its culture of Confucianism but has more to do with the regime's structure and the lack of freedom in the country. In this sense, the situation in North Korea could be better compared to cases of civil society formation in post-communist Central and Eastern European (CEE) countries, as the legacy of the old communist culture is similarly embedded in North Korea. However, as discussed in this chapter, there were waves of civil society mobilisation in CEE countries in the wake of the Soviet Union's collapse because an enabling environment for civil society movements had been created in these countries, which was not observed in North Korea.

Moreover, the case of North Korea is somewhat different from the South Korean case and the CEE cases as the environment is not enabling for ordinary people to develop adequate civil society or to organise mass protests capable of challenging the regime. There have been numerous opposition movements in areas such as Hamhung, Chongjin, Hoeryong, and Musan in North Korea. 'Disorganised resistance against the system's restrictions' has become the norm for North Koreans (Baek, 2016: 224). However, the incidents tend to be easily dismissed as they are 'sporadic, spontaneous, and chaotic, rather than well organised' (Park, 2009: 35). They have occurred on a very small scale due to food shortages or repression of the markets rather than due to political reasons. As seen in the previous chapter, there was public resistance against the 2009 currency reform. However, although the public discontent led to the government abandoning the reform, it did not take the form of mass protest or turn into a social movement that, for example, demanded freedom of trade. The resistance came more from those who had plenty of money as well as a certain amount of power to influence the government. During the marketisation process, for instance, the labour force itself reconciled with reality

DOI: 10.4324/9781003390282-4

and with the bureaucracy by providing the 8•3 deposit rather than organising collective action or unionising (see Chapter 3).

With this in mind, this chapter navigates why the discontent has tended to remain small scale, localised, and/or unorganised, and has not led to an upsurge in collective action in North Korea. It further looks at why it is difficult to create an enabling environment for civil society in this country. The chapter thus seeks the reason for the absence of civil society and/or a mass anti-regime movement even when people seem to be more empowered to influence the government's policy changes than before the marketisation period. In doing so, the chapter examines the existing literature on civil society to provide a better understanding of the term and to assess what might constitute a civil movement against the regime, including an enabling environment for mass protest, through a brief case analysis of CEE countries. The chapter then analyses changes in North Korean society and identifies the factors hindering North Korean civil society from becoming 'the cradle of change from the bottom'.

Understanding Civil Society

For the most part, people understand civil society to mean different political or social interest groups, or even more narrowly, to be equal in meaning to either civil society organisations (CSOs) or non-governmental organisations (NGOs). However, civil society extends beyond this simplistic understanding. Academics such as Edwards (2020), for instance, categorise civil society as a part of society, as a kind of society, and as an arena of social norms, while scholars like Spurk (2010) look at civil society either as a sector or as an intermediate sphere. More commonly, civil society tends to be viewed as institutions, associations, organisations, voices, or movements of people voluntarily participating in the public sphere. The concept of civil society that we use today is heavily influenced by Western European thought and the so-called liberal or neo-liberal tradition. It is noteworthy that 'cultural exchange' between West and East influenced the thinking of CEE civil society (Mastnak, 2005: 327), even though the Western approach was not that important in CEE countries at the time that civil society emerged there.

The contemporary definition of civil society can be understood to rest on two main pillars. First, civil society is an important part of democracy and carries out a political role as it facilitates the participation of citizens in democracy, including through the exercise of free voting rights. In Western Europe, the origins of the democratic character of civil society can be found in the late 18th and early 19th centuries. While civil society was considered part of the state in the 18th century, it emerged as a concept in contrast to the state in the late 18th and early 19th centuries as the power of political groups in civil society challenged European monarchies. In this process, the autonomy of the public political sphere was observed. Then, in the late 19th century, parliamentary democracy came into being based on political parties that worked as a contesting power against the state, which has since developed into the contemporary form of civil society (Bernhard, 1993). In comparison, the evolution of civil society in the context of democracy occurred somewhat differently in CEE countries.

In CEE countries, for instance, in Poland and Czechoslovakia, dissidence (or opposition to communism) emerged in the late 1970s, and dissident revisionists were boosted into the role of resistance groups within civil society against the state (Bernhard, 1993; Mastnak, 2005). The 'state–civil society distinction' was created by activities aiming to recreate an 'independent life of society' and to do so 'from below' (Mastnak, 2005: 333). In this way, civil society existed to challenge the bureaucratic regime in order to restore the political balance of power, but it did not challenge the state itself. In the case of Latin American social movements in the 1980s, in comparison, civil society played the role of a 'parallel democracy' or 'organic grassroots mechanism' that engaged with the state (May, 2005: 3). In the case of CEE countries, civil society was 'equated with democracy per se', with it 'becoming both the aim and the all-embracing actor of the democratic struggle' (Mastnak, 2005: 334). In this sense, it can be said that civil society worked as 'the cradle of democracy', as Purdue (2007: 1) has noted, in the transformation of CEE countries.

Most scholars argue that in the post-Soviet countries, political parties or forum politics functioned as the opposition against communism when civil society did not yet exist, and civil society was then gradually constructed along with the democratisation process (Miller and Klobucar, 2005; Taras, 2005). However, the fact is that the mobilisation of civil society had already been observed in these countries with the pulling down of the Berlin Wall in 1989, led by people from the grassroots (Taras, 2005), confirming the pre-existence of a culture of civil society in these countries. Also, in Hungary, during the 1980s, a new social movement—a new type of political activity—led the participation of about 1,000 people in influencing the existing social-political environment towards transformation (Visegrády, 1992). As Foa and Ekiert (2017: 419) have argued, 'vigorous public spheres and active civil society organisations' were already in place in CEE countries. The transition to democracy in post-communist societies was possible due to civil society mobilisation and civil society resistance activities. Also, there was a wave of civil society revolutions in the region, triggered by Soviet leader Mikhail Gorbachev's policies of *glasnost* (openness) and *perestroika* (restructuring) (Park, 2009; Visegrády, 1992). The role of civil society was important in dismantling communism in the CEE region, and as Mastnak (2005: 324) states, this holds the 'key to understanding recent Eastern European history'.

Second, civil society can be seen as an 'intermediary sphere between family, state, and market', and thus, as a 'sphere of social interactions situated between economy and state' (Zamruzzaman, 2019: 3). This means that civil society can be seen as a 'product of the nation-state and capitalism', mediating social life and the market economy (Edwards, 2020: 2). The notion of civil society or 'the people' encourages the 'development of a civic consciousness or democratic ethos' (May, 2005: 3). In this regard, structuralists argue that economic crises and reforms, such as market liberalisation leading from a socialist to a capitalist system, can result in political pluralism, the emergence of civil society, and thus regime change (Park, 2009).

However, this does not mean that civil society has separate political and economic aspects. As Giner (1995: 304–305) explains, civil society is a 'historically evolved sphere of individual rights, freedoms and voluntary associations' with the market as its structural feature. Civil society is different from the political and economic spheres. Rather, it is an intermediate sphere as it interacts with the state in both the political and economic spheres (Spurk, 2010). It is human nature to pursue good society and to reflect private life into the public sphere. However, this does not imply that all social or public realms can automatically mean civil society. Civil society contains collective public communications or social interactions and requires the collective and voluntary participation of individual members based on individual freedom guaranteed by the state.

While the types, numbers, and intensity levels were different, the outcomes were similar in all the CEE countries as a classical party state system was rapidly transformed into a democratic party system. Communist parties were removed from power, state institutions and constitutions were restructured, and parliaments and governments were redesigned in the democratisation process (Ekiert and Kubik, 1998). However, it is also noteworthy that there was a recurring chain reaction in these so-called non-democratic countries as the waves of civil mobilisation were followed by demobilisation, organisational atrophy, and passivity (Foa and Ekiert, 2017). In other words, civil society revolution or rapid civil society mobilisation itself does not guarantee sustainability. Thus, the gradual cultural development of civil society is required. More importantly, it was observed, for instance, in the case of Slovenia, that 'those who had taken possession of the old power apparatus and organised themselves in political parties, did not need to pose as the embodiment of civil society' (Mastnak, 2005: 349).

In the case of North Korea, the political system does not constitute forum politics nor a multi-party system. North Korea is distinguished by its strong one-party system. Recent marketisation has instilled some hope of change among those who see the potential for people's resistance in it. As seen in the previous chapter, the North Korean economy has adopted a capitalist free market system to some extent. However, even though this free market system exists in North Korea, the entire economy is under state control. For example, certain products, such as foreign media content, are still not free to trade. The 'power of the individual to spread information and mobilise others for change', which made the Arab Spring possible in 2011 (Goldin, 2013: 140), does not seem to be an immediate possibility in the case of North Korea. In light of this, the following discussion focuses on why, paying particular attention to the intermediary sphere between state, market, and family (people, and thus, society) with the marketisation process having been believed to be a trigger for critical changes in North Korea.

State, Market, and Society in North Korea

In North Korea, information is controlled and reframed by the regime. The information supply chain is monopolised by the government, and propaganda and the cult of personality have become the norm in media, films, and even children's animation. Before marketisation, North Koreans were completely blocked by the state from obtaining information from the outside, but the situation has been gradually changing. People are becoming more aware of the gap between the situation inside North Korea and the world outside. As analysed in the previous chapter, a shadow culture has been created from the shadow economy. Smuggled foreign culture is gradually becoming North Koreans' own culture. A culture of distrust in state propaganda has also been created. Not only market actors but also political elites have begun to enjoy foreign videos and music. As people become aware of the cultural dynamics in foreign media and are able to compare them to the messages repeated by the state's propaganda, they emulate foreign cultural status (see Anguelov, 2019). Owing to marketisation, people now have more access to external information and culture. More and more people are realising the dissonance between what the state tells them and what reality is like (Baek, 2016). As Cha and Collins (2018) argue, 'a latent civil society could be emerging around these markets as citizens share information, commerce, and further promote growing autonomy of livelihood through these markets' by using advanced communication technology, such as mobile phones. To some extent, North Korea has shown itself to be on a similar pathway to that which the CEE countries experienced in their transition to democracy.

Many news articles, publications, experts, and defector discussions describe this phenomenon in North Korea as 'revolutionary'. Cultural clashes have been happening in people's minds not only inside North Korea but also outside the North Korean regime's territory. Even though the government controls access to the internet, workers dispatched to other countries by the government have access to it, including to YouTube channels (Kim-M, 2021). An online platform like YouTube has become an avenue to learn about ideological differences and political systems in more detail (Kim, 2022). People come to know more, for example, about life in South Korea, and thus, try to mimic the South Korean lifestyle. As noted by Baek (2016), society is gradually transforming from being a closed space through access to underground information. However, according to one of the workers sent abroad by the regime, entertainment such as K-drama remains just a method of entertainment, and thus, does not dramatically change the mindset of people (Kim, 2022).

Accordingly, it is questionable whether the 'hidden revolution' can become an actual revolution. In other words, the changes do not seem to contribute to the enabling environment for mass movement in state–market–family (people and society) relations, especially in the context of the state's capacity to communicate with its people and society. One could argue that this is because only a small segment of the population has been a beneficiary of technological developments, such as mobile phone communications, and thus, the changes wrought by the related information dissemination and cultural influx have not embraced the entire citizenry. As shown previously, those who enjoy mobile communications or physical mobility comprise less than 20 per cent of the entire population, and most of them have privileged political and/or economic positions in society. Even though mobile phones are now used in 100 cities and towns, compared to 2009 when they were only used in Pyongyang (Kim-S, 2021), the information influx is still limited to some provinces (Lee, 2012). As Yeo (2020) argues, the changes observed through marketisation are mostly limited to Pyongyang and the border regions between China and North Korea. Most rural areas in North Korea are still under the state's heavy control and are thus not a threat to the regime's stability. Likewise, the change is limited to only certain population groups. As a matter of fact, more than 50 per cent of defectors are from the middle and rich economic classes, which are mostly *donju* groups (Kim, 2017: 98). Thus, the regime is concerned about the spread of a disobedient mindset among the elites and youth because they will eventually become the new generation of the party (for example, see Lee-J, 2021), or possible civil society movement leaders who can enlighten the rest of the ordinary populace. As discussed in Chapter 3, the young generation is less loyal to the government and could be completely different from the existing generation, which had to undergo a stricter ideology education programme. Thus, in April 2021, Kim Jong-un sent a letter to the Youth League aiming to 'root out anti-socialist and non-socialist practices, and improve ideological education' (Lim, 2021). To create more youth-friendly conditions, he also changed the name of the youth league from Kimilsungist-Kimjongilist Youth League to Socialist Patriotic Youth League at its 10th congress.

Box 4.1 Kim Jong-un's State Media and Digital Effects: A Case of 'Top Gun'

Source: Korea Central TV, 2022[1]

At the same time, Kim Jong-un is trying to capture people's minds[2] by adopting a so-called Western style so that state media can 'entertain' people while still distributing propaganda. For example, as seen in Box 4.1, Kim Jong-un was recently featured on state TV as if he were part of *Top Gun*, a Hollywood film, through the use of slow and fast motion digital effects, while he was introducing an intercontinental ballistic missile (ICBM) test. The government is also trying to develop new modalities of ideology education, such as patriotism-based mobile games, for the technology-savvy generation that is less interested in state ideology and in public media such as newspapers or TV news (Yoon, 2020: 1492). The government has not only made *Rodong Sinmun* (the North Korean state newspaper) available on mobile phones but it is also feeding people with propaganda through a free short message service (SMS) to mobile phone subscribers while blocking internet access and international calls.

While using new technology to introduce edutainment and a more westernised approach to try and grab public attention for the regime's military development, Kim Jong-un also uses old propaganda methods, such as public lectures, to reach those without full access to new technology. While new technology tends to be used by a limited population in North Korea, most users of the smuggled content are reportedly people in rural areas where censorship tends to be less, who are accessing the content not necessarily with mobile phones but with older technology (Anguelov, 2019). Even though the mobile communication revolution is helping to bring about certain changes in North Korea, traditional styles of communication have not gone away. This is why some NGOs and activists based outside North Korea send out leaflets and use radio broadcast programmes (for example, see Daily NK, 2015). For this reason, the government continues to put pressure on the information sphere in a conventional style. An example of the use of such propaganda is the public lecture titled 'Eliminating All Kinds of Impure Publications That Harm Our Ideas, Our System, and Our Destiny', which was delivered to people in the Sino-North Korean border region (Mun, 2021).

Here, the reason why the North Korean regime has become more alert to the recent information influx from South Korea seems to have to do with the higher level of cultural absorption owing to a shared language. Cultural assimilation can happen much faster than it did in CEE countries because North Koreans share their language with South Koreans. In the case of CEE countries, during the transition period, people mostly obtained Hollywood blockbusters, which were in a language different from their own. In comparison, North Koreans do not need to struggle with a language barrier when listening to or watching K-pop, K-drama, or K-films, although there are some differences in expressions and vocabularies in the shared language (see also Chapter 3). Since the division of the Korean peninsula, the two Koreas have developed along different orthographic routes. While both use *Hangul*—the Korean alphabet—their sound and spelling systems have become differentiated (Chang, 2020). This makes verbal expressions somewhat different, but it does not prevent South and North Koreans from understanding each other. For ordinary Koreans, the dissimilarity is more like speaking in different dialects. It is said that for some South Koreans, the North Korean 'dialect' is easier to understand than the dialect of Jeju Island, which is in the very south of the Korean peninsula. Thus, North Koreans do not need to try to understand the language played through popular media, but they can literally soak up the culture as it is their language, except for certain expressions and vocabularies such as ice-cream and elevator (see Chapter 3). For example, the word *oppa*—meaning older brother—is used not only for siblings or in families but also among friends in South Korea. The same is now used by North Koreans, although they are meant to call each other *dongmu*—meaning comrade. It is evident that South Korean expressions that do not exist in North Korean have become prevalent in North Korean society, with state media officially warning people against using South Korean slang (for example, see BBC, 2021).

In the meantime, the surveillance system to slow down the spread of information has also evolved, reflecting the mobile communication revolution and information and communications technology (ICT) advancement. While mobile communication and ICT developments have created a so-called smartphone era, they have also become a double-edged sword for North Koreans. Mobile phone technology and the digital economy—discussed in the previous chapter—have helped the expansion of markets and provided a solution to mobility barriers, but they also function as new modes of surveillance. The regime often censors the use of mobile phones through measures such as jamming wireless signals at the border and monitoring phone conversations, conducted by the State Security Department (or the Ministry of Social Security in a recent structure). The government promotes mobile phones in which the SD card slot has been blocked during production. Spyware is preloaded onto mobile phones to monitor conversations through the mobile network (Kim, 2014; Kim-S, 2021). The North Korean government reportedly monitors voice calls, text messages, fax messages, web logs, file transfers, and email messages (Williams, 2021). In the defector survey conducted by Choi (2021: 32–33), all respondents said they had not shared important or sensitive issues over a mobile phone but only engaged in ordinary conversation as they had known that their phone calls were monitored by the authority. Also, domestic communication and active dissemination of information through the mobile network have been very limited, mostly remaining at the level of a brief communication due to the high cost that ordinary people, except traders, cannot afford (Kim, 2014; Yoon, 2020). Moreover, the authority has established a new surveillance agency that specialises in monitoring anti-socialist activities (Lee-C, 2021). The government's surveillance strategy does not allow ordinary North Koreans access to the internet. Even privileged groups have only limited access to the state intranet, and not the internet, as discussed in Chapter 3.

Due to the mass surveillance of varied communication methods, such as text messages and hashtags which are critical methods of sharing information and mobilising civil society as they were during the Arab Spring, cannot be utilised in North Korea, as mentioned earlier. Facebook or Twitter access is unimaginable. As the theory holds, a critical requirement for civil society is free public communication or social interaction, but this does not exist in North Korea. As discussed earlier, CEE countries experienced the domino effects of an opening-up movement that started with Gorbachev's *glasnost* and *perestroika* policies. It is highly unlikely for North Koreans to be influenced by external events in a way that can similarly ignite civic movements in the country, not only due to the blocked information inflows from outside into North Korea but also due to the poor conditions for social network sharing. The global K-wave (or *Hallyu*) has arrived in North Korea, but not K-pop standom (at least not yet). While cyberspace platforms have provided opportunities for people around the world to communicate with each other, thereby enabling them to contribute to social and political activism in place (Alsford, 2022), this is not the case in North Korea. It is still very unlikely to find North Korean youth not attending a mass parade in Kim Il-sung Square as part of a boycott of Kim Jong-un that has been organised based on communication through TikTok or Twitter hashtags. This is because possession of knowledge is not automatically followed by action.

The unlikelihood of this happening is not only because such apps (Twitter, TikTok, and the like) are blocked in North Korea but also because ordinary North Koreans do not have freedom of mobility (including to 'not attend'). Civil society requires the collective and voluntary participation of its individual members; however, due to the limits on mobility, North Koreans cannot participate properly in collective voluntary action in the public sphere. The ban on mobility also has an impact on the ability of people to engage in social interactions. This further hinders information exchange between regions. Even though some mobility is tolerated for logistics, such as for the *servicha* system (see Chapter 3), it is still limited (or illegally allowed through bribery). Travel is difficult not only within the country. For ordinary North Koreans, it is impossible to travel abroad. Only government officials under training programmes and those workers who work on government-associated projects are allowed to go abroad. Those who travel abroad are under very strict restrictions on what they can and cannot do in foreign countries. Furthermore, to ensure their loyalty to the regime, some members of their immediate family—mostly children—must remain behind in North Korea. Government officials, meanwhile, do not normally mix with ordinary citizens due to the *songbun* system (North Korea's social classification system as presented in Chapter 3).

Owing to a culture of surveillance, people do not enjoy freedom of expression. The daily lives of North Koreans have been under constant government scrutiny since the birth of the country. The 'owners' of the state—for example, the Kim family and elite groups—engender people's attitudes and behaviours, including the way they speak in public. For example, so-called *chochik saenghwal*—meaning organisational life—has become a unique feature of North Korean society, comparable to other Soviet or Leninist approaches to organisational life. North Korea's organisational life is a 'highly formalised array of surveillance and indoctrination practices that are conducted within a set of networks' controlled by the regime (Lankov, Kwak and Cho, 2012: 194). This organisational life allows the regime to operate a peer surveillance system covering the entirety of residential and work spheres.

The organisational life of North Koreans starts with membership of the *Chosun Sonyeondan* or Chosun Children's Union. Some of us may have seen photos of North Korean boys and girls wearing red ties around their necks. This is typical of members of *Chosun Sonyeondan*. Boys and girls aged between seven and 13 belong to *Chosun Sonyeondan*, usually becoming members between their second and third year of elementary school. Once the children enter middle school, they become members of the Socialist Patriotic Youth League. The entire structure is like that of the military (Kang, 2005; Kim, 2018). Then, if the *songbun* allows, or there are other reasons for it, some become members of the *Chosun Rodongdang* or Korean Workers' Party (KWP). The rest join either the Union of Agricultural Workers of Korea or the General Federation of Trade Unions of Korea. Housewives who have not been allocated to specific workplaces become members of the Socialist Women's Union of Korea (Kim, 2018). While unions are typically an important CSO in democratic systems, those in North Korea provide ideology education, impose loyalty to the regime, and function as a surveillance system, thereby repressing the creation of democratic CSOs in North Korea.

In addition, everyone in North Korea is included in a local *inminban*—a peer surveillance system that exists in every residential neighbourhood. *Inminban* leaders not only serve as agents of state control but also have a role in the performance of basic state functions, such as government surveys, distribution, and labour mobilisation, as well as in ensuring attendance at public lectures. For example, when the July 2002 economic reform was implemented (see Chapter 3), *inminban* leaders, not government officials, conducted the census survey for the government (Kim, 2018). Simply put, the surveillance system is just another part of people's lives in North Korea, which makes it difficult for them to get away from it to any appreciable extent.

In this way, existing ideological indoctrination still prevails in people's minds. Coupled with coercive punishment and the politics of fear, the minds of ordinary people are easily shaped and brainwashed into *Juche* ideology. *Jucheism* (a unique North Korean ideology created by Kim Il-sung) has come to be at the core of people's thoughts and behaviours through mandatory ideology education, along with propaganda activities. The education system teaches people that loyalty to the Kim family is a virtue of their life while not allowing them to learn concepts like human rights or civil society. North Koreans do not fully understand the concept of human rights. In a survey conducted by the Christian Solidarity Worldwide (2018: 22), about 50 per cent of defector respondents answered that they had heard of the term 'human rights', but only 10 per cent responded that they fully understood the term: among them, 21 per cent had heard the term from foreign media; 50 per cent had heard it from friends, family members, neighbours, or colleagues; and 23 per cent from government sources, with some government sources, in turn, having heard it in the context of the international community's criticism of human rights violations in North Korea.

Moreover, there is a lack of awareness in society that people can change the way the system works. North Koreans may rebel in a small group against individual agents of state authority, such as street-level bureaucrats, but not against the regime's system itself. According to Yoon (2016: 181), the North Korean regime has strategically imposed a politics of fear in order to unite society in the absence of state legitimacy and has used societal oppression and physical punishment to restrain the inner solidarity of the labour force. In this process, the working class has become 'atomised', losing the capacity to gather and exercise political power against the government. In other words, the forced mindset of workers, imposed through the politics of fear and ideology, has shrunk even the mere possibility of trade unionism. Also, the existing *songbun* system embedded in people's minds has played the role of a self-suppressing mechanism in North Korean society. For example, the defector interview carried out by Kim (2018: 160) shows that discrimination by the upper class towards the lower classes within society is considered natural, and thus, acceptable in people's minds. Even those who were discriminated within the *songbun* system thought it was nothing wrong. Discrimination in daily life is simply the norm in North Korean society and individuals are thus either eager not to lose their societal status or eager to obtain better status in society. Changing the regime is not in their immediate interests, and people do not want to risk what might come next after a dismantling of the existing system in its entirety.

For this reason, people choose to cope with the existing mechanism between the market and the state. Here, the state for ordinary people does not mean top-level decision-makers, but rather the bureaucrats who implement policy at the street level. For instance, Kwon (2020) explains that the democratisation process pushed forward by the middle class in other societies is not to be expected in the case of North Korea due to the *donju*'s cooperation with authority. This book echoes this view and expands the argument: it is more about the street-level bureaucrats who actually implement top-down policies and can exercise their discretion. Rather than resist against the state, people choose to bribe officials who can turn a blind eye to their 'misdeeds'. At the same time, borrowing from Hastings' (2016: 104–105) culture of entrepreneurialism argument, government officials, who tend to be paid insufficiently, have found a substitute for their economic hardship in the market. They themselves have become a part of the market and demand bribes from the market. This can be confirmed by a more recent study by Carothers (2022: 147): 'marketisation made corruption more beneficial to the regime both as a source of revenue and as an escape valve for public discontent'. According to Yoon (2021), this can be better understood as a societal self-survival system rather than as typical corruption in a somewhat complex manner because, in North Korea, bribery is ironically allowed in socialist values and not entirely excluded. As the state cannot provide rations nor compensate for labour, bribery fills the gap, and it is thus not considered corruption. In contemporary North Korea, not only is the culture of bribery utilised to resolve immediate economic and social issues, but it is also based on societal understanding of the isolation and hardship caused by international sanctions. In other words, a skewed form of solidarity has been created in North Korean society through the adoption of an evolving culture of bribery.

Also, even though changes have been observed in North Korea, this has been through the lens of defectors who escaped by bribing street-level bureaucrats. The earlier generation of defectors comprises those who left the country due to economic reasons related to the famine. It was, more or less, a case of forced defection by the situation or the economic environment in order to survive. However, the later generation of defectors has tended to willingly leave the country to find greater economic freedom, which involves financial costs. Within North Korean neighbourhoods, while *inminban* leaders are supposed to report any anti-regime activities to agents of the Ministry of Social Security (former State Security Department), they are now among those who accept bribes from residents (Draudt, 2020). *Inminban* leaders can be a political power group in the system, occupying a space between the state and its citizens, only when they (mostly women) have financial power (or if their spouses hold political power in the party). Therefore, they tend to increase their financial power by collecting money from residents in the form of bribes. The 8•3 deposit (see Chapter 3) is also used in *inminban* territory to avoid forced labour mobilisation (Kim, 2018). At the individual level, people bribe using different means. Moreover, while paying a high rate of commission to *donju* at *igwanjib* (see Chapter 3), defectors-to-be also bribe bureaucrats. North Koreans choose to seek and create reconciliation with the street-level bureaucrats rather than to resist against the regime: 'the authority set out restrictive policy, then the residents come up with countermeasures' (Kim, 2018: 220).

In this sense, bribery at the street level has become an inducement from the family (people and society), through the market, to the state—or society's countermeasure against state control. As bribery can be committed only by those with financial capacity, the unforeseen layers of social power have created and been thickened by an amalgam of corrupt bureaucrats and the wealthy class. Thus, markets have not become completely independent of the state (David-West, 2013), and *donju* play the role of a veiling layer between the top and the bottom of the market system. As a new class situated between the authority and citizens, *donju*—including those who have financial capacity—enjoy privileges in society, and they do not seem willing to give up this privileged status easily. They do not want to leave North Korea as they know how to make money in the existing system and can even hire others as their handmaidens because they can pay for it (Kim, 2018). They might only decide to defect because their system of bribery did not work in their favour. Unless the state attempts to dismantle this new 'class' in society, it will not rebel but work as a buffer zone to keep the balance among state, market, and family (people and society). *Donju* have learned how to work in concert with the authority and how to use the power of money in the political system, and thus, they do not have strong motivation to change the system. As bribers, *donju* and some who can collect money through remittances have been able to seize political power in the bureaucracy at some level (for example, by having restrictions waived or escaping punishment). They also control the market with their financial power. Unless this new class cooperates with the very bottom level of society and/or associates with political elite leaders as a whole, and organises 'civil society' against the regime's misconduct, a mass social movement is unlikely to occur in North Korea.

Cloaked by Economic Elites

Marketisation was established in the shadow economy, and resistance to minimise the regime's market power remains in the shadows. Those responsible for 'imposing' regulations at the street level are willing to take bribes from businesses as they themselves are suffering due to the broken state supply system. The culture of bribery has thus become their own survival system in the government. Meanwhile, for citizens, rather than create a collision between the state and the market, bribery of the street-level bureaucracy provides an exit from the central government's surveillance system. Thus, forbidden activities are informally acceptable. While the state controls markets, the markets rule over society, and also the state vice versa. The authority is indirectly forced to continue to leverage and balance between market autonomy and state restrictions. In this context, the role of the newly created economically powerful class in the social classification system—for instance, *donju*—has created another layer within society. *Donju* keep changes to a minimum by balancing state control and market autonomy at the individual level rather than gathering as a powerful collective force against the state.

This is because people (and thus society) do not know 'how to' become an empowered civil society. Having knowledge and acting on that knowledge are two distinct things (Kim-S, 2021). Having information may have successfully helped people realise that the current government system is not adequate for them. However, they do not know how to challenge it. Even though people have developed innovative ways to hide illegal activities and improper expressions from the country's surveillance system, they have not reached the point of boycotting the authority. Rather, they use doublespeak to share risky information so that such disobedience activities remain a secret within society (see Chapter 3). While we might be able to observe how soft power is slowly 'winning the hearts and minds' of North Koreans—to borrow Nye's (2008) expression here—this has not yet translated into mass activism. Resistance occurs at the individual level rather than collectively, and the failure of other individuals to join in has resulted in each case of resistance losing its bargaining power (Szalontai and Choi, 2014). Thus, the society is not sufficiently empowered to become a 'civil society' for a democratic transition to occur through the marketisation process. People would rather defect than collectively rebel.

Also, society itself is segmented into different layers of the class system. In the case of social movements, the elites or the educated are typically the ones who can bravely challenge the system and lead resistance to it. However, in North Korea, the elites fear the regime or want to remain within their comfort zone. They do not understand how people in other segments of society live, they do not even think to cooperate with them for further changes, and they do not want to lose their privileges. There is knowledge and there are potential actions that can be taken, but there is no connection between 'leaders' and 'followers' as yet. The existence of *donju* and economic disparity blocks potential actions and has even worsened in society. Communication between the core and the periphery is blocked by a semi-periphery group—an alliance of street-level bureaucrats and a newly created middle-income class, including *donju*.

Hence, this book defines this phenomenon as the creation of a 'cloaked society' by street-level bureaucrats and *donju*—representing a middle-income class—who have become rent-seeking economic elites. In other words, the explanation for the absence of civil society can be found in the cloaking of society, driven by the existing social classification system and the emerging alliance between street-level authority and *donju*. This cloaked society of North Korea is illustrated in Figure 4.1.

This chapter argues that the creation of a cloaked society can be attributed to the bribery between those with financial resources and street-level bureaucrats, which has covered the citizenry with a new semi-peripheral layer. With marketisation, ordinary people established a self-survival system, while a new class group managed to find a way to wedge and hedge between the market's autonomy and the authority's power. The push and pull between the regime and the market resulted in a buffer zone composed of the street-level bureaucracy and those with financial power. According to Lee (2021), it is clear that North Korean society has experienced changes emerging from the marketisation process and we may thus witness an uprising in the future. However, based on a reinterpretation of marketisation in the context of the state's inevitable interaction with it, the findings of this research study suggest that the culture of bribery, coupled with the existing social class system, is a critical obstacle making it difficult for society to move forward. Marketisation did not empower ordinary citizens but empowered economic elites who are not likely to welcome a change to the social structure. The youth are imitating external cultures, like South Korean culture, but this has not linked with the social movement against the regime.

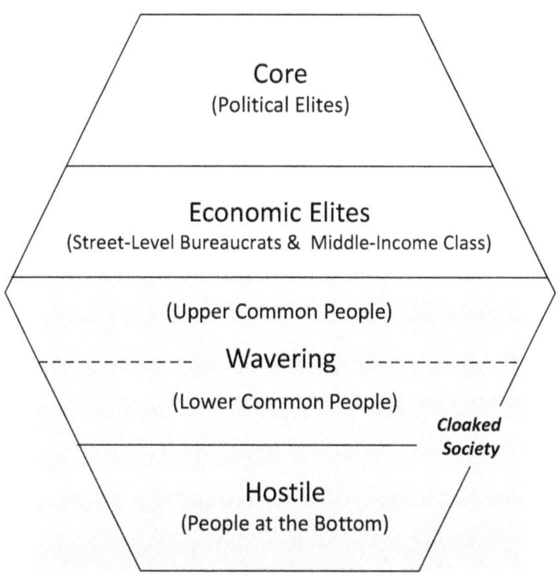

Figure 4.1 New Social Classification in Post-Marketisation North Korea.

Source: Author's own compilation.

Those in the Youth League, whose minds Kim Jong-un is worried about keeping away from foreign media, are also those who are privileged in the *songbun* system.

All in all, the economic elites or the young generation may be capable of 'influencing the values and behaviour of the majority' (Lankov et al., 2012: 210), but that influence does not reach other classes in society. The economic elites and the youth do not even share common interests. Those who have so far resisted against the regime's new restrictions on markets have done so not because they disagree with the existing political system, but because they are unhappy or unsatisfied with the authority's interference in the expansion of their economic power. The millennials and Gen Z are not interested in becoming party members; rather, they want to enjoy the newness of alien cultures. They enjoy popular culture from other countries and become aggrieved if their access to external information is prohibited. However, as long as both groups can still wedge and hedge, they will not easily challenge the existing system due to the way in which they have been nurtured by state propaganda. In any case, those who have been abroad are also those who have benefited from the regime (Park, 2009). If they, who have been abroad, are not intellectuals or workers sent by the government, then they are mostly associated with street-level bureaucrats through bribery. The existing culture of 'selfness' to survive among individuals placed between the market and the regime makes it hard to see the rise of collectively organised civil society in North Korea. Dissent against the human rights violations suffered by the majority remain muttered.

As Dukalskis (2016) concludes, North Korea may see a gradual change in the landscape of its political economy, but not a sudden upsurge in citizen protests. Moreover, as long as the middle layer of the social system, created by collusion between the authority and financially well-resourced citizens, is not challenged by the state, resilience to change will become stronger and the bottom billion will remain left behind in a cloaked society. In the end, resilience is created not only by the state's adaptation to change but also by the unity of rent-seeking economic elites. Marketisation has resulted in the unexpected consequences of enclosure and striving for the right of exclusion by dominant market actors. As the marketisation process in North Korea was unique when compared to the process in capitalist societies, the right to property did not result from income generation, but rather from the exclusive possession of property (Min, 2002: 170).

The COVID-19 lockdown seems to have created a new opportunity for the Kim regime to experiment with rebalancing the state, market, and economic elites (not people or society). The remittances from which the economic elites benefitted have dramatically decreased. Defection routes, which were one of the most effective methods for resolving the predicament of those who lost their financial power to the authority, have been blocked. The entire economic situation has worsened. Opportunities to enjoy foreign media through smuggling have been suspended. However, it is not certain whether the absolute isolation of the country will restructure the dynamics between the state and the market, and the wedging and hedging of the economic elites. For example, in March 2022, prior to re-opening the borders, the central government seemed to be investigating the alliance of street-level bureaucrats and *donju* as a precautionary countermeasure against a resurgence of the influx of information through smuggling. Also, a new phenomenon has been observed with central government officials, not just those at the street level, beginning to request bribes (Mun, 2022). Judging by the length of time that allowed the creation of the alliance between street-level bureaucrats and *donju*, the fact that the existing marketisation process cannot be reversed, and the fact that the government is concerned about and trying to dismantle wealthy businesses, it seems that this phenomenon is likely to continue in North Korea once the COVID-19 border restrictions are lifted.

Whether ordinary citizens will eventually be able to break through the 'ceiling' of the cloaked society as time goes by remains in question. This, in turn, makes it more important for information and cultural influxes to be 'accompanied by' or 'associated with' human exchanges such as in the form of communication with aid workers so that people can develop capacity for 'action' by learning. This does not mean using aid as a tool for 'winning the hearts and minds' of society (see Coyne and Williamson, 2015: 118); rather, it is about 'capacity building' and creating an 'enabling environment' for a culture of civil society. As seen, CEE countries already had a culture of civil society before changes occurred. The expansion of the culture of civil society in those countries was endowed with external aid. Western donors provided ODA directly to local CSOs and NGOs in the context of democratic consolidation, civil society development, and capacity building (Fagan, 2006).

Therefore, it is necessary for the international community to explore and prepare for the time when external aid is allowed to resume in North Korea. As long as people do not voluntarily take collective action in North Korea, structural change in society will not be realised. Seeking a way for development aid to support an enabling environment for civil society and civil society capacity building can be a practical alternative to the repetitive security-first-over-nuclear-programme rhetoric of today. In regard to this, the next chapter examines the international aid regime for North Korea in the past and assesses what was done and what was missed with regard to developing the capacity of civil society in North Korea.

Notes

1 For those who do not have access to Korea Central TV archives, see The Guardian (2022).

2 As we have seen in the 2022 Russia–Ukraine case, ordinary people exposed to Russian state propaganda through the media strongly believe that the Russian invasion of Ukraine is not a war. In one instance, a Ukrainian woman called her mother, who was in Moscow, and explained how Putin's war started, but the mother did not believe her own daughter even though the daughter sent her a video clip showing scenes of the war. The mother remained firm in her belief that the information on Russian state-controlled media platforms was true (Korenyuk and Goodman, 2022). This is but one example showing how strongly state propaganda and the personality cult of a leader can be persistent in the minds of people even when they have access to outside information and the internet, free communication, and use of mobile phones. Putin's war is legitimate in Russian minds as the country's propaganda is still effective. North Koreans have far less freedom than Russians to access information, mobile phones, and the internet.

References

Alsford, Niki J.P. (2022). Stan Activism: Is K-Pop the New Punk? In: Sojin Lim (ed.). *South Korea Popular Culture in the Global Context: Beyond the Fandom*. London: Routledge, pp. 25–38.

Anguelov, Nikolay (2019). Popular Culture in Transitional Societies: An Eastern European Perspective. In: Youna Kim (ed.). *South Korean Popular Culture and North Korea*. New York: Routledge, pp. 67–80.

Baek, Jieun (2016). *North Korea's Hidden Revolution: How the Information Underground is Transforming a Closed Society*. London: Yale University Press.

BBC (2021). North Korea Warns Young People Against Using Slang From the South. 18 July 2021, *BBC News*. https://www.bbc.co.uk/news/world-asia-57881108. Accessed: 15 March 2022.

Bernhard, Michael (1993). Civil Society and Democratic Transition in East Central Europe. *Political Science Quarterly*, 108(2): 307–326.

Carothers, Christopher (2022). The Rise and Fall of Anti-Corruption in North Korea. *Journal of East Asian Studies*, 22: 147–168.

Cha, Victor and Lisa Collins (2018). The Markets: Private Economy and Capitalism in North Korea? 26 August 2018, *Beyond Parallel – CSIS Korea Chair*. https://beyondparallel.csis.org/markets-private-economy-capitalism-north-korea/. Accessed: 15 March 2022.

Chang, Eunha (2020). *The Orthography Between South and North Korea and the Study of Korean Vocabulary*. Seoul: Prunsasang [장은하 (2000). 남북한 맞춤법과 한국어 어휘연구. 서울, 푸른사상].

Choi, Sunkyung (2021). Mobile Phone Use and the 'Trust' Network of Market Activity in North Korea. *Review of North Korean Studies*, 24(1): 7–40 [최선경 (2021). 북한 주민의 휴대폰 사용과 시장 활동에서의 '신뢰' 네트워크. 현대북한연구, 24(1): 7-40].

Christian Solidarity Worldwide (2018). *Movies, Markets and Mass Surveillance: Human Rights in North Korea After a Decade of Change*. Surrey: CSW.

Cotton, James (1991). *'Civil Society' and Nationalism in North Korea: Foundations for Political Change?* Working Paper 1991/7. Australian National University.

Coyne, Christopher J. and Claudia R. Williamson (2015). Foreign Aid and the Culture of Contacting. *Eastern Economic Journal*, 41: 102–125.

Daily NK (2015). *Radio Broadcasts Key to Civil Society in North Korea*. 31 March 2015. https://www.dailynk.com/english/radio-broadcasts-key-to-civil-soci/. Accessed: 15 March 2022.

David-West, Alzo (2013). North Korea and the Contradiction of Inversion: Dictatorship, Markets, Social Reform. *North Korean Review*, 9(1): 100–113.

Draudt, Darcie (2020). People's Groups and Patterns in Neighbourhood Surveillance: Another Tool in State Control over Daily Life. 10 December 2020, *38 North*. https://www.38north.org/2020/12/ddraudt121020/. Accessed: 15 March 2022.

Dukalskis, Alexander (2016). North Korea's Shadow Economy: A Force for Authoritarian Resilience or Corrosion? *Europe-Asia Studies*, 68(3): 487–507.

Edwards, Michael (2020). *Civil Society* (4th edition). Cambridge: Polity Press.

Ekiert, Grzegorz and Jan Kubik (1998). Contentious Politics in New Democracies: East Germany, Hungary, Poland, and Slovakia, 1989–93. *World Politics*, 59(4): 547–581.

Fagan, Adam (2006). Transnational Aid for Civil Society Development in Post-Socialist Europe: Democratic Consolidation or a New Imperialism? *The Journal of Communist Studies and Transition Politics*, 22(1): 115–134.

Foa, Robert Stefan and Grzegorz Ekiert (2017). The Weakness of Postcommunist Civil Society Reassessed. *European Journal of Political Research*, 56(2): 419–439.

Giner, Salvador (1995). Civil Society and Its Future. In: John A. Hall (ed.). *Civil Society: Theory, History, Comparison*. Cambridge: Polity Press, pp. 301–325.

Goldin, Ian (2013). *Divided Nations: Why Global Governance is Failing, and What We Can Do About It*. Oxford: Oxford University Press.

Hastings, Justin V. (2016). *A Most Enterprising Country: North Korea in the Global Economy*. London: Cornell University Press.

Kang, Changseo (2005). What is the Chosun Children's Union? 6 November 2005, *Daily NK* [강창서 (2005). '300만 조선소년단' 뭐하는 단체일까? 데일리 NK, 2005년 11월 6일자] https://www.dailynk.com/300만-조선소년단-뭔하는-단체일까/. Accessed: 15 March 2022.

Kim, Byung-Yeon (2017). *Unveiling the North Korean Economy: Collapse and Transition*. Cambridge: Cambridge University Press.

Kim, Myoungsung (2021). "It is Jangmadang, Not the Party, Who Raised Me": MZ Generation Dancing With BTS Threatening the Regime. 11 June 2021, *Chosunilbo* [김명성 (2021). "날 키운건 당 아닌 장마당" BTS 춤추는 MZ 세대, 北 체제 흔든다. 조선일보, 2021년 6월 11일자] https://www.chosun.com/politics/north_korea/2021/06/11/5XTBF5GIQZHX3MVEZ5ZQF5CSTY/. Accessed: 15 March 2022.

Kim, Seok Hyang (2018). *Story by North Korean Defectors About North Korea*. Seoul: Konrad Adenauer Stftung [김석향 (2018). 북한이탈주민이 들려주는 북녘 땅 고향 이야기. 서울, 콘라드 아데나워 재단].

Kim, Suk-Young (2021). *Millennial North Korea: New Media Technologies and Living Creatively with Surveillance*. Presentation at the 12th Critical Issues Form, Center for Korean Studies at the University of Hawaii. 31 March 2021, Webinar.

Kim, Yonho (2014). *Cell Phones in North Korea: Has North Korea Entered the Telecommunications Revolution?* Washington, D.C.: US Korea Institute at SAIS and Voice of America.

Kim, Youngkwon (2022). North Korean 2030 Generation and Youtube. 4 February 2022, *VOA* [김영권 (2022). 북한 2030 세대 "북한 유튜브 들어가면 획기적 변화, 평양 청년들 김정은에게 억지 충성". VOA, 2022년 2월 4일자] https://www.voakorea.com/a/6426174.html. Accessed: 15 March 2022.

Korea Central TV (2022). *8 PM News*. 20 March 2022. https://kcnawatch-org.eu1.proxy.openathens.net/kctv-archive/623dc6638ba1d/. Accessed: 20 March 2022.

Korenyuk, Maria and Jack Goodman (2022). Ukraine War: 'My City's Being Shelled, But Mum Won't Believe Me'. 4 March 2022, *BBC News*. https://www.bbc.co.uk/news/world-europe-60600487. Accessed: 15 March 2022.

Kwon, Ji Min (2020). A Study on the Growth of 'Donju' and Transition of the Political System in North Korea: Focusing on the Theory of Modernisation. *Discourse and Policy in Social Science*, 13(2): 89–108 [권지민 (2020). 북한에서 '돈주'의 성장과 정치체제이행 고찰 : 근대화 이론을 중심으로. 사회과학 담론과 정책, 13(2): 89-108].

Lankov, Andrei Nikolaevich, In-ok Kwak and Choong-Bin Cho (2012). The Organizational Life: Daily Surveillance and Daily Resistance in North Korea. *Journal of East Asian Studies*, 12(2): 193–214.

Lee, Chae Eun (2021). North Korean Sweeping Anti-Socialist Citizens. 16 March 2021, *Daily NK* [이채은 (2021). 北, 주민에 반사회주의 소탕 작전 천명, "무자비하게 쓸어버릴것". 데일리NK, 2021년 3월 16일자] https://www.dailynk.com/北-주민에-반사회주의-소탕-작전-천명-부자비하게/. Accessed: 15 March 2022.

Lee, Jeehee (2021). Unification Within 20 Years With the Youth in Leadership in North Korea. 27 December 2021, *UniKorea Foundation* [이지희 (2021). 北 20-30대가 요직 차지하는 20년 안에 통일 올 것. 통일과 나눔, 2021년 12월 27일자] http://www.tongnastory.com/news/articleView.html?idxno=97. Accessed: 15 March 2022.

Lee, Sang-soo (2012). Paradox of Neoliberalism: Arab Spring's Implications on North Korea. *North Korean Review*, 8(1): 53–66.

Lim, Sojin (2021). North Korea Food Shortage: Kim Jong-un's COVID-19 Policy Could Lead to Mass Starvation. 24 June 2021, *The Conversation*. https://theconversation.com/north-korea-food-shortage-kim-jong-uns-covid-19-policy-could-lead-to-mass-starvation-162966. Accessed: 15 March 2022.

Mastnak, Tomaž (2005). The Reinvention of Civil Society: Through the Looking Glass of Democracy. *European Journal of Sociology*, 46(2): 323–355.

May, Rachel A. (2005). Human Rights NGOs and the Role of Civil Society in Democratization. In: Rachel A. May and Andrew K. Milton (eds.). *(Un)Civil Societies: Human Rights and Democratic Transitions in Eastern Europe and Latin America*. Plymouth: Lexington Books, pp. 1–10.

Miller, Arthur H. and Thomas Klobucar (2005). Partisan Development and Differentiation in Post-Soviet Russia and Ukraine. In: Rachel A. May and Andrew K. Milton (eds.). *(Un)Civil Societies: Human Rights and Democratic Transitions in Eastern Europe and Latin America*. Plymouth: Lexington Books, pp. 239–265.

Min, Young-ki (2002). *Money and Market in North Korea: Supreme Leader, Money, Market*. Seoul: Hanul Academy [민영기 (2002). 북한의 화폐와 시장 : 수령, 돈, 시장. 서울, 한울 아카데미].

Mun, Dong Hui (2021). North Korean Illegal Propaganda Possessions. 23 March 2021, *Daily NK* [문동희 (2021). 北 불법선전물 소지자 자수 회유, "죄 백지화, 사회생활 지장 無". 데일리NK, 2021년 3월 23일자] https://www.dailynk.com/北-불법선전물-소지자-자수-회유-죄-백지화-사회생/. Accessed: 15 March 2022.

Mun, Dong Hui (2022). North Korea Ratchets Up Crackdowns on Wealthy Business People Amid Concerns Over Smuggling. 23 March 2022, *Daily NK* [문동희 (2022). "신의주서 돈주, 보위부 집중 단속", 중앙 검열단도 '뇌물' 요구. 데일리NK, 2022년 3월 23일자] https://www.dailynk.com/20220321-4/. Accessed: 23 March 2022.

Nye, Joseph (2008). Public Diplomacy and Soft Power. *The Annals of the American Academy of Political and Social Science*, 626(1): 94–109.

Park, Kyung-Ae (2009). Regime Change in North Korea?: Economic Reform and Political Opportunity Structures. *North Korea Review*, 5(1): 23–45.

Purdue, Derrick (2007). Introduction: Dimensions of Civil Society. In: Derrick Purdue (ed.). *Civil Societies and Social Movements: Potentials and Problems*. New York: Routledge, pp. 1–16.

Spurk, Christoph (2010). Understanding Civil Society. In: Thania Paffenholz (ed.). *Civil Society and Peacebuilding: A Critical Assessment*. London: Lynne Rienner Publishers, pp. 3–28.

Szalontai, Balázs and Changyong Choi (2014). Immunity to Resistance? State-Society Relations and Political Stability in North Korea in a Comparative Perspective. *North Korean Review*, 10(1): 55–70.

Taras, Ray (2005). Civil Society, Human Rights, and the Shaping of Postcommunist Europe's Identity Politics. In: Rachel A. May and Andrew K. Milton (eds.). *(Un)Civil Societies: Human Rights and Democratic Transitions in Eastern Europe and Latin America*. Plymouth: Lexington Books, pp. 31–50.

The Guardian (2022). *Kim Jong-un Gets Top Gun Treatment in North Korea's Missile Coverage*. 25 March 2022. https://www.theguardian.com/world/2022/mar/25/kim-jong-un-gets-top-gun-treatment-in-north-korea-missile-coverage. Accessed: 25 March 2022.

Visegrády, Antal (1992). Transition to Democracy in Central and Eastern Europe: Experiences of a Model Country – Hungary. *Illiam and Mary Bill of Rights Journal*, 1(2): 245–266.

Williams, Martyn (2021). Pegasus-Style Surveillance is Everyday Life in North Korea. 21 July 2021, *North Korea Tech*. https://www.northkoreatech.org/2021/07/21/pegasus-style-surveillance-is-everyday-life-in-north-korea/. Accessed: 15 March 2022.

Yeo, Andrew (2020). Assessing Domestic Change and Continuity in North Korea. *Asian Studies Review*, 44(4): 641–651.

Yoon, Boyoung (2021). Changes in the Social Context of Bribery in North Korea. *Korean Journal of Cultural Sociology*, 29(1): 39–90 [윤보영 (2021). 북한사회 뇌물의 사회적 맥락. 문화와 사회, 29(1): 39–90].

Yoon, Cheol Gee (2016). Change of Class-System and Working-Class Ideological Identity After Marketisation in North Korea. *Review of North Korean Studies*, 19(2): 155–189 [윤철기 (2016). 북한 시장화 이후 계급체계와 노동계급의 이데올로기적 정체성 변화. 현대북한연구, 19(2): 155–189]

Yoon, Sunny (2020). Mobile Media and Its Impacts on Social Change and Human Rights in North Korea. *International Journal of Communication*, 14: 1480–1497.

Zamruzzaman, Palash (2019). Introduction – Civil Society in the Global South. In: Palash Zamruzzaman (ed.). *Civil Society in the Global South*. New York: Routledge, pp. 1–24.

5 International Aid and Uncloaking Society

In almost all cases, Western aid pushed civil society forward in Central and Eastern European (CEE) countries during the democratic transition period, including by improving the transparency and accountability of both state and civil society (Mandel, 2001). International aid contributed to the expansion of market-associated changes for civil society empowerment. For example, after the collapse of the Soviet Union, United States (US) development assistance to Ukraine was more focused on political, economic, and social restructuring than on economic growth and humanitarian relief. In this way, aid supported an enabling environment for institutional capacity building, empowerment, and the sustainability of civil society (Pishchikova, 2007). In other words, by supporting the capacity development of the state, international aid can also provide an opportunity for building up the capacity of civil society. The role of aid can thus become critical in the context of state capacity development. However, in this regard, little research has been done in the case of North Korea. In addition, full consideration has not been given to how development aid could support North Korean citizens as agents for regime change. The reason for this is rather simple: the country is under sanctions. Under the pretext of the prolonged sanctions on the country, scholarship has tended to ignore the argument on the need for development aid to North Korea, especially to its cloaked society. Studies dealing with aid issues in North Korea are very limited.

As seen in the previous chapter, it is doubtful whether ordinary citizens can voluntarily organise a powerful resistance against the regime. While sanctions have not been effective in bringing about behavioural change in the Kim regime, civil society cannot contribute to bringing this about either due to its ignorance of systemic changes. Economic elites—the middle-income class and street-level bureaucrats—are seemingly the most likely and feasible kingmakers in North Korea, if they want to bring about structural changes at all. If not, the impetus for regime change could be found among elite groups in the party system—for example, political elites—who could lead members from the different layers of society in the *songbun* system. However, they do not seem to have any incentives for regime change. Even if external aid were to be provided to improve lives and livelihoods, it would most likely be concentrated on the economic and political elites, without fully reaching the end beneficiaries who actually need aid in society.

According to Cartier-Bresson (2012: 501), 'the behaviour of elites is both the problem and the solution' for successful aid programmes. This can be interpreted

DOI: 10.4324/9781003390282-5

to mean that the elites who lead a country or society should be accountable for external aid. Otherwise, aid will not become a contributor to actual socio-political-economic development, but rather deepen inequality due to its failure to provide an equal and fair supply of public goods. Therefore, it is critical to create a culture of accountability within the state system that expects equal distribution of public goods by developing state capacity (Lim, 2021b). The argument for accountability is not limited to development aid, but applies to all kinds of assistance, including humanitarian aid. At the same time, the role of civil society is important in preventing further corruption and widening the gap in society, and for aid to have positive consequences. Furthermore, aid can become an important engine for building and enhancing a culture of accountability and institutional capacity through carrying out monitoring and evaluation.

This chapter thus assesses how aid has been provided to North Korea, by examining whether aid provision had any impact on society and on state capacity development and whether aid monitoring influenced the culture of accountability and communication between the government and citizens. To that end, the chapter begins with a brief overview of aid mechanisms, before discussing what has been done and what has been missed, and what needs to be considered to bring about change in North Korea.

Understanding International Aid Mechanisms

Bilateral aid, especially in the form of official development assistance (ODA), means aid from one government to another, while multilateral aid is provided by international organisations (IOs), such as the United Nations (UN), and multilateral development banks (MDBs), such as the World Bank or the Asian Development Bank, to a recipient government. In general, the funds from IOs or MDBs are composed of individual government contributions, a pooled or basket budget, or multi-donor trust funds. That is, for example, when bilateral aid flows from high-income countries (HICs) to low-income countries (LICs), HIC donors disburse their ODA budgets indirectly to LICs, through IOs or MDBs, with or without earmarking sectors or development projects. If bilateral donors earmark their aid contributions to IOs or MDBs for specific purposes, we call it multi-bi aid. Normally, UN bodies provide grant aid, while MDBs execute loan aid, along with a relatively lower amount of grant aid, to developing countries. Bilateral aid donors provide both grant and loan aid.

Grant aid can play a very effective role as 'seed' financing, contributing to the development of state capacity for the economic take-off of a country, including through soft infrastructure development by means of technical cooperation and policy development consultations, among other things. Loan aid can boost economic growth and industrialisation processes on a larger scale through hard infrastructure development, such as highway or dam construction. For example, after the Korean War, South Korea was a war-torn fragile state, but its economy took off with early industrialisation benefitting from the vast influx of international aid into the country (Lim, 2021a). The case of South Korea illustrates an interesting developmental pathway as the aid that it received in the initial stage of development was mainly grant aid, which met the nation's need for institutional capacity building (soft infrastructure), including education and industrial human resource development. In and after the economic take-off stage, South Korea received more concessional loans (loan aid) than grant aid to which its hard infrastructure development can be attributed. This example shows the importance of grant aid in the early stage of economic development, especially for recipient countries—including fragile states—that do not have debt repayment capability, while loan aid becomes more critical for development projects on a larger scale once the state has greater capacity for industrialisation in later stages. At the same time, a state's absorptive capacity should be considered in aid management. The capacity to repay debt on aid loans is equally important.

Both bilateral and multilateral donors channel their aid through civil society organisations (CSOs), including non-governmental organisations (NGOs). NGOs not only mobilise resources for their budgets through donations, but they also implement humanitarian and development projects financed by aid donors—both governments and IOs. Contributions to NGOs in the Global South reportedly exceed the amount of UN aid. About 13 per cent of development aid and almost 50 per cent of humanitarian aid, excluding food aid, have been distributed or implemented by NGOs. If we include food aid, more than half of the world's humanitarian aid has been provided by NGOs to developing countries (Duffield, 2014: 53). More recently, philanthropists and business entities have also become participants in development projects and programmes in developing countries, joining governments and IOs in the format of blended finance to maximise impact.

Here, it is necessary to note the difference between development aid and humanitarian aid. In situations such as conflict and immediate post-conflict states, humanitarian aid in the form of emergency relief typically arrives first. Humanitarian aid is also provided in the aftermath of natural disasters, such as tsunamis and floods. As it is intended to serve as emergency relief, humanitarian assistance normally remains at a 'minimum' level during the specific crisis period. According to the UN Office for the Coordination of Humanitarian Affairs (UN OCHA), 'humanitarian actions often aim to build resilience at the community level' (OCHA, 2011: 5). Thus, humanitarian assistance tends to be limited to food, medicine, water, and sanitation sectors as grant aid, while development aid projects and programmes vary as in both grant and loan aid. Yet, this does not necessarily mean that the absolute amount of humanitarian relief is small, but that it is relatively smaller than the amount of development aid, especially loan aid. This means that humanitarian aid is not normally provided on a sufficiently large scale to help states build up the required state institutional capacity or escape the trap of extreme poverty. This, in turn, indicates that humanitarian aid is usually targeted at emergent incidents. Thus, it does not contribute to development per se. Meanwhile, development aid targets institutional capacity building and industrialisation processes, which can lead to sustainable development and a resilient society in developing countries. In a nutshell, the role of development assistance lies in state capacity development, linked to long-term socio-political-economic development and resilience to climate change–related natural disaster shocks, while the role of humanitarian aid receives greater emphasis in the prevention of civilian casualties during crises.

Humanitarian assistance is mostly provided due to an ethical obligation, and thus remains limited to providing minimum capacity building as it is 'guided by the core principles of humanity, impartiality, neutrality, and independence' (Cartier-Bresson, 2012: 501; OCHA, 2011: 4). Accordingly, it tends to be detached from donors' motivations for providing ODA. The distribution of ODA, which normally comes with conditions or purposeful reasons, cannot be understood apart from donors' national interests (Lancaster, 2007; Lim, 2019), with some exceptions. For example, like-minded Nordic countries tend to provide more altruistic aid than other donors. For this reason, it is unlikely for a single donor country to provide a massive amount of aid to a single recipient country as a form of humanitarian assistance without conditions. This is why some criticise the motivation of, and national interests behind, bilateral aid and instead argue that multilateral aid is more effective in humanitarian aid as well as development aid discourses. The reason why some researchers, such as Milner and Tingley (2013), imply that multilateral aid is more poverty driven than bilateral aid can be understood in the context of donor motivations and national interests. However, this chapter does not intend to compare the effectiveness of bilateral and multilateral aid, as it is not the focus of the analysis here.

Because humanitarian aid plays the role of an immediate response to urgent situations, such as natural disasters, it normally does not become a vehicle for a country's development (OECD, 2018: 11). However, this does not completely limit the role of humanitarian aid. Rather, it is crucial to link 'relief and development' in a way that overcomes the humanitarian crisis and achieves development (JICA, 2017; Macrae and Harmer, 2004). With hindsight, we can see South Korea as a case of good practice of linking humanitarian aid to development assistance. Emergency relief funding in response to the post-war crisis was expanded to development assistance from donors to which the country's economic take-off can be attributed. In the South Korean case, it is clear that grant aid was poured into the country at the starting stage of the aid regime, which was changed to loan aid in later stages with rapid industrialisation (Lim, 2021a). However, its sister country, North Korea, has been the opposite case in terms of linking humanitarian aid to development assistance into which this chapter looks in more detail.

Aid Regime for North Korea

Russia (Soviet Union) and China

External financial support to North Korea began with the Soviet Union providing loan aid. Building upon the existing infrastructure that had been established by the Japanese during the colonial period, North Korea was able to jump-start its economic growth with the support of the Soviet loan aid. When the Korean War broke out, other communist countries also began providing aid—both grant and

Table 5.1 Bilateral Aid Volume to North Korea Before the 1990s—Set 1 (USD Millions)

	Russia (Soviet Union)		*China*		*East Germany*		*Other Eastern European Countries*		*Total*	
	Grant	*Loan*	*Grant*	*Loan*	*Grant*	*Loan*	*Grant*	*Loan*	*Grant*	*Loan*
1945–1949	—	53	—	—	—	—	—	—	—	53
1950–1960	515	199	336	173	101	—	326	4	1,278	376
1961–1969	—	197	—	105	—	35	—	—	—	337
1970–1976	—	906		2	—	—	—	—	—	908
1978–1984	—	—	259	—	—	—	—	—	259	—
Total	515	1,355	595	280	101	35	326	4	1,537	1,674
Grand Total	1,870		875		136		330		3,211	

Source: Revised from Ford, 2018: 76.

loan aid—to North Korea, as seen in Table 5.1. Then, in the post-war period, North Korea became heavily reliant on Soviet aid, which later changed to a dependency on Chinese aid.

Here, it is noteworthy that there are some data discrepancies in the scholarship as early aid flows into North Korea were not officially consolidated at the international level or in open access sources. As a result, some variation in the figures have been observed, as presented in Tables 5.1 and 5.2. The segregation of time in the two tables is not identical, and this leaves some room for variance or assumption in the absence of exact figures in statistics. Table 5.1 shows that the Soviet Union provided USD 515 million in grant aid between 1950 and 1960 (ten years). Meanwhile, according to Table 5.2, USD 325 million in grant aid was provided by the Soviets between 1953 and 1960 (seven years). Based on the difference between the figures in the two tables, and without access to raw data from (now) Russia or North Korea, we can only assume that Soviet grant aid support to North Korea amounted to USD 190 million between 1950 and 1952 (during the Korean War). The situation is not much different in the case of Chinese aid to North Korea during this period.

Having said that, it may be necessary to investigate the data sources further to reduce any misinterpretations or discrepancies. Although sources are included for the data contained in the two tables in the original works, they show the data to be second-hand rather than raw data. In other words, we know that the data in Table 5.1 was published in 1986 by the Statistics of North Korean Economy of the South Korean National Unification Board, the predecessor of the Ministry of Unification, and that the data in Table 5.2 was presented in 1996 by the Korea Development Institute (KDI) North Korean Economic Indicators. However, we do not know how the raw data was collected. Here, for greater accuracy, this chapter attempts to locate the original data sources for both the South Korean National Unification Board's Statistics of North Korean Economy and the KDI North Korean Economic Indicators.

While it was not feasible to interview the officials who produced the datasets, it was possible to find a published interview with the KDI Office of North Korean Economic Studies in 2020 (see Lee and Cho, 2021). According to this interview, the National Unification Board collected quasi-statistics and data from available sources, such as official North Korean statements and media reports, and compiled and published them as its statistics on North Korea. Around the time of the Soviet collapse in the late 1980s and early 1990s, the South Korean government became more attentive to capturing information about economic conditions in North Korea. Accordingly, the KDI Office of North Korean Economic Studies was founded. Not only the National Unification Board but also other agencies such as the Bank of Korea (BOK) and the Korea Trade-Investment Promotion Agency (KOTRA) began to produce regular statistical data on North Korea. Since then, BOK has published yearly estimates of the North Korean gross national income (GNI) growth rate, while KOTRA has gathered mirror data from North Korea's trade partners, such as China. The Rural Development Administration (RDA) also began to systematically collect data on North Korea's grain production and supply to

Table 5.2 Bilateral Aid Volume to North Korea Before the 1990s—Set 2 (USD Millions)

	Russia (Soviet Union)		*China*		*Other Socialist Countries*		*Total*	
	Grant	*Loan*	*Grant*	*Loan*	*Grant*	*Loan*	*Grant*	*Loan*
1945–1949	53.0	—	—	—	—	—	53.0	—
1953–1960	325.0	284.0	287.1	172.5	364.9	—	977.0	456.5
1961–1970	558.3	—	157.4	—	159.0	—	874.7	—
1971–1980	682.1	—	300.0	—	—	—	982.1	—
1981–1990	508.4	—	500.0	—	—	—	1,008.4	—
Total	2,410.8		1,417.0		523.9		4,351.7	

Source: Revised from Kim, 2014: 431.

produce an annual estimate of grain production in North Korea. Similar efforts were made by other agencies in South Korea, including the KDI, with Statistics Korea publishing *Major Statistics Indicators of North Korea* yearly based on the data gathered and analysed by various agencies. These are the main South Korean data sources on North Korea that we use today (Lee and Cho, 2021). Other sources include statistics produced by IOs and MDBs.

In addition to bilateral aid, as shown in Table 5.3, there was technical cooperation with North Korea, which cannot be measured in exact numbers. Here, it is unclear whether there are any overlaps across the different datasets. It is also not obvious whether the assistance that North Korea received in the health sector from the Soviet Union, China, and other Soviet bloc countries has been included in the existing records. For example, between 1945 and 1958, while China provided Chinese medicines, the Soviet Union and allied countries provided assistance in varied forms, such as vaccine distribution, health sector policy advice, and medical education, as well as the establishment of a Soviet Red Cross hospital and the development of a pharmaceutical factory, infectious disease research institute, and so on. Some of the assistance was described as technical assistance, which was mostly knowledge transfer, while other assistance took the form of medical surgeries and treatment directly carried out by medical teams dispatched from those countries to North Korea (see Kim and Moon, 2019). However, it is unclear whether these activities are fully reflected in the datasets and statistics found in existing research.

Like Russia, China is not a member of the Organisation for Economic Cooperation and Development's (OECD) Development Assistance Committee (DAC), which is a group of ODA providers. Neither is an OECD member yet. Thus, it is not only the early aid data but also recent assistance data for North Korea that has not been recorded officially in a consolidated manner in an international statistical system such as the OECD ODA Creditor Reporting System (CRS). All DAC member countries provide data on ODA and other official flows (OOF),

Table 5.3 Non-Financial Term Bilateral Aid to North Korea Before the 1990s (USD Millions)

	Technical Assistance or In-Kinds (not measurable in financial terms)
Russia (Soviet Union)	Training programs (North Koreans going to Russia) Military equipment Oil Technicians (more than 5,000)
China	Volunteers
East Germany	350 engineers and technicians
East European Countries in all	Training programmes (North Koreans going to East European countries)
Czech	Buses
Albania	Asphalt
Mongolia	Horses (10,000)

Source: Author's own compilation based on Seth, 2018: 70–71 & 165.

including export credits, to the CRS. Especially in the case of China, it is only relatively recently that the Chinese government has started to officially share its development aid allocation. Before 2011, Beijing tended to keep a veil on its aid distribution due to domestic concerns and tensions between the government's lack of assistance to the poor within China and its aid to other countries. Also, Chinese aid is associated with trade cooperation, and thus, it is not easy to separate the trade and development assistance data in some cases. Therefore, any data on Chinese aid before 2011 was collected by individual research projects. However, since 2011, Beijing has published White Papers on 'China's Foreign Aid'—in 2011, 2014, and 2021—in English (see State Council Information Office, 2011, 2014 & 2021). While these three White Papers do not include detailed data segregation, they clearly state that China began providing foreign aid in 1950, starting with North Korea and Vietnam (State Council Information Office, 2011). Figure 5.1 shows Chinese aid to North Korea between 1995 and 2005.

There was a time when North Korea's economic situation was not as bad as it is now. Pyongyang even provided aid to countries in West Africa in the 1960s, which continued until the 1970s. For example, North Korea provided *Juche* farming methods to Ghana even though its own agricultural situation had already reached a nadir (Fahy, 2019b). But then North Korea experienced the great famine in the 1990s, and for the first time in its history, in 1995, the North Korean government asked for international aid support from non-socialist countries as well as IOs. Between 1996 and 2001, 5.94 million tonnes of food aid were provided to North Korea, mostly by the US, South Korea, and Japan: the US distributed 1.7 million tonnes; South Korea 0.67 million tonnes; and Japan 0.81 million tonnes. In comparison, China disbursed 1.3 million tonnes of food aid during this period

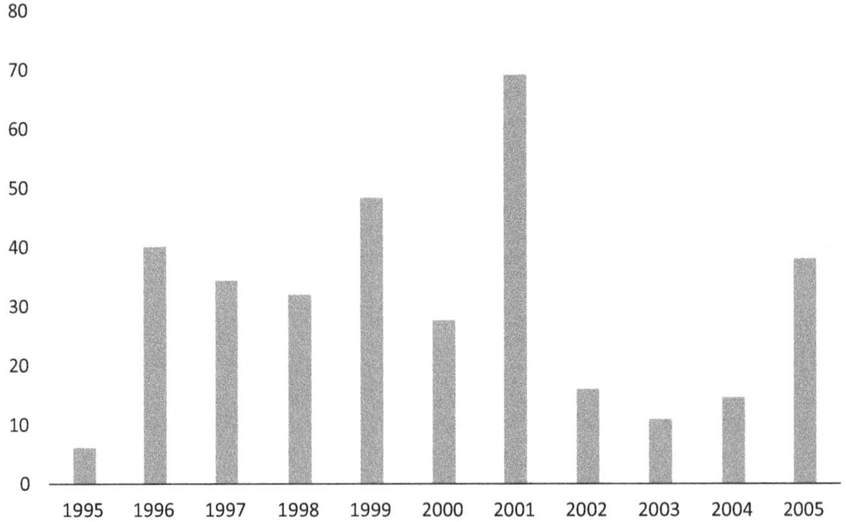

Figure 5.1 Chinese Bilateral Aid to North Korea, 1995–2005 (USD Millions)

Source: Author's own compilation based on Söderbert, 2006: 450.

(Lankov, 2015: 186). If we expand the time span to include the years between 1995 and 2012, China becomes the second largest aid donor to North Korea in the form of multi-bi food aid through the World Food Programme (WFP): China provided 3.27 million tonnes; South Korea 3.31 million tonnes; and the US 2.4 million tonnes (Reilly, 2014: 1171). While the exact figures for China's bilateral aid to North Korea are unknown, the WFP officially reported on its multi-bi aid amounts during this period (Reilly, 2014).

International Organisations

Owing to the seriousness and urgency of the situation generated by the famine, and in response to Pyongyang's call for international assistance, the WFP, the United Nations Children's Fund (UNICEF), and the United Nations Development Programme (UNDP) began providing food aid to North Korea. Between 1995 and 2005, the WFP provided 4 million tonnes of food aid, equivalent to USD 1.7 billion, which reached more than 25 per cent of the North Korean population (Ford, 2018: 107). The WFP disbursed around USD 300 million worth of food aid per year in the late 1990s. Between 1995 and 1998, more than 1 million tonnes of food aid was provided by humanitarian aid organisations (Hazel, 2015: 201). By 2000, 40 per cent of the food supply in North Korea was from aid agencies (Seth, 2018: 202). In 2003, the WFP reported that its aid to North Korea had reached 85 per cent of the population, especially women and children in need. An increase in primary school attendance from 75 per cent to 95 per cent was attributed to the successful distribution of biscuits in schools. This was confirmed by UNICEF stating in its report that food aid was delivered to the most vulnerable populations in North Korea between 1998 and 2002 (Ford, 2018: 110–111).

Unfortunately, consolidated data on the humanitarian aid provided to North Korea early in the famine period is only available in the research done by other scholars as of April 2022, as some early data provided by IOs is no longer shared in publicly accessible websites. However, since 2000, UN OCHA has provided humanitarian aid statistics for North Korea through its Financial Tracking Service (FTS). The FTS was established in 1992, based on UN General Assembly resolution 46/182, and is managed by UN OCHA. The FTS statistics are fully downloadable from its website,[1] which is regularly updated. Humanitarian aid flows, including flows to North Korea, from bilateral donors, IOs, NGOs, and other humanitarian actors are captured by the FTS based on the data submitted by these humanitarian actors (OCHA, 2022). Apart from this UN OCHA database, historical data on food aid provided to North Korea through the WFP can be found on the International Food Aid Information System (INTERFAIS or FAIS),[2] which was discontinued in the late 2000s. Figure 5.2 depicts humanitarian aid flows to North Korea between 2000 and 2021. It includes all bilateral donors, IOs, and humanitarian NGOs. During this period, humanitarian assistance from the international donor community to North Korea amounted to USD 377,599,330 at its highest and stood at USD 1,017,640 in 2021. The data includes both commitments and disbursements.

Figure 5.2 Humanitarian Aid Flows to North Korea, 2000–2021 (USD Thousands).

Source: Author's own compilation based on OCHA FTS (Data extracted on 11 February 2022).[3]

Some governments provided humanitarian aid to North Korea directly, but most of them disbursed their aid budgets through IOs and/or NGOs, which then implemented aid projects in North Korea. Before analysing the aid regime for North Korea in more detail, Figure 5.3 delineates aid statistics, segregated by channel, from the FTS. In the figure, 'bilateral donors' means individual governments that directly implemented aid projects in North Korea, while the data for multilateral organisations includes contributions from bilateral donor governments to IOs, including multi-bi aid. 'NGOs' means both national and international NGOs and other humanitarian organisations with part-funding from bilateral donor governments and IOs in addition to their own budgetary resources.

European Union

In Europe, ODA donors, including the European Union (EU), disbursed their aid budgets for North Korea through the WFP's humanitarian food scheme. For instance, the EU provided food aid worth Euro 50 million (USD 44 million) to North Korea through the WFP (Ford, 2018: 238), along with aid worth Euro 344 million (USD 430 million) that was dispatched by the European Commission between 1995 and 2005 (Ford, 2018: 109). While EU aid to North Korea was based on humanitarian assistance, mostly comprising emergency food aid, during this period, it also included in-kind support such as fertiliser and technical support for the agricultural and health sectors (Ford, 2018: 110). In addition, the EU provided energy aid to North Korea through the European Atomic Energy Community (Euratom) by joining the Korean Peninsula Energy Development Organization (KEDO) (EC, 1997). Including the Euratom budget, the EU provided about USD 121.4 million to KEDO for nine years

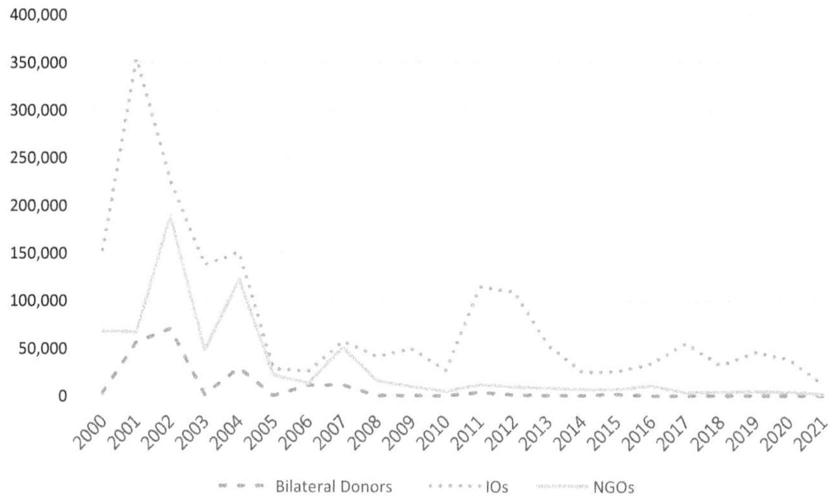

Figure 5.3 Humanitarian Aid to North Korea by Channel, 2000–2021 (USD Thousands).
Source: Author's own compilation based on OCHA FTS (Data extracted on 11 February 2022).

(Hautecouverture, 2020: 8). The EU was the fourth biggest bilateral donor to North Korea, after the US, South Korea, and China (Ford, 2018: 109).

The EU continued to provide aid amid the nuclear crisis in 2005, giving Euro 10.7 million (USD 13.5 million) to the health sector (Ford, 2018: 110), and this continued even when UN aid agencies had to leave the country at the request of the North Korean government. In comparison, most others ceased providing aid during the nuclear crisis as discussed later (see also Chapter 2). The North Korean government requested aid agencies to leave by the end of 2005, but the EU successfully persuaded Pyongyang of the need to continue food aid already in place. Accordingly, the EU, along with European NGOs, continued to provide humanitarian assistance until 2011. The total amount that the EU provided to North Korea during this period was Euro 500 million (USD 630 million), with Euro 10 million (USD 13 million) provided in emergency aid format in 2011 (Ford, 2018: 112). The legacy of this period still exists in the EU's aid focus on food security and deforestation in North Korea.

United States

Including the WFP, the largest donor to UN multilateral aid for North Korea during this period was the US (Ford, 2018). Figure 5.4 shows US multi-bi aid to North Korea through the years. Between 1995 and 2010, US aid to North Korea, in the form of food and energy aid, amounted to over USD 1.3 billion, as shown in Table 5.4.

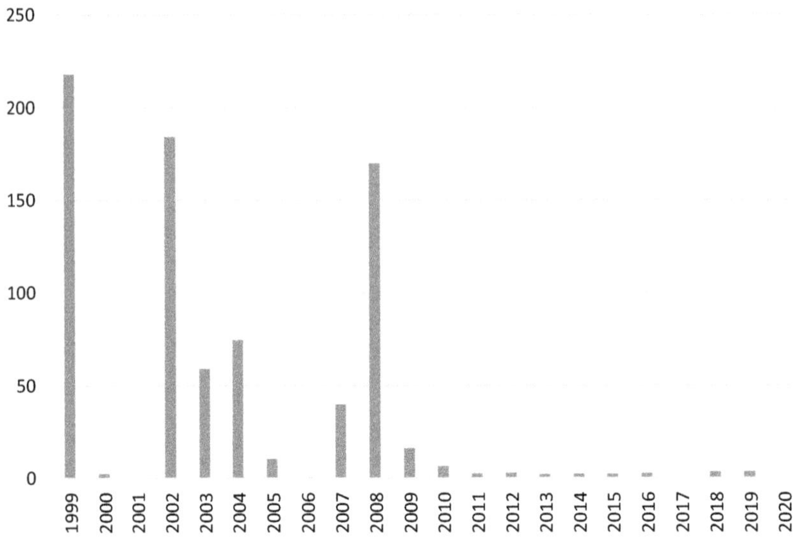

Figure 5.4 US ODA to North Korea (Disbursement) (USD Millions).

Source: Author's own compilation based on OECD statistics (Data extracted on 18 April 2022).

Table 5.4 US Aid to North Korea 1995–2010 (In-kind Support and All Channels) (USD Millions)

Financial Year	*Food Aid*	*Energy Aid*	*Total*
1995	—	9.50	9.50
1996	8.30	22.00	30.30
1997	52.40	25.00	77.40
1998	72.90	50.00	122.90
1999	222.10	65.10	287.20
2000	74.30	64.40	138.70
2001	58.07	74.90	132.97
2002	50.40	90.50	140.90
2003	25.48	2.30	27.78
2004	36.30	—	36.30
2005	5.70	—	5.70
2006	—	—	—
2007	—	45.00	45.00
2008	93.70	131.00	224.70
2009	5.60	15.00	20.60
2010	2.90*	—	2.90
Total	708.15	594.70	1,302.85

Source: Revised from Manyin and Nikitin, 2012: 224.

*USD 2.9 million in the 2010 financial year represents a budgetary adjustment for contributions provided in the 2008 financial year.

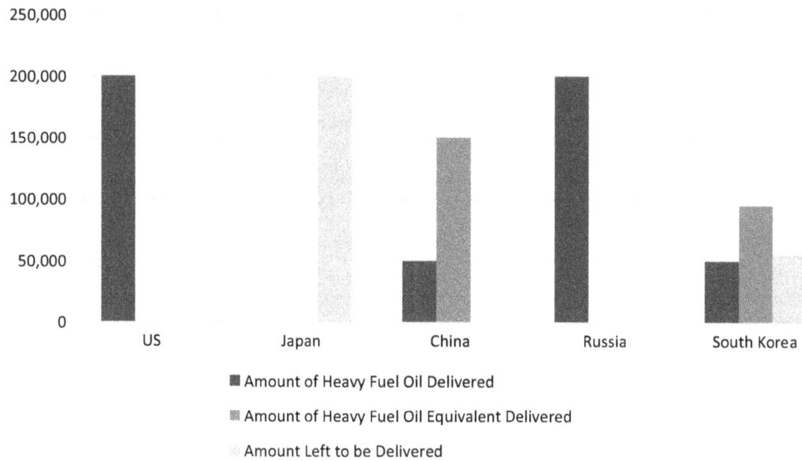

Figure 5.5 Energy Assistance to North Korea, 2007–2009 (Tonnes).

Source: Author's own compilation based on Manyin and Nikitin, 2012: 231.

Energy aid was included under the 1994 Agreed Framework establishing KEDO between 1995 and 2003, and fuel oil and technical assistance to assist nuclear disarmament by North Korea under the aegis of the Six-Party Talks between 2007 and 2009 (see Chapter 2). A small amount of medical assistance, including medical equipment and training, has also been provided by the US to North Korea (Manyin and Nikitin, 2012). However, since 2011, the US has not disbursed any aid to North Korea, except some exempt humanitarian assistance, due to sanctions on the country for its nuclear programme. (For more details about KEDO and North Korea's nuclear development programme, see Chapter 2.)

Figure 5.5 depicts the energy assistance that North Korea received from the five other participating countries in the Six-Party Talks—the US, China, Russia, Japan, and South Korea—between 2007 and 2009. All five countries agreed to provide 200,000 metric tonnes of heavy fuel oil, or its equivalent, each. However, as can be seen, Japan did not deliver any of its promised energy aid to North Korea during this period. Apart from humanitarian support, no further support was provided by Japan to North Korea due to increasing conflict over the abduction of Japanese citizens by the North Korean government and the resulting difficulty in normalising relations (Hughes, 2006; Lankov, 2015; Manyin and Nikitin, 2012; Söderbert, 2006).

Japan

Japan did not provide aid to North Korea until the famine period in the 1990s, but did to South Korea, which received USD 300 million in grant aid and USD 200 million in loan aid from Tokyo (Lim, 2021a: 121). The Japanese aid to South Korea has been defined by Seoul as 'property claim payments' as

Table 5.5 Japanese Aid to North Korea During the 1990s Famine Period (Including In-kind Support)

Year	*Bilateral Assistance*	*Through Multilateral Channels*
1995	Rice 500,000 tonnes	USD 500,000 (UNICEF, UNDP, WHO)
1996	Medical supplies USD 750,000	USD 5,250,000 (WFP, UNICEF)
1997	Rice 67,000 tonnes	JPY 94,000,000 (NGO)
2000	N/A	Rice 600,000 tonnes (WFP)
2004	N/A	USD 47,100,000 (WHO, WFP, UNICEF, WHO)

Source: Revised from Söderbert, 2006: 451.

compensation for the colonial period, but it was categorised by Tokyo as economic cooperation (Lim, 2021a; Söderbert, 2006). North Korea continuously demanded aid from Japan as compensation for colonial rule; however, Tokyo first requested the normalisation of relations between Japan and North Korea, and then rejected the claim for compensation but informed Pyongyang that it had to be in the form of economic cooperation (Söderbert, 2006). When KEDO was established in 1995, Japan agreed to provide support to North Korea (Hughes, 2006; Söderbert, 2006), which coincided with international food aid support to deal with the famine in North Korea. As shown in Table 5.5, Japan provided humanitarian aid to North Korea between 1995 and 2004.

Japan's provisional aid support plan under KEDO was suspended when North Korea fired a Taepodong missile in 1998 (Söderbert, 2006). According to Seth (2018: 203), the Japanese withdrawal of its aid programme was also due to lack of access in North Korea. Food aid was resumed after negotiations for normalising relations in 1999, but the relationship had to be put on hold once again between 2001 and 2003 due to increasing tensions between the US and North Korea over the latter's nuclear development programme. Bilateral relations between Tokyo and Pyongyang improved again when the Japan–North Korea's Pyongyang Declaration was agreed in 2002 (Hughes, 2006; Söderbert, 2006). Based on this improvement in relations, Japan provided food aid to North Korea again in 2004, as shown in Table 5.5. However, owing to North Korea's continuing nuclear development programme and to increasing conflict over the issue of abductions, Tokyo then imposed sanctions on Pyongyang. There is no record of Japan providing any ODA to North Korea in the CRS.

South Korea

South Korea replaced the US as the leading donor to North Korea, apart from China, in the late 1990s (Seth, 2018). Between 1995 and 1998, South Korea provided USD 316 million worth of aid to North Korea, which was more than 30 per cent of the total aid provided to North Korea (Ford, 2018: 107). However, it is somewhat unclear whether this figure included bilateral aid from South Korea to North Korea or whether it was calculated based on the data reported in humanitarian aid records. South Korea's bilateral aid to North Korea, with the exception of multi-bi aid, is not included in DAC statistics because Seoul does not report this aid as ODA. Under article 3 of the South Korean Constitution, North Korea is part of South Korea's territory. Bearing in mind that ODA is aid from one government to another, South Korean aid to North Korea thus does not constitute ODA as the latter is not a foreign sovereignty under the South Korean Constitution. Instead, the South Korean Ministry of Unification provides detailed statistics on aid from South Korea to North Korea. Figure 5.6 shows the trends in South Korean humanitarian aid to North Korea.

Like other donor countries, South Korea began providing humanitarian aid to North Korea in 1995. However, as shown in Figure 5.6, South Korean humanitarian aid to North Korea dropped to almost nil in the second year because President Kim Young-sam considered North Korea's request for humanitarian assistance to be exaggerated. The assistance resumed and increased during the ten years of progressive government under President Kim Dae-jung, from 1998 to 2003, and President Roh Moo-hyun, from 2003 to 2008. Then, it dramatically decreased during the conservative governments of President Lee Myung-bak, from 2008 to 2013, and President Park Geun-hye, from 2013 to 2017. It dropped down to almost nil again in 2016 and 2017 after North Korea's fifth and sixth nuclear tests. In theory, South Korean aid to North Korea should have increased again under the progressive government of President Moon Jae-in between 2017 and 2022.

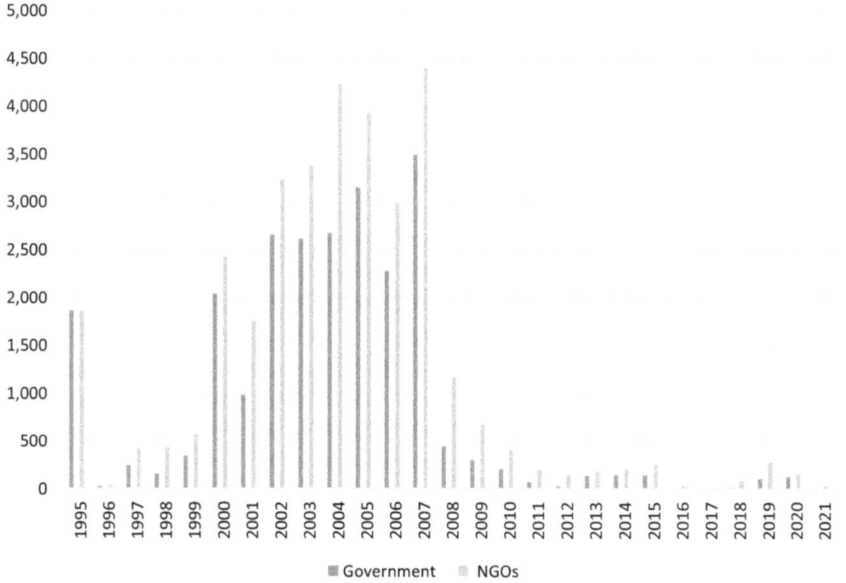

Figure 5.6 Trends in Humanitarian Aid from South Korea to North Korea (KRW 100 Millions).

Source: Author's own compilation based on Ministry of Unification dataset (Data extracted on 18 April 2022).

However, there was only a slight increase, and then almost no aid disbursement between 2020 and 2021 due to North Korea's COVID-19 border closure. In the later period, South Korean aid to North Korea focused more on development than on humanitarian assistance. Figure 5.6 thus does not necessarily include the total amount of aid from South Korea to North Korea. However, it does include bilateral and multi-bi grant aid, food loan aid, and aid to NGOs implementing aid projects in or for North Korea.

The South Korean government runs the Inter-Korean Cooperation Fund (IKCF) which provides an ODA-like fund. The IKCF was established in March 1991, following the passage of the Inter-Korean Cooperation Fund Act in 1990. While the Ministry of Unification is the governing body of the IKCF, the fund is administered by the Export-Import Bank of Korea (KEXIM Bank), with the government having commissioned KEXIM to operate the IKCF. South Korean companies and institutions willing to trade with North Korean businesses or to open businesses in North Korea can apply for grants and loans through the IKCF (KEXIM Bank, 2022c). For instance, companies running businesses in Kaesong Industrial Park took loans from the IKCF, and when the industrial park closed, KEXIM dealt with the insurance issues of those companies based on IKCF insurance. The IKCF also covers cultural, academic, and athletic events if they are co-hosted by South and North Korea, while a part of the fund goes towards humanitarian aid to North Korea. Between 1991 and 2020, the government of South Korea spent KRW 7.71 trillion (about USD 5.75 billion) of the IKCF budget (KEXIM Bank, 2022b). Only about 0.2 per cent of the IKCF was allocated to humanitarian aid to North Korea. Loans for KEDO were included in the IKCF budget (see KEXIM Bank, 2022a).

Other Donors

How other donor countries—apart from those already discussed—have provided aid to North Korea is not widely discussed in the literature, but the UN OCHA dataset presented earlier shows that countries including Switzerland, Sweden, Italy, and Russia have provided aid to North Korea. At the individual donor level, it is known that Denmark committed food aid worth USD 1 million to North Korea in 1996 (Tae, 2018: 100). The United Kingdom contributed about 18–20 per cent of the EU's humanitarian aid to North Korea around 2005, which was worth about GBP 2 million annually (Tae, 2018: 252). Also, Switzerland has continuously provided aid to North Korea, mainly through the UNICEF water, sanitation, and hygiene (WASH) programme, which is detailed later in this section.

According to the existing research, and as mentioned earlier, Western countries, IOs, and NGOs provided international aid to North Korea for the first time in the country's history in 1995. However, OECD statistics show that North Korea received ODA from 1985. According to the data from the KDI, there were already aid flows from OECD countries to North Korea in the 1960s (see Kim, 2014: 431, table 2). Furthermore, ODA has been continuously provided to North Korea, even under sanctions, mostly in the form of humanitarian aid. Figure 5.7 shows the ODA records of OECD donors to North Korea. Although OECD statistics include ODA

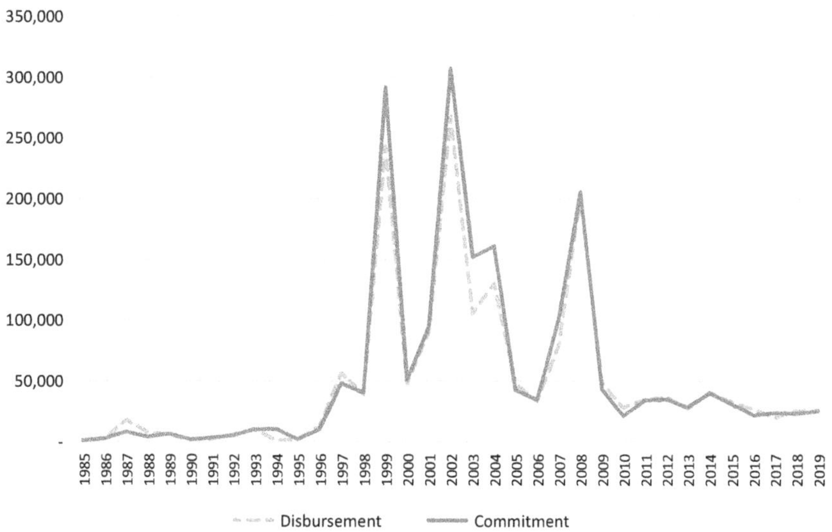

Figure 5.7 OECD Donor ODA Flows to North Korea (USD Thousands).

Source: Author's own compilation based on OECD statistics (Data extracted on 7 April 2022).

data from South Korea, Figure 5.7 does not include the complete data on aid from South Korea to North Korea because Seoul, as mentioned earlier, does not report its bilateral ODA to North Korea to the OECD CRS. However, South Korean aid that has been channelled through international organisations is included in the CRS. This data also does not include Chinese data—despite China being one of North Korea's largest bilateral donors—as it is not an OECD member country.

Notably, Switzerland has committed to providing aid for WASH and COVID-19-related nutrition programmes through UNICEF, until 2025. In addition to food aid, water aid has also been provided, mostly through the UNICEF WASH programme (Lee, 2019). Canada, South Korea, and Sweden have been the major donors to WASH programmes in North Korea, along with the UN Central Emergency Response Fund (CERF), the UNICEF Global Humanitarian Thematic Fund, and the Global Fund (UNICEF, 2020). Water supply facilities in North Korea were mostly built as part of industrialisation in the 1950s, and piped water supply systems were established in the 1970s; however, owing to the economic downturn in the 1980s, the government has not properly maintained the water supply system or invested in rehabilitation (Lee, 2019; UNICEF DPRK, 2022). The UNICEF WASH programme has been in place since 1995, but 39 per cent of the North Korean population still does not have access to clean water (UNICEF DPRK, 2022). Because of the COVID-19 border closure, all UNICEF international staff had left North Korea by December 2020, but the programme is still being managed by local members at the country office—for example, seconded national staff—with remote management by international staff. However, this has reduced the capacity for activities in North Korea during the COVID-19 pandemic, even though access to clean water is a greater need than ever before (UNICEF DPRK, 2020).

Non-Governmental Organisations

The trend in NGO assistance to North Korea is almost identical with the trends in aid provided by bilateral donor governments and multilateral organisations as NGOs are not eligible to provide aid to North Korea under international sanctions. NGOs began providing assistance to North Korea in 1995 at the same time as governments began disbursing humanitarian aid during the famine period. For instance, as the government of Denmark provided food aid to North Korea in 1996, Danish NGOs, such as the Danish Red Cross and Caritas Denmark, also provided food assistance (see Tae, 2018: 102). The trend of NGO aid following government aid to North Korea can be confirmed with the example of South Korea (see Figure 5.6). The full numerical picture of NGO aid to North Korea is not available; however, some useful comparisons can be found in the existing research. For example, in terms of humanitarian assistance, as a group, South Korean NGOs provided more food aid to North Korea than other groups of NGOs between 1996 and 2001. During this period, South Korean NGOs provided between 262,747 and 292,289 tonnes of food aid to North Korea, accounting for 48.8 per cent of all NGO food aid to the country. In comparison, European NGOs sent 261,065 tonnes of food aid (48.4 per cent), while US NGOs provided between 12,024 and 13,024 tonnes (2.4 per cent) and Japanese NGOs distributed 2,095 tonnes (0.4 per cent), according to data from the WFP (Flake, 2003: 23 & 36).

Aid Management and State Capacity in North Korea

As shown in Figures 5.3 and 5.6, international humanitarian aid to North Korea began to decrease sharply after 2002, with aid from South Korea the exception (see Figure 5.6). In 2002, multiple donors made political decisions against the North Korean regime, as mentioned earlier. This also coincided with the increasing attention on Afghanistan. Only 50 per cent of the target amount of 61,100 tonnes of food aid reached North Korea because of this situation (Kondro, 2002). Amid this decrease in humanitarian assistance, in 2005, the North Korean government announced that it no longer wanted humanitarian support while the country was still in need of aid. Instead, it requested development aid and technical assistance (Ford, 2018). As mentioned earlier, humanitarian aid is not designed to contribute to socio-economic changes at the macro level in a country's development pathway; rather, it plays the role of addressing urgent situations resulting, for example, from natural disasters. Accordingly, the North Korean government announced that it no longer needed humanitarian assistance, pointing to improved harvests, and that it now wanted development assistance. However, the actual reason for this request had less to do with the North Korean regime's desire to implement economic development projects but more to do with its concern about the foreign information influx reaching ordinary citizens (Lankov, 2015). Seemingly, the authority knew that no international development aid would be forthcoming due to increasing conflict over security issues. It also seemingly knew that the South Korean progressive government would become its saviour. On the donor side, there was hesitancy to provide development aid due to concern about the lack of transparency and accountability in place. Eventually, most international aid to North Korea was stopped in 2005. In the case of South Korea, aid to North Korea decreased, starting in 2008 when the conservative government of President Lee Myung-bak took office.

Among the donor community, there was increasing suspicion that aid to North Korea was not being used to meet the people's needs but was being provided to and used for the armed forces (Fahy, 2019b; Seth, 2018). Tae Yong-ho—the former North Korean diplomat who defected from the North Korean embassy in London to South Korea—noted in his testimonial book that Danish cheese intended for children was sent to military camps as a present from Kim Jong-il in the 1990s. Denmark sent 3,200 tonnes of feta cheese to North Korea—worth USD 33 million including shipment—which had been originally intended for Iran but was then blocked from being sent there by EU sanctions (Tae, 2018: 117–118 & 123). Also, general distribution did not equally reach all parts of the country. For instance, the most common form of aid that was provided, food aid from the WFP, tended to stay in the west of the country while remaining lacking on the east coast due to restrictions placed by the North Korean government (Fahy, 2019a; Seth, 2018). This was due, in part, to the basic conditions for distribution logistics. For example, roads, energy supplies, and basic resources for aid delivery were reportedly problematic, and delays were thus inevitable. However, the uneven distribution was also due to the government's tactic of distributing food to those who showed loyalty to the regime, and not to those in need, in order to maintain people's allegiance to the regime (Fahy, 2019a; Ford, 2018). Upon realising this, NGOs such as Care International, Oxfam, Action Against Hunger, Doctors Without Borders (Médecins Sans Frontières), and Doctors of the World ceased the programmes they had been implementing in North Korea (Fahy, 2019a; Ford, 2018).

It was difficult for aid workers to reach deep into the country to rural places not only due to the poor transport infrastructure but also due to the high level of restrictions imposed by the North Korean government, which sought to control aid workers in order to limit the influx of information from them to people at the grassroots. Korean-speaking personnel were not allowed in international aid teams, and aid workers were prohibited from learning the Korean language (Fahy, 2019b; Ford, 2018; Seth, 2018). This then caused confusion in translation and interpretation (Fahy, 2019a & 2019b; Seth, 2018). In other words, the North Korean government made the assessment that greater engagement by foreigners in the country endangered national security, and thus, demanded that aid agencies leave the country, except those with ongoing projects, under the pretext of its request for development aid. The situation was not much different for NGOs. When the UNICEF, WFP, and EU teams were not allowed to access the north-eastern part of North Korea to examine children's nutrition status, NGOs like the Red Cross were also not able to enter those provinces (Fahy, 2019a).

Another issue was observed beyond the country. Aid agencies provided financial support to North Korean embassies abroad intending to cover the costs of domestic distribution. However, this was not spent as planned, but used to cover the costs of running the embassies as the North Korean government could not afford these costs due to its economic difficulties (Tae, 2018). As Haggard and Noland (2017) explain, trust did not exist from the beginning and was absent throughout the period that the food aid programme was implemented in the 1990s. Furthermore, rice from Japan and South Korea was reportedly resold in the market (Seth, 2018). On one occasion, North Korea even demanded that South Korea should provide the aid in unmarked rice bags (Fahy, 2019a). Admittedly, the reselling of goods provided by donors is not an uncommon practice among aid recipients when there is a weak culture of accountability and transparency. Earlier on, accountability was not a common concept at the international level either. In many African countries, for example, untagged medicines, with the donor aid agencies' logos on them, were easily observed being resold in local pharmacies or markets, despite having been provided for free as part of grant aid packages by the donor organisations. However, the distinguishing feature of the North Korean case was that limited physical accessibility to places within the country made it difficult to confirm the end beneficiaries of aid.

Due to the lack of access to data and official information, aid workers were limited in terms of not only having accurate baseline surveys but also conducting monitoring and evaluation of their programmes. This made it difficult for them to measure the effectiveness of their aid programmes. In 1998, UNICEF, the WFP, and the European Commission were able to assess the nutrition status in North Korea and reported that about 60 per cent of children were suffering from chronic malnutrition while about 15 per cent were severely malnourished (Fahy, 2019a: 50; Smith, 2015: 205). The WFP reported that children were at risk of death from malnutrition in some areas of North Korea in 1997 (Smith, 2015: 205). A joint assessment by the Food and Agriculture Organization (FAO) and the WFP was also conducted and it found that 2.1 million children and 500,000 pregnant women were suffering from starvation (Ford, 2018: 107). However, these were not accurate statistics as the organisations were not allowed to assess the entire population of children. For example, the north-eastern provinces of North Korea were known to be the worst affected by the famine as most people living there belonged to the lower level of the *songbun* system, with access to 200–300 per cent less food than those belonging to higher *songbun* levels. The assessment team was only allowed partial access to these provinces, and only after Tun Myat, a senior WFP official, warned the North Korean government that they could stop the programme. Some aid workers' recollections of their experiences in North Korea from this period were based on these partial observations of lived reality, without access to about 15 per cent of the population (Fahy, 2019a: 51).

Yet, it is not impossible to negotiate for monitoring aid projects in North Korea. Indeed, the North Korean government accepted, to some extent, the donor community's request for monitoring in order to receive humanitarian aid to deal with food shortages in 2011, following floods in 2010. Specifically, Pyongyang accepted field-based observation by the WFP prior to the delivery of food aid this time (Dong, 2011). According to the former US special envoy for North Korean human right issues, Ambassador Robert King, he and his North Korean counterpart 'reached an agreement that satisfied US requirements but was also acceptable to the North Korean government' in terms of US legal requirements for assessing and monitoring assistance between 2011 and 2012. However, all this was halted due to the leadership change in North Korea (King, 2018). Therefore, concerns about aid distribution and accountability could be mitigated through negotiation.

When natural disaster hit again in 2017, the UN committed USD 6 million in support of drought-affected North Korea and conducted a USD 111 million campaign to deal with the country's food insecurity a year later (Ford, 2018: 233), despite the heavy sanctions imposed against Pyongyang. However, the plan had to be halted due to North Korea's COVID-19 border closure. Even before the COVID-19 lockdown by the North Korean government, humanitarian aid and education activities permitted under UN sanctions had already been blocked. For example, no US aid workers were allowed to travel to North Korea due to the 2017 US sanctions. Exemptions were given, but only in very rare cases, and even then, the exemption process was very slow (King, 2018). The US travel ban was in place and then the COVID-19 border closure began at the beginning of 2020. Only 9 per cent of the required aid was disbursed in 2018 (UN, 2018). Also, even in the case of exemptions granted by the US, monitoring activity was not included in the exemption list, and thus, no monitoring trips could be made (Zadeh-Cumming and Harris, 2020).

In 2018, North Korea was reported to be in need of USD 111 million in humanitarian aid for about 6 million vulnerable civilians, while 50 per cent of children in the country's rural areas were without access to safe drinking water and about 30 per cent of children under five were stunted (King, 2018; UN, 2018). Critical medicines were severely lacking. For example, in 2018, in one hospital in North Korea, there were 140 patients with tuberculosis but only 40 of them could be treated due to the lack of medicine (King, 2018). These were the 'unintended consequences of the sanctions' (UN, 2018). In addition, even though humanitarian aid could have been continued, as pointed out earlier, it would have provided a very minimal level of support in the form of ad hoc measures. If USD 111 million—possibly more—was the amount required for urgent basic needs, such as water, health, sanitation, and food, the amount needed for state capacity building, and further for economic and social development, would have been much higher.

Furthermore, a culture of accountability needs to be built up in countries like North Korea, so that they can implement aid effectively (see Lim, 2021b). Data collection and information sharing are critical aspects of monitoring and evaluation, especially within the culture of accountability. However, access to data has been very limited in the case of North Korea, making it difficult for any aid actor to put accountability in place. Also, the country has weak data collection capacity. Recalling the CEE cases that were mentioned at the beginning of this chapter, it is evident that aid can bring about changes by improving the transparency and accountability of both state and society. Based on the experience of CEE countries, we can also see that lack of attention to aid management capacity and accountability can have some adverse results (see Fagan, 2006).

While donor governments, as well as IOs and MDBs, tend to work at the national and local levels of the recipient government, NGOs implement aid programmes and projects at a more grassroots level, usually with local communities. It has been evident in the existing research that NGO activities can contribute to local capacity development (for example, see Yeo, 2017). Especially in countries with state fragility, like North Korea, the government can easily fail to provide adequate basic health services in remote rural areas, thus building the capacity of local communities is equally important in such fragile states. Fragile states exhibit some common features: they are often unable or unwilling to provide services to people, and political accountability does not exist (Alagiah et al., 2012). Thus, in many fragile states, international or local NGOs complement government efforts, for instance, to improve the effectiveness and efficiency of community healthcare systems (Baldursdóttir, Gunnlaugsson and Einarsdóttir, 2018; Rosales et al., 2015). Likewise, there was a brief attempt at local capacity building in North Korea by training people in the use of new agricultural technologies in rural areas during the first aid-provision period. However, due to the reasons discussed earlier, the project was left unfinished, which otherwise could have helped people 'in the impoverished rural communities' (Seliger, 2006: 18). Providing development aid, whether at the macro level or through a people-to-people approach at the micro level, does not mean that aid workers directly tell local beneficiaries what to do. Rather, it is more about building and developing capacity in the political, economic, and social spheres and in local communities, so that both state and society can function with accountability.

However, in the case of North Korea, there has been an almost complete lack of opportunities for aid workers to engage at the people-to-people level with those at the very bottom level of society. According to Masood Hyder, a former UN humanitarian coordinator in North Korea, 'North Korea knows how aid works, but has no idea about development assistance. It is no good just listing shortages, the bureaucracy will need to understand accountability, transparency, and debt management' (Watts, 2004: 1031). Countries with weak capacity, like North Korea, require differentiated approaches throughout the aid project cycle. In other words, when providing aid to fragile countries—where the state does not function properly—we need to take customised approaches, including to the monitoring and evaluation process (Lim, 2021b; Von Engelhardt, 2018). However, this thinking did not yet exist in the international aid regime when donors were providing assistance to North Korea during the famine period. Therefore, it is highly likely that donors did not consider taking tailored approaches, but rather imposed the standard general framework of the aid cycle on the dysfunctional North Korean state. Countries like North Korea need international aid that is 'concerned first and foremost with facilitating local processes to enable them to foster the cohesive societies and widely accepted institutions necessary for societal governing systems to work effectively', and it is because they are fragile in the context producing 'an institutional structure that its people regard as legitimate is unlikely to foster the conditions necessary for development' (Kaplan, 2008: 50).

In light of this, the North Korean regime does not function for its people. In the discourse of aid management, the regime even blocks opportunities for the capacity development of the state, market, and society. Therefore, this book argues that we need to provide international aid to North Korea to uncover and realise the potential of its cloaked society with capacity building and development. To that end, the existing aid regime for North Korea needs to be redesigned by considering the country in the context of approaches to fragile states. The next chapter continues the discussion, dealing with the question of whether North Korea is a fragile state, given that the Kim regime has survived and remained resilient through difficult times.

Notes

1 https://fts.unocha.org/.
2 https://www.wfp.org/fais.
3 At the time of writing this book, the OCHA FTS database stated that 'Trends from 2008 to 2018 data are currently under review. Reliable annual data can be found in the Country Page by year. The amount per year might change based on daily reports received and processed in the system'.

References

Alagiah, Adam, Daria Oulianova, Elena Pietschmann and Vasundhra Thakur (2012). *Accountability in Fragile States: Lessons From Nepal and Uganda.* Development in Practice: International Development Advisory Services Africa Impact Paper 7.

Baldursdóttir, Sigríður, Geir Gunnlaugsson and Jónína Einarsdóttir (2018). Donor Dilemmas in a Fragile State: NGO-iszation of Community Healthcare in Guinea-Bissau. *Development Studies Research*, 5(S1): S27–S39.

Cartier-Bresson, Jean (2012). Official Development Assistance in Fragile States. *Crime Law Social Change*, 58: 495–507.

Dong, Yong-Sueng (2011). Behind North Korea's Plea for Emergency Food Aid. *SERI Quarterly*: 127–130.

Duffield, Mark (2014). *Global Governance and the New Wars: The Merging of Development and Security.* New York: Zed Books.

EC (1997). European Union Joins North Korean Nuclear Security Body. 22 September 1997, *European Commission.* https://cordis.europa.eu/article/id/9049-european-union-joins-north-korean-nuclear-security-body. Accessed: 18 February 2022.

Fagan, Adam (2006). Transnational Aid for Civil Society Development in Post-Socialist Europe: Democratic Consolidation or a New Imperialism? *The Journal of Communist Studies and Transition Politics*, 22(1): 115–134.

Fahy, Sandra (2019a). *Dying for Rights: Putting North Korea's Human Rights Abuses on the Record.* New York: Columbia University Press.

Fahy, Sandra (2019b). *Marching Through Suffering: Loss and Survival in North Korea.* New York: Columbia University Press.

Flake, L. Gordon (2003). The Experience of US NGOs in North Korea. In: L. Gordon Flake and Scott Snyder (eds.). *Paved With Good Intentions: The NGOs Experience in North Korea*. Westport: Praeger Publishers, pp. 15–46.

Ford, Glyn (2018). *Talking to North Korea: Ending the Nuclear Standoff*. London: Pluto Press.

Haggard, Stephan and Marcus Noland (2017). *Hard Target: Sanctions, Inducements, and the Case of North Korea*. Stanford: Stanford University Press.

Hautecouverture, Benjamin (2020). *A Look Back on KEDO: The European Involvement*. Researchs and Documents 20/2020. Paris: Fondation Pour La Recherche Stratégique.

Hughes, Christopher W. (2006). The Political Economic of Japanese Sanctions Towards North Korea: Domestic Coalitions and International Systemic Pressures. *Pacific Affairs*, 79(3): 455–481.

JICA (2017). Linking Humanitarian Aid and Development Aid: A Lively Discussion With Julia Steets and Other Experts. 16 January 2017, *JICA Ogata Sadako Research Institute for Peace and Development News and Topics*. https://www.jica.go.jp/jica-ri/news/topics/20161212_01.html. Accessed: 18 February 2022.

Kaplan, Seth D. (2008). *Fixing Fragile States: A New Paradigm for Development*. Westport, CT: Praeger Security International.

KEXIM Bank (2022a). *About IKCF: Annual Disbursement Statistics* [한국수출입은행 (2022) 남북협력기금: 연도별 기금현황]. https://www.koreaexim.go.kr/se/HPHFSE055M01#tab1. Accessed: 18 April 2022.

KEXIM Bank (2022b). *About IKCF: Assistance Activities*. https://www.koreaexim.go.kr/he/HPHEOM005M01#tab2. Accessed: 18 April 2022.

KEXIM Bank (2022c). *About IKCF: Overview*. https://www.koreaexim.go.kr/he/HPHEOM004M01. Accessed: 18 April 2022.

Kim, Jin-hyouk andMi-ra Moon (2019). The Socialist Camps North Korean Medical Support and Exchange (1945–1958): Between Learning From the Soviet Union and Independent Course. *Korean Journal of Medical History*, 28(1): 139–189 [김진혁, 문미라 (2019). 사회주의 진영의 북한 의료지원과 교류 (1945–1958) : 소련배우기의 주체적 발전의 틈새에서. 의사학, 28(1): 139–189].

Kim, Jiyoung (2014). The Politics of Foreign Aid in North Korea. *The Korean Journal of International Studies*, 12(2): 425–450.

King, Robert R. (2018). Humanitarian Engagement With North Korea – Great Need But Increasingly Difficult. 4 September 2018, *Center for Strategic & International Studies (CSIS) Commentary*. https://www.csis.org/analysis/humanitarian-engagement-north-korea-great-need-increasingly-difficult. Accessed: 9 February 2020.

Kondro, Wayne (2002). Shortfall in Food Aid for North Korea. *The Lancet*, 359: 1679.

Lancaster, Carol (2007). *Foreign Aid: Diplomacy, Development, Domestic Politics*. London: University of Chicago Press.

Lankov, Andrei (2015). *The Real North Korea: Life and Politics in the Failed Stalinist Utopia*. New York: Oxford University Press.

Lee, Kyunghee (2019). A Study on Water Governance Transition in DPRK. *The Korean Journal of International Studies*, 59(3): 347–379 [이경희 (2019). 북한의 물 거버넌스 변화 연구 : 북한과 유니세프의 물 협력 실증 분석을 중심으로. 국제정치논총, 59(3): 347–379].

Lee, Suk and Byoungkoo Cho (2021). *North Korean Statistics and Research on the North Korean Economy*. Dialogue on the North Korea Economy No. April 2021. Sejong: Korea Development Institute.

Lim, Sojin (2019). Determinants of Aid Modalities: A Case of South Korea on Triangular Cooperation and its Implication towards North Korea. *North Korean Review*, 2019: 73–93.

Lim, Sojin (2021a). The Evolution Story of South Korea From a Fragile State to an International Actor. In: Sojin Lim and Niki Alsford (eds.). *Routledge Handbook of Contemporary South Korea*. London: Routledge, pp. 118–135.

Lim, Sojin (2021b). The Paradox of Unsustainability in UN Sustainable Development Goals (SDGs): The North Korean Case in the Context of Accountability and the Fragile States Under Sanctions. *Journal of Peace and Unification*, 11(1): 55–78.

Macrae, Joanna and Adele Harmer (2004). *Beyond the Continuum: An Overview of the Changing Role of Aid Policy in Protracted Crises.* HPG Research Briefing Number 16. London: Overseas Development Institute.

Mandel, Ruth (2001). Seeding Civil Society. In: C.M. Hann (ed.). *Postsocialism: Ideal, Ideologies and Practices in Eurasia*. London: Routledge, pp. 279–296.

Manyin, Mark E. and Mary Beth Nikitin (2012). Foreign Assistance to North Korea. *Current Politics and Economics of Northern and Western Asia*, 21(2): 221–254.

Milner, Helen V. and Dustin Tingley (2013). The Choice for Multilateralism: Foreign Aid and American Foreign Policy. *Review of International Organizations*, 8(3): 313–341.

OCHA (2011). *Peacebuilding and Linkages With Humanitarian Action: Key Emerging Trends and Challenges.* OCHA Occasional Policy Briefing Series No. 7. New York: OCHA.

OCHA (2022). *What is the Financial Tracking Service (FTS) and How to Use It?* https://fts.unocha.org/content/what-financial-tracking-service-fts-and-how-use-it. Accessed: 11 February 2022.

OECD (2018). *States pf Fragility 2018. Highlights*. Paris: OECD.

Pishchikova, Kateryna (2007). What Happened After the 'End of History'? Foreign Aid and Civic Organisations in Ukraine. In: Derrick Purdue (ed.). *Civil Societies and Social Movements: Potentials and Problems*. New York: Routledge, pp. 35–52.

Reilly, James (2014). The Curious Case of China's Aid to North Korea. *Asian Survey*, 54(6): 1158–1183.

Rosales, Alfonso C., Elizabeth Walumbe, Frank W. J. Anderson, Juli A. Hedrick, Dennis T. Cherian and Rhonda Holloway (2015). Role of International Non-Governmental Organisation in Strengthening Health System in Fragile-State Context: Evaluation Results From South Sudan. *African Evaluation Journal*, 3(2): 1–7.

Seliger, Bernhard (2006). Income, Wealth, and Political Power in North Korea. *North Korean Review*: 5–22.

Seth, Michael J. (2018). *North Korea: A History*. London: Palgrave.

Smith, Hazel (2015). *North Korea: Markets and Military Rule*. Cambridge: Cambridge University Press.

Söderbert, Marie (2006). Can Japanese Foreign Aid to North Korea Create Peace and Stability? *Pacific Affairs*, 79(3): 433–454.

State Council Information Office (2011). *China's Foreign Aid.* Beijing: State Council Information Office of the People's Republic of China. http://english.www.gov.cn/archive/white_paper/2014/09/09/content_281474986284620.htm. Accessed: 15 February 2021.

State Council Information Office (2014). *China's Foreign Aid.* Beijing: State Council Information Office of the People's Republic of China. http://english.www.gov.cn/archive/white_paper/2014/08/23/content_281474982986592.htm. Accessed: 15 February 2021.

State Council Information Office (2021). *China's International Development Cooperation in the New Era*. Beijing: State Council Information Office of the People's Republic of China.

Tae, Yong-ho (2018). *Testimonial of Former First Minister of the Embassy of the Democratic People's Republic of Korea in the United Kingdom, Tae Yong-ho*. Seoul: Giparang [태영호 (2018). 전 영국 주재 북한공사 태영호의 증언 : 3층 서기실의 암호. 서울, 기파랑].

UN (2018). Interview: UN's Top Official in North Korea Foresees 'Surge' in Humanitarian Aid. 28 June 2018, *UN News*. https://news.un.org/en/interview/2018/06/1013432. Accessed: 9 February 2022.

UNICEF DPRK (2020). *UNICEF DPRK Humanitarian Situation Report No. 2*.

UNICEF DPRK (2022). *Water, Sanitation and Hygiene*. https://www.unicef.org/dprk/water-sanitation-hygiene. Accessed: 11 February 2022.

Von Engelhardt, Marie (2018). *International Development Organizations and Fragile States: Law and Order*. Cham: Palgrave MacMillan.

Watt, Jonathan (2004). Profile: Masood Hyder, UN Humanitarian Coordinator in North Korea. *The Lancet*, 364: 1031.

Yeo, Andrew I. (2017). Engagement With North Korea: Evaluating the Scope of People-to-People Engagement in North Korea, 1995–2012. *Asian Perspective*, 42(2071): 309–339.

Zadeh-Cummings, Nazanin and Lauren Harris (2020). The Impact of Sanctions Against North Korea on Humanitarian Aid. *Journal of Humanitarian Affairs*, 2(1): 44–52.

6 Strong Regime but Dysfunctional State Capacity

According to the Organisation for Economic Co-operation and Development (OECD), the main objective of providing official development assistance (ODA) is to promote 'economic development and welfare of developing countries' (OECD, 2021: 11). However, the actual spectrum of factors that development aid can influence extends beyond economic development and welfare, especially in the recent paradigm of sustainable development in line with the framework of the United Nations (UN) Sustainable Development Goals (SDGs). The concept of development is no longer limited to economic and social development but includes areas such as climate change and the environment as well as peace and security. Thus, more stakeholders—private sector organisations as well as civil society organisations and non-governmental organisations, in addition to bilateral donor governments and international organisations—are engaged in development processes. Consequently, a greater number and variety of financial vehicles can contribute to development, more broadly.

In this context, the donor community has created tailored approaches to countries struggling with implementing globally agreed development goals. A key lesson learned from the implementation of the Millennium Development Goals (MDGs) has been that donors need to consider differentiated approaches to providing aid to some countries, like fragile states, whose state capacity is not similar to that of other developing countries. As the SDGs are more demanding than the MDGs, with a longer list of goals and indicators to achieve, they require more financial resources and state capacity to implement. Thus, countries that lagged in MDG implementation seem to struggle more with implementing the SDGs. This means that aid has a rather specific role when it comes to countries with fragility. The objectives of aid to these countries need to be able to address the fundamental causes of fragility in each recipient country. For example, in a situation of conflict, there can be no socio-economic–political development unless peace and state stability are achieved. Also, it becomes more important to focus on improving state capacity when providing aid for the delivery of basic needs, public goods, and services to people in these countries (Cartier-Bresson, 2012; Muchadenyika, 2016). This can help the government gain legitimacy and build mutual trust between state and society (Muchadenyika, 2016). A country like Burundi was able to exit the category of most capacity-challenged fragile states in 2016, thanks to

DOI: 10.4324/9781003390282-6

development aid from international organisations such as the World Bank and the United Nations Children's Fund (UNICEF) (Carment et al., 2017).

However, common ground on a definition of 'fragile states' is yet to be found (Nussbaum Zorbas and Koros, 2012), with the term continuing to be a subject of scholarly debates and practical policy discussions alike. Not only that, but consensus is also absent on how to define terms. As Engelhardt (2018: 18) observes, 'the different terms often describe the same phenomenon in the same vague manner'. Accordingly, this chapter examines existing definitions and fragility indices to provide a better understanding of fragile states or the fragility of states. Based on an in-depth understanding of fragile states, the chapter then discusses the paradoxical case of North Korea in the context of discussion on fragile states. In the end, the chapter supports the argument put forward in previous chapters that North Korea is a fragile state in that it is a dysfunctional state but cloaked by the image of a strong regime and that we thus need to redirect our rhetoric and narratives from a focus on nuclear and security issues to a more productive stance that involves taking a differentiated approach to the aid regime for North Korea. Taking this more productive stance could lead to 'state capacity' development of government for its people, thus creating an enabling environment for resilient civil society—especially if the timing is right.

Defining Fragile States

The concept of fragile states can be understood in various ways, while different approaches can use different terms for the concept. The terms 'weak states' and 'failed states' tend to be more familiar to, and used more by, international security experts and academics. In comparison, the terms 'state fragility' and 'fragile states' seem to be more welcome to international development policymakers and practitioners, and in the development studies discipline. The term 'weak states' originated in 1915 when the United States (US) government used it to refer to the weakness of countries that were 'politically incompetent to prevent outbreaks of internal violence' (Lemay-Hébert, 2019: 78). The main reason that the term 'weak states' is used more than the term 'fragile states' in international security debates lies in the continuing dichotomy between weak states and so-called strong or stronger states such as the US and the United Kingdom (UK), or group of strong states such as the European Union (EU). To protect against the spillover effect of state weakness or state failure and its aftermath, strong or stronger countries tend to seek to prevent threats emanating from weak or failed states, such as 'crime, terrorism, disease, uncontrolled migration, and energy insecurity' (Patrick, 2011: 5). In other words, security policymakers see weak or failing states as threats to regional or global security and to countries like the US.

However, the interpretation of such states is different in the international development discourse. In this discourse, these countries are not seen as threats that need to be addressed to prevent or mitigate conflict, but more as the targets of assistance that can reduce the causes of fragility, and thus, help these countries achieve sustainable development and resilience. In the development studies discipline, fragile states are those identified as having the 'development challenges of weak capacity' of state (see von Engelhardt, 2018). Therefore, countries like the US or the UK provide financial support to fragile states or illegitimate states with weak institutions due to the nexus between fragility and poverty, or due to the economic disconnection resulting from the political disconnection between state and society (Kaplan, 2008; Lemay-Hébert, 2019). In general, aid donors tend to focus on the lack of state capacity, institutional resilience to external shocks, and state legitimacy in the case of fragile states (Hout, 2010).

Here, this use of different concepts does not mean that there is complete polarisation between security and/or international relations and development discourses. Rather, it merely indicates a continuing tendency. For example, we can accept that the concept of fragile states has roots in the concept of weak states. The latter developed into the concept of failed states, which then evolved into fragile states, state fragility, or states of fragility, and then more recently, further into state resilience (for example, see Lemay-Hébert, 2019). However, despite the conceptual evolution, the terms 'weak states' or 'failed states' are still used interchangeably with the concept of fragile states in current affairs. For instance, in 2002, US President George W. Bush announced, 'America is now threatened less by conquering states than we are by failing ones'. Then, in 2003, the US State Department's Director of Policy Planning, Richard Haass, speaking at the School of Foreign Service, noted, 'the attacks of 9/11, 2011, reminded us that weak states can threaten our security as much as strong ones' (Patrick, 2011: 4).

In 2007, then Senator Barak Obama also used the term 'weak states', along with the term 'ungoverned states', in his remarks to the Chicago Council on Global Affairs, when he referred to 'weak and ungoverned states that have become the most fertile breeding grounds for transnational threats like terror and pandemic disease and the smuggling of deadly weapons' (Patrick, 2011: 3). Here, Obama's understanding of weak and ungoverned states as a threat to national security cannot be clearly detached from the concept of illegitimate states with weak national institutions, defined as fragile states, in international development discussions. Similarly, US Secretary of State Condoleezza Rice spoke about weak states in her speech at the Launch of the Civilian Response Corps in Washington DC in 2008, while her successor, Hillary Clinton, noted the chaos generated by failed states in her testimony before the US Senate Committee on Foreign Relations in 2009 (Patrick, 2011: 3). Rice identified weak or poorly governed states as countries 'on the verge of failure or have already failed', putting weak states, fragile states, and failed states into the same box. Clinton, who was seen to take a more traditional security line, interpreted fragile states as threats to national security. As just discussed, Obama used the term 'weak states' in the same context.

The use of the term 'weak states' by the US government, beginning in the 1910s, gave way to the term 'failed states' in the mid-1990s. Then, the international community in the 1990s saw the divergence of the concept in traditional security and development. Eventually, security experts began to familiarise themselves with the term 'fragile states' rather than use the term 'failed states' by adopting development approaches based on the notion of security as 'the result of and the precondition for development' (Lemay-Hébert, 2019: 79). This concept was then further developed into the idea of state fragility when the events of 11 September 2001 (hereinafter 9/11) occurred in the US. However, there is still no clear consensus on the concept of fragile states.

One of the main reasons we do not have a concrete theoretical understanding of fragile states is that each fragile state tells a unique story (Carment, Prest and Samy, 2010). For example, according to Kaplan's (2008: 35) definition of fragile states, the 'divided natures of fragile states have left them with no unifying identities, no unifying institutions, and no unifying governance systems with which to bind their peoples together'. However, this definition of fragile states cannot explain country cases like North Korea. While most post-colonial countries have borders that were artificially drawn without regard for their histories, traditions, ethnicities, and so on, not all of them became fragile for this reason. Post-colonial countries are mostly agriculture-based economies, with state-building pathways that are irrelevant or absent. Thus, it is more likely that states become fragile due to lack of structural capacity to function properly for their people. Also, the colonial powers did not pay attention to nation-building processes in these countries (Brock et al., 2012). This could be why the recent phenomenon of conceptualising fragile states is not simply about categorising countries as conflict or post-conflict countries (see Alonso, Cortez and Klasen, 2014).

At the same time, various criteria, such as the capability of the state to hold its society, define state fragility (Lemay-Hébert and Mathieu, 2014). While the meaning of collapsed states is derived from the consequences of collapse, the concept of failing, fragile, or failed states focuses more on the intermediary stages (Engelhardt, 2018). Thus, various organisations and institutions distinguish fragile states based on the main 'causes' of state fragility (Alonso et al., 2014; Engelhardt, 2018). In other words, the fragility of a state is not simply comprised of whether the state will collapse or not. Rather, fragility is to be found in the state's capacity to function for its people. For example, the OECD, which includes most of the leading aid donors in its Development Assistance Committee (DAC), defines fragile states as follows.

> States are fragile when governments and state structures lack capacity—or in some cases, political will—to deliver public safety, good governance and poverty reduction to their citizens… the capability of states to fulfil their core functions is essential in order to reduce poverty. Priority functions include: ensuring security and justice; establishing an enabling environment for basic service delivery, strong economic performance and employment generation.
>
> (Cited in Simpson and Hawkins, 2018: 22)

Looking at the various existing fragile states indices, as the following section does, it becomes even clearer that the concept of fragile states or state fragility is understood in a more specific way, based on indicators such as human security, peacebuilding, development performance, governance, corruption, conflict, legitimacy, economic management, and other related factors—in a way that is far more specific than other categorisations of developing countries (Alonso et al., 2014; Nussbaum, Zorbas and Koros, 2012).

Understanding Fragile States through Indices

There are several global indices that measure the fragility of countries. They include the Fragile States Index (FSI) produced by the Fund for Peace (FFP), the Index of State Weakness in the Developing World (ISW) by the Brookings Institution, the Global Peace Index by the Institute for Economics and Peace, the Fragility Index by the Country Indicators for Foreign Policy (CIFP) project, the Fragility Index by the Center for Systemic Peace (CSP), the State Weakness Index by the Bertelsmann Transformation Index project, the Peace and Conflict Instability Ledger by the University of Maryland, the Political Instability Index by the Economist Intelligence Unit, the State Fragility Index by George Mason University, States of Fragility (index) by the OECD, and Country Policy and Institutional Assessment (CPIA) by the World Bank (Lim, 2021; Mata and Ziaja, 2009). Among these, this chapter mainly focuses on those either regularly produced or widely cited in existing studies.

World Bank: Country Policy and Institutional Assessment

The World Bank's CPIA is the 'most widely reproduced index of state fragility', according to De Siqueira (2014: 271). The CPIA uses 16 criteria, grouped in four clusters—economic management, structural policies, policies for social inclusion, and public sector management and institutions—to assess state policy and institutional frameworks, and thus, state fragility (World Bank, 2010). The CPIA measures the capacity of a state (Lemay-Hébert, 2019). It was originally designed to measure a country's financial capacity for resource allocation by the World Bank. Conflict-affected and weakly governed states were therefore categorised as countries 'under stress' (Nay, 2014). In other words, the CPIA is not a fragile states index itself but recognises fragile states through its assessment. In 2005, the term 'under stress' was changed to 'fragile' and countries with a CPIA score of 3.2 or less were identified as 'fragile states' (De Siqueira, 2014; Nay, 2014). Furthermore, given its genesis, the CPIA does not include countries like North Korea that are not eligible for ODA from the World Bank's International Development Association (Rice and Patrick, 2008), which is a limitation of the CPIA. Also, fragile states indices produced by international organisations, such as the World Bank, have been criticised due to their nexus with politics (see Lim, 2021). For example, the concept of fragile states itself cannot be free from political perceptions and government intentions (Nay, 2014: 211). Furthermore, it is not evident that the CPIA has been reproduced most widely as it does not include countries like North Korea.

Country Indicators for Foreign Policy: Fragility Index

In its recent Fragility Index, the CIFP project team clearly states that the project is 'less concerned about producing a specific list of Fragile and Conflict Affected

States as OECD or World Bank Group have done' and that it views 'fragility as a matter of degree, not kind' (Carment, Muñoz, and Samy, 2020: 2). The CIFP's Fragility Index was inspired by Joel Migdal's 'dual nature of the state', which distinguishes between two concepts: the 'image of the state'; and the 'practices of states' (Carment, Prest and Samy, 2011: 84). This implies that the strong image of a state does not necessarily mean that the actual capacity of the state is also strong. Based on this understanding, the CIFP's Fragility Index comprises the three dimensions of 'authority, legitimacy, and capacity (ALC)' (Carment and Samy, 2012). The ALC dimensions are detailed in Table 6.1, which also shows North Korea's rank in each dimension in 2006. Except for the 2006 report, the CIFP's Fragility Index reports only provide the country's overall rank, and not its rank in each dimension, including the case of North Korea. While the CIFP project claims to conduct annual assessments, not all the assessments seem to have been publicly shared. Of those that have been published in an annual Fragility Index report, only four include North Korea's fragility rankings, which can be seen in Table 6.2.

Table 6.1 The ALC Framework of the CIFP Fragility Index, and the Case of North Korea in 2006

Dimension	*Definition*	*Rank of North Korea*
Authority	The extent to which a state processes the ability to enact binding legislation over its population, to exercise coercive force over its sovereign territory, to provide core public goods, and to provide a stable and secure environment to its citizens and communities	58 (out of 189)
Legitimacy	The extent to which a particular government commands public loyalty to the governing regime, and to generate domestic support for that government's legislation and policy	7 (out of 189)
Capacity	The potential for a state to mobilise and employ resources towards productive ends	55 (out of 189)

Source: Author's own compilation based on Carment et al., 2011: 92; Carment and Samy, 2012.

Table 6.2 North Korea's Fragility Ranking Between 2006 and 2015 in the CIFP Fragility Index

Year	*Fragility Rank of North Korea*
2006	32 (out of 189)
2011	56 (out of 197)
2012	57 (out of 190)
2015	38 (out of 198)

Source: Author's own compilation based on Carment, Langlois-Bertrand and Samy, 2014: 6, 2016: 6, Carment et al., 2011: 92; Carment and Samy, 2012.

Since 2015, the CIFP project has not provided a full global rankings list but has tended to focus on the top 20–30 fragile countries in its latest reports, mentioning North Korea in its 2017 report with the country's cluster scores. Alongside the ALC framework, the CIFP assesses performance in seven clusters: governance; economics; security and crime; human development; demography; environment; and gender (Carment and Samy, 2012). In the 2017 report, North Korea was ranked fifth in the top nine poorest performing countries in the East Asia and Pacific region based on its cluster scores. In the governance cluster, North Korea had a score of almost 8 (Carment et al., 2017: 16). In the CIFP's most recent report, in 2020, North Korea ranked 13th in the list of top 20 legitimacy scores. The country also featured again among the top 10 poorest performers in the East Asia and Pacific region based on its cluster scores, ranking seventh (Carment et al., 2020: 8 & 14).

Fund for Peace: Fragile States Index

Similarly, North Korea was a persistently fragile state between 2006 and 2021, according to the FFP's FSI, as shown in Table 6.3. While North Korea was found to be a fragile state by both the CIFP project and the FFP, its rank occupied a

Table 6.3 North Korea Between 2006 and 2021 in the FFP FSI

Year	*Fragility Rank of North Korea*
2006	14 (out of 178)
2007	13 (out of 178)
2008	15 (out of 178)
2009	17 (out of 178)
2010	19 (out of 178)
2011	22 (out of 178)
2012	22 (out of 178)
2013	23 (out of 178)
2014	26 (out of 178)
2015	29 (out of 178)
2016	30 (out of 178)
2017	30 (out of 178)
2018	28 (out of 178)
2019	26 (out of 178)
2020	30 (out of 178)
2021	30 (out of 179)

Source: Author's own compilation based on Fund for Peace, 2015, 2016, 2017a, 2018a, 2018b, 2019, 2020 and 2021

Note: The number of countries for the assessment increased from 178 to 179 in 2021 by adding Eswatini to the list.

slightly different range in their respective indices. The CIFP ranked North Korea between 32nd and 57th out of 198 countries, while the FFP ranked it between 13th and 30th out of 179 countries. The FFP produces the FSI annually based on its Conflict Assessment System Tool (CAST). The CAST assesses both the qualitative and quantitative data for each country against indicators and uses expert validation and triangulation (Fund for Peace, 2017b & 2021). The FFP promotes 'sustainable security through research, training and education, engagement of civil society, building bridges across diverse sectors, and developing innovative technologies and tools for policy makers' (Fund for Peace, 2017b: 2). The FFP's FSI not only provides fragility rankings and scores, but also shows its analysis of each country's performance and compares its performance over two consecutive years in each report. For instance, the FSI shows whether a country improved or worsened over the previous year.

Even though the FSI's methodology itself has not changed, its categories and indicators, as well as its ordering of categories, have been revised constantly. As Table 6.4 delineates, the latest version of the FSI has 12 indicators grouped in four categories: cohesion; economic; political; and social and cross-cutting. Each indicator contains sub-indicators for more detailed analysis.

Brookings Institution: Index of State Weakness

Brookings' ISW was published in 2008, and it has been widely used in existing studies even though it is not published continually on a yearly basis. This index was developed based on an examination of the landscape of the field of fragile states definitions and indices and defined fragile states as weak states in the sense of lack of capacity. Unlike the CIFP and FFP's indices, Brookings' ISW did not assess all countries but 141 developing countries which were low-income and middle-income countries (Rice and Patrick, 2008). As Table 6.5 demonstrates, this index also had dimensions and indicators, and used the latest available data from existing sources, such as the World Bank and the Food and Agriculture Organization (FAO). Table 6.5 shows the scores for North Korea, which was ranked as the 15th weakest developing country in the world out of 141 (Rice and Patrick, 2008: 11).

Center for Systemic Peace: Fragility Index

The Global Report series on conflict, governance, and state fragility, produced by the CSP assessed North Korea as a fragile state but with a low level of fragility. The CSP published its Global Report in 2007, 2008, 2009, 2011, 2014, and 2017. It rates state fragility based on quantitative analysis of existing data from international and governmental organisations (Marshall and Elzinga-Marshall, 2017). The eight indicators and two main categories of the CSP's Fragility Index and matrix can be found in Table 6.6. In 2017, for example, North Korea received a score of 7, while the most fragile country—the Democratic Republic of the Congo—had a score of 24 (Marshall and Elzinga-Marshall, 2017: 45–48).

Table 6.4 Development of the FFP FSI Categories and Indicators, and the Case of North Korea

Period	*Category*	*Indicator*	*Average Score of North Korea*
2015–2016	Social	Demographic Pressures	7.8
		Refugees and Internally Displaced Persons (IDPs)	4.45
		Group Grievance	6.15
		Human Flight and Brain Drain	4.15
	Economic	Uneven Economic Development	7.85
		Poverty and Economic Decline	8.95
	Political and Military	State Legitimacy	10.0
		Public Services	8.85
		Human Rights and Rule of Law	9.65
		Security Apparatus	8.55
		Factionalised Elites	8.5
		External Intervention	9.05
2017–2018	Cohesion	Security Apparatus	8.3
		Factionalised Elites	8.65
		Group Grievance	5.8
	Economic	Economic Decline (and Poverty)[a]	8.9
		Uneven Development	7.5
		Human Flight and Brain Drain	4.4
	Political	State Legitimacy	10
		Public Services	8.6
		Human Rights and Rule of Law	9.4
	Social	Demographic Pressures	7.45
		Refugees and IDPs	4.4
	Cross-Cutting	External Intervention	9.85
2019–2021	Cohesion	Security Apparatus	8.27
		Factionalised Elites	8.6
		Group Grievance	5.5
	Economic	Economic Decline	8.8
		Uneven Development	7.3
		Human Flight and Brain Drain	4.1
	Political	State Legitimacy	9.93
		Public Services	8.5
		Human Rights and Rule of Law	9.4
	Social and Cross-Cutting	Demographic Pressures	7
		Refugees and IDPs	4.1
		External Intervention	9.5

Source: Author's own compilation based on Fund for Peace, 2015, 2016, 2017a, 2018a, 2019, 2020 and 2021.
Note: A higher score means more fragile, and 10 points is the highest score for each indicator.
[a] 'and poverty' was removed in 2018.

Table 6.5 Brookings' ISW and the Case of North Korea

Basket	*Indicator*	*Score of North Korea*
Economic	GNI per capita	0
	GDP Growth	0
	Income Inequality	0
	Inflation	0
	Regulatory Quality	0.47
Political	Government Effectiveness	1.42
	Rule of Law	3.38
	Voice and Accountability	0.26
	Control of Corruption	0.24
	Freedom	0
Security	Conflict Intensity	10
	Gross Human Rights Abuses	2.54
	Territory Affected by Conflict	10
	Incidence of Coups	10
	Political Stability and Absence of Violence	6.22
Social Welfare	Child Mortality	8.25
	Access to Improved Water and Sanitation	7.52
	Undernourishment	5.79
	Primary School Completion	0
	Life Expectancy	6.58

Source: Revised by the author based on Rice and Patrick, 2008: 43.
Note: A lower score means worse, while a higher score means better. Also, a point of zero indicates the worst score.

Table 6.6 The CSP Fragility Index Categories and Indicators, and the Case of North Korea

Indicator	*Score of North Korea*	*Category*	*Score of North Korea*	*Fragility Index of North Korea*
Security Effectiveness	0	Effectiveness	2	7
Political Effectiveness	0			
Economic Effectiveness	2			
Social Effectiveness	0			
Security Legitimacy	3	Legitimacy	5	
Political Legitimacy	1			
Economic Legitimacy	1			
Social Legitimacy	0			

Source: Author's own compilation based on Marshall and Elzinga-Marshall, 2017: 44 & 48.
Note: A score of 4 means for extreme fragility, 3 for high fragility, 2 for moderate fragility, 1 for low fragility, and zero for no fragility.

Comparative Analysis of Fragile States Indices

The indicators used by the CSP for its fragility matrix are not too different from those of the FFP's FSI, and the databases used are more or less similar to those of Brookings' ISW. Nevertheless, differences exist, and the reason for this can be found in the qualitative and contextual discussions in the analyses. Looking at the different fragile states indices which include the case of North Korea, it seems that the greater the qualitative analysis included, the higher the fragility scores for North Korea. Similarly, the more detailed the context for indicators when scoring, the higher the fragility ranking of North Korea. For example, in the indices including social indicators, on most of them, except child mortality, North Korea showed as fragile—except in the CSP's index, which gave North Korea a score of zero, meaning 'no fragility', for both social effectiveness and legitimacy. This is obviously due to differences in the components and data sources of indicators. Table 6.7 compares the social indicators of three different fragile indices: FFP's FSI; Brooking's ISW; and CSP's Fragility Index. In the case of the FFP's FSI, the indicator for group grievance from the cohesion category has also been included as FSI indicators are not exclusive to a category, and group grievance as an indicator has an important social aspect as noted in the component section of the indicator.

Moreover, how state fragility is defined or considered affects the ranking results. Three of the indices clearly define North Korea as a seriously fragile state: the CIFP's Fragility Index considers fragility in terms of the functional capacity of a state (for example, see Carment et al., 2017: 2); the FFP's FSI understands it in terms of a state's capacities and resilience (for instance, see Fund for Peace, 2021: 40); and Brookings' ISW interprets fragility as weakness in the sense of lack of state capacity to fulfil the functions of statehood (see Rice and Patrick, 2008: 8). Also, their indicator definitions include factors impacting the lives of ordinary people, and do not only assess the regime's sustainability. In comparison, the CSP's fragility matrix tends to look at whether a state or a regime has failed or is failing by focusing on security and political conditions (see Marshall and Elzinga-Marshall, 2017: 44). In accordance with the CSP's Fragility Index, North Korea seems to be a fragile state, but not extremely, if we focus on security and political factors. However, it becomes a seriously fragile state if we extend our consideration of state stability to social and economic aspects, according to most of the fragile states indices.

North Korea: A Dysfunctional Fragile State Under a Strong Regime

As seen, an understanding of the concept of fragile states and existing fragile states indices indicates that North Korea is fragile. Fragile states are not defined entirely by regime failure or by their failure to provide strong security if we think about how states function. State security or stability is only one of core criteria for measuring state fragility. Based not only on the different dimensions and indicators used in fragile states indices to measure fragility but also on the conceptualisation of state fragility, it is obvious that North Korea is a fragile state. Yet, in order to

Table 6.7 Comparison of the Social Indicator Components of Fragility Indices

Index	*Indicator*	*Component*	*Data Source*
FFP FSI	Demographic Pressures	Pressures on the state deriving from the population itself or the environment around it in order to analyse population pressures related to food supply, access to safe water, and other life-sustaining resources, or health, such as prevalence of disease and epidemics	• Raw Data: data provided by a commercial content aggregator, including media articles, research reports, and other qualitative data points collected from over 10,000 different English language sources around the world • Quantitative Data: pre-existing datasets from international and multilateral statistical agencies, such as the UN, the World Bank, and the World Health Organization • Qualitative Data: social science researchers' independent reviews, in comparison with previous year's key events in that year
		Demographic characteristics, such as pressures from high population growth rates or skewed population distributions, such as a youth or age bulge, or sharply divergent rates of population growth among competing communal groups as such effects can have profound social, economic, and political effects	
		Pressures stemming from natural disasters	
		Pressures on the population from environmental hazards	
	Refugees and IDPs	Pressure on states caused by the forced displacement of large communities as a result of social, political, environmental, or other causes, measuring displacement within countries, as well as refugee flows into others	
		Refugees by country of asylum because population inflows can put additional pressure on public services, and can sometimes create broader humanitarian and security challenges for the receiving state if that state does not have the absorption capacity and adequate resources	
		IDPs and refugees by country of origin, which signifies internal state pressures as a result of violence, environmental or other factors such as health epidemics	
	Group Grievance	Division and schisms between different groups in society—particularly divisions based on social or political characteristics—and their role in access to services or resources, and inclusion in the political process	
		Historical component, where aggrieved communal groups cite injustices of the past, sometimes going back centuries, that influence and shape that group's role in society and relations with other groups	
		Specific groups who are singled out by state authorities, or by dominant groups, for persecution or repression, or where there is public scapegoating of groups believed to have acquired wealth, status, or power illegitimately, which may manifest itself in the emergence of fiery rhetoric, such as through hate radio, pamphleteering, and stereotypical or nationalistic political speech	

(*Continued*)

Table 6.7 Continued

Index	*Indicator*	*Component*	*Data Source*
Brookings' ISW	Child Mortality	Annual probability (per 1,000 live births) of a child dying before reaching five years of age in order to measure a state's ability to provide a wide range of public services, including health care, environmental quality, and maternal education	• UNICEF State of the World's Children
	Primary School Completion	Proportion of pupils starting in Grade 1 who reach Grade 5 in order to provide a direct measure of a state's ability and/or will to fulfil its responsibility to provide education for its citizens, and essential public service	• World Bank Development Indicators
	Prevalence of Undernourishment	Percentage of the population whose food intake is insufficient to meet dietary energy requirements continuously in order to measure a state's ability and/or will to meet the basic food requirements of its people	• FAO
	Access to Improved Water Sources and Improved Sanitation Facilities	Simple average of a country's available data on the percentage of the population with access to improved sanitation facilities and improved water sources in order to measure a state's capacity and will to provide social welfare services across the entire population of that country	• World Bank Development Indicators
	Life expectance	Life expectancy at birth in order to measure a state's capacity and will to provide services and an environment conducive to human survival	• World Bank Development Indicators
CSP Fragility Index	Social Effectiveness	Human Capital Development	• United Nations Development Programme (UNDP) Human Development Report • Human Development Index
	Social Legitimacy	Human Capital Care	• US Census Bureau International Database • Infant Mortality Rate

Source: Author's own compilation based on Fund for Peace, 2021: 38, 42, 47; Marshall and Elzinga-Marshall, 2017: 54; Rice and Patrick, 2008: 35–36.

conclude that North Korea is a fragile state, there are a couple of points we must discuss further.

First, the validity of the data used in the fragile state indices could be challenged—especially in the case of North Korea, for which information and data access are very scarce. In other words, it could be argued that the lack of data access dilutes the credibility of the fragility analyses of North Korea. Based on this reasoning, some scholars do not fully accept the results of the analysis under each indicator in the indices. Rather, they tend to insist that North Korea is not a fragile state by pointing out its nuclear programme and strong military regime. However, according to Cho (2018: 117–118), military experts tend to find that North Korea's vehicles and weaponry are outdated, and thus, without a nuclear programme, it may not be very strong militarily. This could be discussed further in the context of Russia's war in Ukraine in 2022. Seen through the lens of the world's media, Russian military equipment was revealed not to be as effective as had been believed, and morale among Russian soldiers was weak due, for example, to the lack of quality food provided to them. Beyond Pyongyang's nuclear armaments programme, it is not difficult to conclude that North Korean military equipment is inferior compared to technologically advanced Western armaments. North Korean soldiers are sent to work on construction sites and agricultural farms rather than be properly trained as soldiers. The food situation and the rationing of necessities in military camps are not much different from the nationwide situation in North Korea (Lee, 2022). In addition, as mentioned earlier, the image of a state as a strong regime does not amount to a strong capacity to function as a state.

Also, it would not be appropriate to simply ignore existing indices just because of the challenges in data collection. Most fragile states, not just North Korea, have similar issues of data quality and accessibility. The Brookings Institution clearly stated that Somalia, not North Korea, was missing the most data, and then explained how the problem was mitigated. In the case of Somalia in the Brookings's ISW, the authors reported that '96 percent of the potential data points' were available (Rice and Patrick, 2008: 36). As a matter of fact, the authors of all the fragile states indices discussed in the previous section claim to have developed potential ways to test data samples. The FFP employed the triangulation method in its analysis to increase data validity and reliability. Thus, simply denying the finding of these indices that North Korea is a fragile state due to the issue of data accessibility is not a strong argument.

Second, North Korea looks far from fragile, or vulnerable, when it comes to national security and regime strength. The country is indeed a threat to international security with its nuclear programme and cyber security attacks. Recently, US President Joe Biden also confirmed that North Korea is the 'biggest foreign policy threat' to the US (Salama, 2021). While developing its nuclear programme and conducting missile tests (see Chapter 2), North Korea has also steadily built up its cyber technology (see Chapter 3). It is now a widely known fact that the country's cyber hacking capacity is well advanced. However, paradoxically, North Korea is fragile according to definitions of fragile states in the policymakers' statements discussed at the beginning of this chapter, in the context of international security.

As seen, failed or weak states, and thus fragile states, are threats to the national security of other states as well as to international security. Here, policymakers tend to take failed states to mean those with weak institutional governance.

Yet, it seems that the image of a 'threat' to international security has come to define how North Korea is generally seen, as being either a 'bad' country or a 'strong' country. This image has also made it difficult for international organisations to justify providing not just development aid but also humanitarian assistance to North Korea (Cheng, 2018). Aid officials at international organisations with a specialised and theoretical understanding of state fragility do not seem to be any different. For example, officials at the United Nations Development Programme (UNDP), which uses its own definition of fragility, do not necessarily categorise North Korea as a fragile country (Lim, 2021). Also, let us look at countries like Pakistan or Iran. Some might consider them to be 'strong' countries, yet both have been ranked as fragile states in the aforementioned indices. The case of Pakistan especially has been explored as a fragile state in many research projects (for example, see Carment et al., 2010). The key to seeing that the stereotyped image of a country can be different from the actual condition of its society lies in recognising the difference between a regime and the state. The Kim regime may be strong, but not the state itself. A particular regime can fail, but people in society can cope with a new regime.

The main reason some reject the claim that North Korea is a fragile state—despite existing fragile states indices and definitions of fragile states indicating it to be one—could be that the country does not look vulnerable due to its arguably strong defences (Lim, 2021). If we focus on the security effectiveness of North Korea, it is not a fragile country. The CSP's Fragility Index scored North Korea's security effectiveness as zero, meaning 'non-fragile' (see Table 6.6). Also, the country received a score of 10, meaning 'better' than others, under the criteria of conflict intensity, territory affected by conflict, and incidence of coups in Brookings' ISW (see Table 6.5). However, in both cases, these security criteria are only a minor component of the total measure of a state's fragility. By reflecting on the results across all criteria, we can see that all the indices define North Korea as a fragile state. The general state system does not function for the welfare of the people or have accountable institutions.

This would be in line with the World Bank's CPIA. As mentioned earlier, the CPIA does not assess North Korea; however, if we were to apply its criteria of 'capacity' to the North Korean case, the country would score high in national security. Thus, some security experts tend to focus on state failure as a measure of fragility based on a government's capacity to control national security. Accordingly, countries in conflict or in immediate post-conflict situations are more likely to be categorised as fragile in both security and development fields (Lemay-Hébert, 2019). However, it is evident from fragile states indices such as Brookings' ISW and the CSP's Fragility Index that this approach is only one part of the whole picture. North Korea scored zero on six indicators in the same index: gross national income (GNI) per capita; gross domestic product (GDP) growth; income inequality; inflation; freedom; and primary school completion. Also, its scores on another three indicators (regulatory quality, voice and accountability, and control of corruption) were almost zero. When the FFP changed the name of its index, from 'Failed States Index' to 'Fragile States Index', in 2014, it explained that the change was made to acknowledge the fact that 'all states, to different degrees, face conditions that threaten the livelihoods of their citizens' (Lemay-Hébert, 2019: 79–80). The FSI aims to provide a platform to understand the capacities and pressures of a country in the context of fragility and resilience (Fund for Peace, 2017b). This confirms that state fragility is not simply about 'international security' but more about 'citizens within the territory'. The EU tends to accept this understanding and has categorised North Korea as a fragile state by considering its 'internal' economic, political, environmental, and social development conditions (Lim, 2021: 67).

At the same time, North Korea is not easily acknowledged as being fragile or weak due to perceptions of the country as a strong dictatorship based on a stereotyped image that has survived for three generations amid famine and harsh sanctions (Lim, 2021). As the following quote illustrates, the story of the North Korean regime indeed seems to be one of survival.

> The regime, created in 1948 out of the division of the Korean Peninsula by US and Soviet occupation forces at the beginning of the Cold War, has outlasted anyone's expectations. Even after the mighty Soviet Union and other communist regimes collapsed some two decades ago, this enigmatic Asian nation continues to hang on. Today, we witness an Arab Spring, where dictators in Egypt, Tunisia, Yemen, and Libya, ensconced in power much longer than North Korea's leadership, have been ousted, and yet the Dear Leader Kim Jong-il, until his death in late 2011, sat happily in Pyongyang, as does his son, Kim Jong-un, declaring 2012 as the year of a 'powerful and prosperous nation'. The regime remains intact despite famine, global economic sanctions, a collapsed economy, and almost complete isolation from the rest of the world. By any metric, this poor, backward, and isolated place should have been relegated to history's graveyard. It is a hermetically sealed Cold War anachronism.
>
> (Cha, 2012: 7)

Here, again, the survival of an authoritarian 'regime' does not mean that the 'state' itself is strong. As the so-called Western state model itself holds, 'the state is founded on a social contract between the rulers and the ruled' (social contract theory, whose proponents included John Locke and Jean-Jacques Rousseau), and 'the state relies on a bureaucratic apparatus with the ability to maintain a claim to the monopoly of the legitimate use of force' (a key element of Max Weber's definition of the monopoly of the legitimate use of force) (Engelhardt, 2018: 21). As Fukuyama (2004: 21, cited in Brock et al., 2012: 16) explains, enforcement—understood as 'the capacity to make people comply with the state's laws'—is the essence of statehood. It 'cannot be based only on coercion understood as the state's power over society. It is also based on legitimacy, that is power through society', as Weber emphasises (Brock et al., 2012: 16).

In this sense, the North Korean 'regime' may be referred to as strong, but—borrowing Cha's (2012) words—it is impossible for North Korea's current system to sustain itself as a 'state'. Rather, it constitutes weak 'statehood' due to its weak capacity to fulfil the functions of a state, especially towards its society and people. The concept of weak governance, and thus state fragility, is associated with a country's chronic underdevelopment (Engelhardt, 2018). That being so, if one wants to define North Korea as a non-fragile state, they need to reconsider how the regime manages the state's institutional functions and its society. This is why the state's legitimacy under the Kim family's dictatorship has been recorded as being 'most fragile'. For example, the FFP's FIS gives North Korea a score of 10 (out of 10), meaning 'most fragile', on state legitimacy (see Table 6.4). Most importantly, a 'country that cannot produce an institutional structure that its people regard as legitimate is unlikely to foster the conditions necessary for development', given that this is the most basic prerequisite for state-building (Kaplan, 2008: 50).

This chapter thus argues that North Korea is a fragile state in terms of the state's capacity to function for its population, encompassing factors such as governance deficit, absence of civil society, and abnormal state function especially in response to disruptive shocks. State fragility is not a concept limited to conflict-affected or post-conflict countries. North Korea as a state is not strong, while its regime may be. The North Korean government has focused on its security and military abilities, leaving society insecure amid increasing inequality. While the regime does not have a strong connection with society, the international community sees the country only through the lens of the strong regime narrative, not looking underneath this blanket narrative for actual society and for required (but lacking) state functions. This chapter has therefore adopted the term 'fragile states' rather than the concept of weak and strong states, not only because organisational definitions and indices are oriented more towards development than towards aspects of security although they include factors affected by international or domestic security, but also because the case of North Korea needs to be examined as this chapter has sought to do from non-traditional security perspectives.

Some may further argue that North Korea is not fragile because it has not, or will not, collapse as it has a strong political system due, ironically, to dictatorship. However, as mentioned, 'state fragility' is not based on the likelihood of, or potential for, collapse. Even though the country has been under increasingly severe sanctions since 2016 and has been sealed off by the COVID-19 border closure since 2020, there have been no signs of collapse (yet). Indeed, in a nutshell, the regime looks strong and the country seems sustainable, and thus, it is understandable how North Korea does not look like a fragile country in some ways. However, it is still questionable as to whether North Korean society would be able to remain in the current status quo. North Korea is currently facing another very difficult situation, which could turn out to be worse than the famine period in the 1990s. Due not only to the sanctions but also to the COVID-19 pandemic and border closure, already in April 2021, Kim Jong-un warned North Korean officials of a 'more difficult "Arduous March" in order to relieve our people of the difficulty' (Bicker, 2021). During the famine in the 1990s, his father, Kim Jong-il, called for food aid, and this not only helped relieve the emergency situation in the country but also led to the opening of diplomatic relations with European countries. Following his defection to South Korea, the former North Korean diplomat Tae Young-ho revealed, in his testimonial book, that in the 1990s, Kim Jong-il had ordered all North Korean diplomats to secure food and medicines for the people of their country who were experiencing the Arduous March (Tae, 2018).

Kim Jong-un does not seem to be taking the same approach as his father due to the different circumstances that he faces. Kim Jong-un's regime has been under the severest sanctions measures, which have now coincided with COVID-19 isolation. As seen in the previous chapters, compared to previous generations, the new generation—the youth—have been more influenced by external information, mostly by the influx of South Korean culture, and have had a less strict ideology education. With marketisation, financial power can be at times more important to them than loyalty to the Kim family. Joining the economic elites is more important than becoming a member of the political elites. The future of North Korea might, therefore, be different from what the stereotyped image suggests. Until now, there has been a lack of strong belief in the prospect of coups or uprisings, like the Arab Spring, in North Korea. However, contrary to conventional belief, there have already been attempted coups in North Korea during Kim Jong-il's Arduous March. The situation was quickly brought under control by the government then, but it will not be as easy for Kim Jong-un. Not only does North Korea's young generation have growing resentment towards lack of free access to external culture, but it also now has access to mobile phones, and with this, greater power to mobilise. But these will not lead to action, and thus regime change, unless the common understanding and mass action link up with members in other layers of the *songbun* system.

References

Alonso, Jose Antonio, Ana Luiza Cortez and Stephan Klasen (2014). *LDC and Other Country Groupings: How Useful Are Current Approaches to Classify Countries in a More Heterogeneous Developing World?* CDP Back-ground Paper, No 21. ST/ESA/2014/21. Department of Economic and Social Affairs. New York: United Nations.

Bicker, Laura (2021). Kim Jong-un Warns of North Korea Crisis Similar to Deadly 90s Famine. 9 April 2021, *BBC News*. https://www.bbc.co.uk/news/world-asia-56685356. Accessed: 1 February 2022.

Brock, Lothar, Hans-Henrik Holm, Georg Sørensen and Michael Stohl (2012). *Fragile States: Violence and the Failure of Intervention*. Cambridge: Polity Press.

Carment, David, Kyle Muñoz and Yiagadeesen Samy (2020). *Fragile and Conflict-Affected States in the Age of COVID-19: A 2020 Country Indicators for Foreign Policy Report*. Ottawa: Carleton University.

Carment, David, Peter Tikuisis, Yiagadeesen Samy and James Floch (2017). *The CIFP Fragility Index: New Trends and Categorizations: A 2017 Country Indicators for Foreign Policy Report*. Ottawa: Carleton University.

Carment, David, Simon Langlois-Bertrand and Yiagadeesen Samy (2014). *Assessing State Fragility, With a Focus on the Middle East and North Africa Region: A 2014 Country Indicators for Foreign Policy Report*. Ottawa: Carleton University.

Carment, David, Simon Langlois-Bertrand and Yiagadeesen Samy (2016). *Assessing State Fragility, With a Focus on Climate Change and Refugees: A 2016 Country Indicators for Foreign Policy Report*. Ottawa: Carleton University.

Carment, David, Stewart Prest and Yiagadeesen Samy (2010). *Security, Development, and the Fragile State: Bridging the Gap Between Theory and Policy*. New York: Routledge.

Carment, David, Stewart Prest and Yiagadeesen Samy (2011). *Security, Development, and the Fragile State: Bridging the Gap Between Theory and Policy*. New York: Routledge.

Carment, David and Yiagadeesen Samy (2012). *Assessing State Fragility: A Country Indicators for Foreign Policy Report Commissioned by the Canadian International Development Agency*. Ottawa: Carleton University.

Cartier-Bresson, Jean (2012). Official Development Assistance in Fragile States. *Crime Law Social Change*, 58: 495–507.

Cha, Victor (2012). *The Impossible State: North Korea, Past and Future*. London: Vintage.

Cheng, Jonathan (2018). UN Appeals for Aid to North Korea as Donations Drop. 13 April 2018, *The Wall Street Journal*. https://www.wsj.com/articles/u-n-appeals-for-aid-to-north-korea-as-donations-drop-1523609690. Accessed: 9 February 2022.

Cho, Dong-sin (2018). *North Korea in 100 Questions*. Seoul: Sejong Books. Translated from Juliette Morillot and Dorian Malovic (2016). La Coree due Nord en 100 Questions. Paris: Editions Tallandier [조동신 (2018). 100가지 질문으로 본 북한. 서울, 세종서적(주)].

De Siqueira, Isabel Rocha (2014). Measuring and Managing 'State Fragility': The Production of Statistics by the World Bank, Timor-Leste and the g7+. *Third World Quarterly*, 35(2): 268–283.

Engelhardt, Marie von (2018). *International Development Organizations and Fragile States: Law and Disorder*. Cham: Palgrave Macmillan.

Fund for Peace (2015). *Fragile States Index 2015*. Washington, D.C.: The Fund for Peace.

Fund for Peace (2016). *Fragile States Index 2016*. Washington, D.C.: The Fund for Peace.

Fund for Peace (2017a). *Fragile States Index 2017*. Washington, D.C.: The Fund for Peace.

Fund for Peace (2017b). *Fragile States Index Methodology and Cast Frameworks*. Washington, D.C.: The Fund for Peace.

Fund for Peace (2018a). *Fragile States Index 2018*. Washington, D.C.: The Fund for Peace.

Fund for Peace (2018b). *Fragile States Index Data*. https://fragilestatesindex.org/excel/. Accessed: 21 January 2022.

Fund for Peace (2019). *Fragile States Index 2019*. Washington, D.C.: The Fund for Peace.

Fund for Peace (2020). *Fragile States Index 2020*. Washington, D.C.: The Fund for Peace.

Fund for Peace (2021). *Fragile States Index 2021*. Washington, D.C.: The Fund for Peace.

Hout, Wil (2010). Between Development and Security: The European Union, Governance and Fragile States. *Third World Quarterly*, 31(1): 141–157.

Kaplan, Seth D. (2008). *Fixing Fragile States: A New Paradigm for Development*. Westport, CT: Praeger Security International.

Lee, Seungju (2022). *Prisoners in Military Uniform: Human Rights in the North Korean Military*. NKDB Report 2022–01. Seoul: Database Center for North Korean Human Rights [이승주 (2022). 군복 입은 수감자 : 김정은 집권기 북한 군 인권 실태. NKDB 리포트 2022-01. 서울, 북한인권정보센터].

Lemay-Hébert, Nicolas (2019). From Saving Failed States to Managing Risks: Reinterpreting Fragility Through Resilience. In: John Idriss Lahai, Karin Von Strokirch, Howard Brasted and Helen Ware (eds.). *Governance and Political Adaptation in Fragile States*. Cham: Palgrave Macmillan, pp. 75–101.

Lemay-Hébert, Nicolas and Xavier Mathieu (2014). The OECD's Discourse on Fragile States: Expertise and the Normalisation of Knowledge Production. *Third World Quarterly*, 35(2): 232–251.

Lim, Sojin (2021). The Paradox of Unsustainability in UN Sustainable Development Goals (SDGs): The North Korean Case in the Context of Accountability and the Fragile States Under Sanctions. *Journal of Peace and Unification*, 10(3): 55–78.

Marshall, Monty G. and Gabrielle C. Elzinga-Marshall (2017). *Global Report 2017: Conflict, Governance, and State Fragility*. Vienna: Center for Systemic Peace.

Mata, Javier Fabra and Sebstian Ziaja (2009). *Users' Guide on Measuring Fragility*. Bonn and Oslo: German Development Institute (DIE) and UNDP.

Muchadenyika, Davison (2016). Multi-donor Trust Funds and Fragile States: Assessing the Aid Effectiveness of the Zimbabwe Multi-Donor Trust Fund. *Journal of International Development*, 28: 1337–1357.

Nay, Olivier (2014). International Organisations and the Production of Hegemonic Knowledge: How the World Bank and the OECD Helped Invent the Fragile State Concept. *Third World Quarterly*, 35(2): 210–231.

Nussbaum, Tobias, Eugenia Zorbas and Michael Koros (2012). A New Deal for Engagement in Fragile States. *Conflict, Security & Development*, 12(5): 559–586.

OECD. (2021). *DAC Working Party on Development Finance Statistics: Converged Statistical Reporting Directives for the Creditor Reporting System (CRS) and the Annual DAC Questionnaire*. DCD/DAC/STAT(220)44/ADD2/FINAL. Paris: OECD.

Patrick, Stewart (2011). *Weak Links: Fragile States, Global Threats, and International Security*. New York: Oxford University Press.

Rice, Susan E. and Stewart Patrick (2008). *Index of State Weakness in the Developing World*. Washington, D.C.: Brookings Institute.

Salama, Vivian (2021). Biden Sees North Korea as Biggest Foreign-Policy Threat. 25 March 2021, *The Wall Street Journal*. https://www.wsj.com/livecoverage/biden-press-conference-live-updates-analysis/card/W9wyilDsb86eqzEySPCI. Accessed: 2 February 2022.

Simpson, Mark and Tony Hawkins (2018). *The Primacy of Regime Survival: State Fragility and Economic Destruction in Zimbabwe*. Cham: Palgrave Macmillan.

Tae, Young-ho (2018). *Testimonial of Former First Minister of the Embassy of the Democratic People's Republic of Korea in the United Kingdom, Tae Young-ho. Seoul: Giparang* [태영호 (2018). 전 영국 주재 북한공사 태영호의 증언 : 3층 서기실의 암호. 서울, 기파랑].

Von Engelhardt, Marie (2018). *International Development Organizations and Fragile States: Law and Order*. Cham: Palgrave MacMillan.

World Bank (2010). *The World Bank's Country Policy and Institutional Assessment: An Evaluation*. Washington, D.C.: World Bank.

7 Conclusion

While scholarly interest in North Korea has increased, as noted in Chapter 1, research tends to focus either on security and international relations or marketisation and the scenario of state collapse due to poor economic growth. More recently, North Korea has also come to occupy the minds of ordinary people, albeit in a lighter way. Owing to the Trump–Kim relationship during the 2018–2019 period of gesture politics, people have become more interested in the Kim family and Pyongyang's nuclear capabilities. They have not been drawn to political, economic, or social perspectives on the country, but have been more interested in whether Kim Jong-un has lost weight or who his potential successor, Kim Yo-jong, is. Some have given their attention to human rights issues by having repeatedly heard sensational stories in various media. It seems that the world has a better understanding of the Kim family and the economic situation in North Korea. However, ordinary people at the very bottom of North Korean society remain almost invisible to policymakers and security experts. Those voicing concern about human rights in North Korea do not relate this concern to the situation that ordinary people find themselves in due to increasing sanctions. Advocacy activities for the human rights of North Koreans tend to be held outside of the country. In other words, a dichotomic rhetoric of denuclearisation and human rights keeps repeating by virtue of being trapped in the paradigm of nuclear deterrence. Not only is North Korea developing its nuclear facilities, but it is also involved in the trading of arms including chemical weapons. Yet, it is not on the radar of policymakers, who have only focused on the nuclear issue, which shows the unbalanced approach to North Korea in policymaking processes. It is indeed a dilemma for policymakers as to whether to put security or people first. Likewise, the United Nations (UN) agenda for sustainable development seems to be failing from the outset in the case of North Korea as it leaves people behind due to its own sanctions regime.

In light of this, the book has posed the question as to whether there are any alternative narratives on North Korea that we can navigate. In conclusion, the four main findings of the research can be summarised. First, marketisation in North Korea has not resulted in changes to the capitalist free market system, but has established another layer in the societal structure composed of economic elites between street-level bureaucrats and middle-income class members, represented by *donju* who have benefitted from the marketisation process. Second, North Korean society is cloaked not only by the regime's repression and the *songbun* system,

DOI: 10.4324/9781003390282-7

but also by the alliance between political elites and the newly created economic elites. Third, the state is dysfunctional, and thus fragile in terms of its capacity to enable sustainable development for its people, in contradiction to its stereotyped image as a 'strong' regime owing to its nuclear programme. Fourth, development aid could thus become an agent for social change and civil society development in North Korea by focusing on both state and local community capacity building and development.

Existing research claiming the ineffectiveness and inefficacy of the sanctions regime against North Korea has not influenced a wider discussion on alternative narratives as they tend to emphasise the adverse humanitarian consequences of sanctions without suggestions. With the North Korean government failing to provide basic services to its people, a tradition of self-reliance in conditions of chronic hardship has become embedded in people's minds, leading them to cope with the dysfunctional system. Rather than coming together in voluntary and collective action, they have tended to decide individually to defect amid uncertainty about the result of any dramatic changes. Among political elites, those who could lead change by organising mass protests, some decide to defect instead because they fear the prospect of occupation by external actors in the event of regime change. The economic elites who have gained financial power in society prefer to support regime stability rather than to organise resistance. Also, those unable to compromise with the government decide to defect rather than seek to take collective action with others in similar situations due to the lack of trust created by the surveillance system. People tend to keep their resentment to themselves, and not share it in the public sphere. Given the long duration of the sanctions, the country has learned how to mitigate and adapt to hardship. In the absence of external engagement, for example, through development aid activities, people have had no opportunities to seriously consider their ability as members of society to bring about changes.

Therefore, this book argues that providing development aid using a tailored approach could be a practical alternative. Some might criticise this conclusion as naïve as it requires at least a partial lifting of sanctions before denuclearisation. Others might worry about the possibility of a scenario in which aid supports civil servants, and thus elite groups, in becoming more powerful in the process of economic development even as they continue to neglect the wider population. Yet, this is why development aid could create room for an enabling environment for civil society. For example, in its Voluntary National Review of Sustainable Development Goals (SDGs) implementation, the North Korean government noted the need for support to build its national statistical capacity that would enable it to conduct appropriate monitoring and evaluation. This could be a potential and practical starting point. By focusing on building the state's statistical capacity for monitoring and evaluation of aid directed towards SDG implementation, a culture of accountability could come to be gradually shared within the government system through the aid activities. This would not necessarily be the exact intention of the North Korean government, but it would be able to contribute to the gradual capacity development of the state as well as the people. With this culture of accountability promoting communication among the state, market, and society, it could become a platform for overcoming the existing blockage between different classes in the country's *songbun* system. What is needed in North Korea is social integration, which is currently absent from the state capacity, and which could be built on the foundation of an accountability mechanism.

While it may perhaps be too early to conclude that the sanctions against North Korea have failed, it could never be too early to acknowledge the adverse effects of the sanctions on innocent people. The UN paradoxically abandoned North Koreans against its own SDG value of 'leave no one behind', and against the principles of the Universal Declaration of Human Rights when it imposed multilateral sanctions. In each resolution, the UN made it clear that the sanctions were not designed to have an adverse humanitarian impact on civilians. However, it is a fact that the sanctions have had a huge and negative impact on the humanitarian aid regime for North Korea (Zadeh-Cummings and Harris, 2020). Even before the COVID-19 pandemic, it was estimated that 3,968 deaths could have been prevented in North Korea if humanitarian access was allowed. The human cost of sanctions has been very high, while there has been no sign of changes in the behaviour of the Kim regime (Korea Peace Now, 2019: 12). It has been obvious that it is the sanctions, rather than natural disasters and the pandemic, that have dismantled the society. Yet, the UN Security Council (UNSC) and individual countries, like the United States (US), have only increased the pressure of sanctions due to Pyongyang's continuing armament and nuclear programme development, while ignoring or accepting human suffering as an inevitable adverse consequence, despite this being unethical. It would seem that the Protocol Additional to the Geneva Conventions of 12 August 1949, which prohibits the starvation of a civilian population, is not universal as it does not seem to apply to the people of North Korea (also see Smith, 2020).

As seen in Chapter 2, the UNSC has adopted 11 resolutions addressing North Korea's nuclear programme development to date, except for the first resolution (resolution 825). These UNSC resolutions have only increased the level of sanctions against North Korea. Most of the resolutions used the 'strongest terms' at the time of adoption, which shows that the scale of sanctions strengthened as North Korea's nuclear programme development progressed. Also, a series of resolutions have repeatedly urged North Korea to stop further launches of ballistic missiles, nuclear tests, and other provocations, to suspend the relevant programmes, and to abandon its nuclear weapons programme. However, we are yet to see any changes in the behaviour of the Kim regime. Despite the UN sanctions imposed on the country after its first nuclear test, North Korea conducted its second nuclear test in 2009 and continued with its nuclear development until the announcement of its self-moratorium in 2018. Then, with the end of Kim Jong-un's experiment of gesture politics in 2019, the regime resumed its missile tests. This clearly shows that the UNSC resolutions have not been effective, except for the period of engagement in gesture politics, and are more or less unlikely to achieve their goal of bringing about behavioural or policy changes in North Korea. Meanwhile, both the rhetoric of denuclearisation and the pursuit of nuclear capabilities continue.

Upon his inauguration, US President Joe Biden made it clear that his administration was ready to resume diplomacy with North Korea, but only for the purpose of denuclearisation, and that it would thus keep the current sanctions against North Korea in place. On 16 April 2022, North Korea tested a nuclear-capable tactical guided missile, following several missile tests earlier in the year.

What continues to be missing in existing discussions on the sanctions regime against North Korea is any attention to the conditions of the target country. For instance, the sanctions imposed on Russia for its invasion of Ukraine in February 2022 were smart sanctions. This obviously signalled and sent a powerful message to Russia as to the level of opposition to its invasion. Also, it could be said that many of the targeted individuals and firms have been deterred by the sanctions. However, the conditions are not even close to being similar in countries like North Korea. Both the size of the North Korean economy and its number of international trade partners are very small. Thus, economic sanctions have not had a significant impact on the regime itself. But they have harmed ordinary North Koreans. Despite this, people have not sought to engage in collective actions, but have found individual means of survival amid the chronic poverty. It is similarly not clear whether diplomatic sanctions have harmed the regime. Diplomatic sanctions are designed to undermine the so-called 'rally round the flag' effect; however, they can actually strengthen rather than weaken the political unity of the target country (Gray and Lee, 2021; Maass, 2011). In the case of North Korea, some diplomatic relations with countries such as Angola, Uganda, and Tanzania were affected by the sanctions; however, new relationships with countries such as Malawi, Gabon, and Niger have been established despite the sanctions (Grzelczyk, 2019). The international community has also shown how it can easily turn to courting North Korea in response to a gesture of engagement from Pyongyang, as we observed during the period of the Trump–Kim gesture politics between 2018 and 2019.

Moreover, North Korea has a strong trade partner who does not abide by the international sanctions on the regime—China. Chinese sanctions violations have supported the expansion of the shadow economy and semi-official trading in the country. When 'third-party spoilers undermine their implementation', sanctions cannot be effective (Wertz, 2020: 27). Also, when South Korea closed Kaesong Industrial Park in 2016 in order to deter North Korea from acquiring foreign currency in line with international sanctions, this did not work as intended. North Korea found an alternative route, which replaced the South Korean market. North Korea's post-Kaesong trade increased as its trade activities with China increased (Lee, 2018). The reports of the UN Panel of Experts have continually revealed multiple instances of sanctions evasion, including a continuing illegal trade in oil. Sanctions evasion has been observed not only in the realm of finance but also in the realm of technology in North Korea's recent cyberattacks and its development of chemical weapons. Other countries like Palestine, which are isolated, have found a way to benefit from advanced cyber technology by using their high education levels to provide outsourced game design or programming services to Silicon Valley (Lim, 2014). However, North Korea has behaved in quite the opposite manner. As explored in Chapter 3, advanced technology has allowed North Korea to conduct cyberattacks and collect cryptocurrency. There has been no evidence of advancements in technology being utilised positively for society and economic development. Rather, it has been proved that the North Korean regime is spending the funds illicitly obtained through technology-based sanctions evasion on its nuclear programme.

Narratives about the effectiveness of sanctions can be understood somewhat differently if we apply different criteria to measure their effectiveness. Sanctions can be assessed in terms of their purpose: to change or constrain behaviour through coercion; to deter or signal a target; or even just for them to be a symbolic action. According to Hufbauer et al. (2019), the case of North Korea can be seen to have been successful if US sanctions had a symbolic purpose or had aimed to signal a need for dismantling the country's nuclear programme. But they can be seen to have failed if we had to assess their effectiveness against the purpose of bringing about behavioural change through coercion. This book agrees with Hufbauer et al.'s (2019) argument that we cannot boldly conclude that sanctions never work; however, it does not agree with the suggestion that symbolism can be sufficient as a purpose of sanctions 'at the cost of civilian lives'. Sanctions cannot be justified merely to 'signal' or serve a 'symbolic' purpose when they 'punish ordinary people' who are unable to express their opinions against the regime. Sanctions against North Korea are a failure from the point of view of morality as they harm civilians while not bringing about any behavioural change in the regime. Ordinary people could be accountable for a regime's misconduct if they were aware that its actions were wrong and had the capacity to protest it. However, this is not the case in every country. Countries like North Korea do not have a culture of protest as people are habitually repressed by a mass surveillance system. While state propaganda might blind people, they could still raise their voices if they had the capacity to act collectively. For instance, in the case of Russia in 2022, when people experienced the negative impact of sanctions on their access to cash and other sources of livelihood, they came out onto the streets to protest against Moscow's illegitimate war despite the strong role of state propaganda in society. Yet, this has not been the case in North Korea.

If the purpose of the sanctions has been to impact the lives of ordinary people in order to encourage them to collectively raise their voices for change from the bottom up, this will not happen in North Korea. As Amartya Sen (1999: 3 & 8) has written, 'development can be seen as a process of expanding the real freedoms that people enjoy', while 'economic unfreedom can breed social unfreedom, just as social or political unfreedom can also foster economic unfreedom'. Ordinary North Koreans are not economically, socially, and politically free. As discussed in Chapter 5, development aid can support the country's transitional society by helping to build up its capacity and develop a civil society–friendly environment, especially in a situation in which the state cannot communicate with the market and the society. Human contacts could plant the seeds of change. However, sanctions have only resulted in a lost opportunity for development aid. To create an enabling environment that facilitates a role for civil society in North Korea, which can produce real change from below, we should not leave the people of this country on their own. Sanctions may be needed to isolate the regime but not the people. Therefore, it is time for us to seek alternative approaches, driven by people-to-people connections, that can uncloak North Korean society and unlock its potential. 'Connections' in this context means not only creating networks but also developing capacity to turn knowledge into action for change.

Bearing in mind Giner's (1995) definition of civil society, which was delineated in Chapter 4, dawn may have arrived for civil society in North Korea, but only just. However, even though there is increasing evidence that North Koreans are beginning to express their grievances behind the scenes and even though the use of so-called doubletalk is being increasingly observed, it seems that an environment for actual civil society actions does not yet exist. North Koreans tend to be quiet in the public sphere and to prefer to act individually because they do not know how to link their thoughts to actions on a sufficient scale to influence the regime. North Korean society is also cloaked in two layers: by the regime's repression, supported by political elites; and by the ring-fencing of limited market freedom by economic elites. As seen in Chapter 3, the digital economy, along with mobile phone usage, has benefitted information exchange and flows between North Korea and the world beyond; however, this has not necessarily empowered society. Rather, it has led to the creation of a new class that has sealed off society at large in North Korea because advanced technology is only affordable for the privileged groups in society. In other words, the recent testimonials that have been collected from defectors have mostly been from political and economic elites, who represent a small proportion of financially well-resourced groups in the population and who are framed in terms of marketisation from below, while the real bottom levels of the *songbun* system remain cloaked by their narratives. Those who have lived in North Korea—as diplomats, aid workers, or educators—tend to admit that their contact with North Koreans remained limited. Thus, the changes that we believe are happening in society seem to be very limited. As Chapters 3 and 4 have shown, the benefit of marketisation has not been equally shared in society. As market actors have used bribery to hedge and wedge between state regulations and autonomy, they have preferred to bandwagon with the politically powerful at street level in order to become economic elites themselves. Given the long tradition of economic hardship that has become the norm in people's lives and the abnormal balance between state and market, the Kim regime has sustained its political and economic resilience amid sanctions.

In this regard, this book has revisited this notion of marketisation by people, and based on its research findings, challenged existing images about associated changes occurring from below. North Korean marketisation was started by people but soon became regulated by the state. Since the first Arduous March in the late 1990s, people have adopted marketisation as a survival strategy, and the government has allowed a parallel system composed of an official socialist economic system from the top and a capitalist market system at the bottom to remain in place. However, as discussed in Chapter 4, the government's monitoring of people with new technology and its existing surveillance system have still limited freedom. People in North Korea enjoy neither economic freedom nor social freedom yet. As the government has increased its countermeasures against the market's economic freedom, more creative ways to share information within society have been developed. However, these creative ways tend to be limited to the rent-seeking economic haves who want privilege and property and who have thus become another obstacle to economic and social freedom. Also, sanctions have limited the 'ability' of ordinary North Koreans to 'develop their economy' (Korea Peace Now, 2019: 31). The sanctions' negative impact on people and society has not automatically brought about the intended result of the sanctions, for example, regime behaviour change, as the regime does not take them seriously. In other words, for the Kim regime, the suffering at the bottom of society is not a deterrent because the upper layers of society have efficiently cloaked any potential for a rebellious mass movement.

As mentioned in Chapter 1, one the main challenges in research on North Korea is data validity and generalisation. Participatory observation or direct interviews with people at the lowest level of the *songbun* system, or with members below the newly created economic elite groups, are lacking. Hence, the 'below' in the expression of 'marketisation from below' does not represent the real bottom of society. Rather, the 'below' is a symbolic metaphor in the expression to capture a phenomenon (marketisation) that was not initiated by the government but created by people (market actors). This research thus argues that while those who contributed to marketisation at the beginning of the famine period could be mixed in among the real bottom of the population, the main force behind the wedging and hedging between the market and the state in the more recent marketisation period has been the newly created 'economic elites' of street-level bureaucrats and middle-income class, represented by *donju*. In light of this, North Korea's real society has been blanketed by the political elites, who officially conceal North Korean society from the outside world, and by the economic elites, who unofficially bandwagon with the authority and obstruct possible changes by the people at the real bottom, who are not market actors and who are discriminated against by the system due to their low *songbun*. Thus, despite the changes that have been observed, it is unclear whether or not we can generalise that the extent of the changes is a widespread phenomenon.

In other words, what we have overlooked is the environment for civil society, for instance, whether it is enabling. For example, a trade union, freely organised and run as a membership-based civil society organisation, performs a major function in society by protecting and promoting the human rights of workers. It represents the voice of workers, and thus, places pressure on the government to respect their rights. However, such a difficult role for a trade union cannot even be discussed as trade unionism occurs in a complete vacuum in North Korea. Especially in the context of fragile states, the challenge of building an effective alliance to retain the autonomy of trade unions so that they can protect workers' rights is a commonly observed one (Stirling, 2011). In the case of North Korea, the alliance between street-level bureaucrats and *donju* with the autonomy granted by the marketisation process has, on the contrary, become an obstacle to the creation of civil society. As discussed in Chapter 4, everyday resistance against street-level bureaucrats may have increased, but it is easily dissolved through bribery. As explored, political elites strategically tolerate economic elites as they could become a genuine threat to the regime. Economic elites, for their part, have jumped on the bandwagon rather than seeking to take the form of civil society. Such elites can be a driver for change or its opposite. In North Korea, they have chosen to be the latter. It tends to be relatively easier to change military regimes than to change personalist regimes. Personalist regime leaders have the power to rotate political elites (Chow and Easley, 2019). Thus, the Kim family, which created a personalist regime in North Korea, has maintained its influence over the political elites, and the political elites have been able to cascade this influence through society by using the economic elites as agents to impede any fundamental shift in society.

Continuing the argument of this book, the most likely alternative to the elites for bringing about societal change is to be found in development aid and in building the capacity of people. That is, it is critical for us to focus on a bottom-up method in this paradoxical and unique situation. Accepting North Korea as a case of a fragile state with weak state capacity to function for its people and society, as discussed in Chapter 6, we need to reframe the way in which we deliver aid and monitor aid activities. Markets and market actors can bring about social transformation if the appropriate institutions are in place. Given that the state is unable and unwilling to perform the function for its people in North Korea, the aid community needs first to focus on capacity building and the environment and then to ask the government to comply with its standards (Cartier-Bresson, 2012: 504). As a fragile state, North Korea should be given aid using customised and tailored approaches rather than the standard aid project management framework, as discussed in Chapter 5. It has become the new norm to admit that North Korea is a de facto nuclear state not only because it has nuclear capabilities but also because it would not give up its nuclear programme, no matter the sanctions imposed on it. While sanctions are intended to change the Kim regime's behaviour with regard to its nuclear programme, the regime has no incentives to do so from the viewpoint of its desire to remain in power. The recent resumption of missile tests, amid hardship while the country remains completely disconnected from the outside world, shows that North Korea is capable of developing nuclear armaments no matter what, and the continuing sanctions will only cause more harm to the people and society, not the regime. The Kim regime has developed an abnormal capacity as a state. The state does not exist for its people and society, but for 'Pyongyang' and its elites.

A parallel and unique approach is required in North Korea that opens the way to building up a civil society mechanism and state capacity for accountability, which is perhaps possible from below. The first step in this direction could be to tailor development aid to the fragile situation of the country. We need to look for a way to minimise the human suffering caused by the existing sanctions regime, and thus, to redirect our focus to methods of human engagement through development aid. In doing so, we can expect to build up the civil society capacity of people in local communities while having a better functioning state that can support an enabling environment. Changes are possible in this impossible state as North Korean society has shown through the change in the market system, even though the leading groups have become more favourable towards the government. External information and cultural influxes have also shown us the possibility of change, even though they are being monitored and constantly challenged by the state surveillance system. In this regard, North Koreans have simply not yet had opportunities to interact and engage with external actors. Thus, alternative narratives could be found in the people's hands again, but this time they need to find a way to break through the cloaking layers above them with the help of customised development aid engagement at the grassroots level.

However, in the end, a crucial question remains as to whether the North Korean government would be willing to open its door to development cooperation ever again. It rejected international offers of COVID-19 vaccines and it has still not asked for any aid despite the suspension of its unofficial trade with China due to national COVID-19 isolation measures, including against vaccines. The UN's Global Humanitarian Overview 2022 notes that North Korea is 'facing acute food insecurity situations, which are likely to deteriorate further by the year's end' (OCHA, 2022: 81). Meanwhile, the international community revoked its initial decision to allocate COVID-19 vaccines to North Korea, following the Kim regime's continued rejection of the offer (Lee and Kim, 2022). As of April 2022, North Korea is one of two countries, along with Eritrea, with no vaccines in circulation among its population. The people of North Korea are thus completely isolated. As we have seen in Chapter 5, the North Korean government is aware of how people-to-people connections can spur changes in society, from its actual bottom level up (also see Park, 2009). Even though North Korea is slowly reopening its border for trade with China, the level of control over any information influx is known to have been seriously increased. It seems that the Kim regime has used the time during the COVID-19 lockdown to reshuffle the balance in its favour against the market. However, as long as the regime can keep its grip on control over the economic elites, they will not gather to challenge its authority. Therefore, to convince the regime to change its position from aid rejection to aid acceptance, a (partial) lifting of sanctions, with room for negotiation and engagement, needs to be considered. It is better to be inclusive than to be exclusive. The key to unlocking the potential of North Korea's cloaked society does not lie in sanctions, whose inefficacy is obvious, but is to be found in engagement with development aid. In doing so, the development of local capacity for action as well as the information and cultural influxes can become synergetic instruments for the people left behind in cloaked society. We will not know whether the power of autonomy in North Korea is alive or dead 'until we open the box'.

References

Cartier-Bresson, Jean (2012). Official Development Assistance in Fragile States. *Crime Law Social Change*, 58: 495–507.

Chow, Jonathan T. and Leif-Eric Easley (2019). Renegotiating Pariah State Partnerships: Why Myanmar and North Korea Respond Differently to Chinese Influence. *Contemporary Security Policy*, 40(4): 502–525.

Gray, Kevin and Jong-Woon Lee (2021). *North Korea and the Geopolitics of Development*. Cambridge: Cambridge University Press.

Grzelczyk, Virginie (2019). From Balancing to Bandwagoning: Evaluating the Impact of the Sanction Regime on North Korea-Africa Relationships. *North Korean Review*, 15(1): 9–33.

Hufbauer, Gary Clyde, Jeffrey J. Schott, Kimberly Ann Elliott and Barbara Oegg (2019). *Economic Sanctions Reconsidered (third edition)*. Washington D.C.: Peterson Institute for International Economics.

Korea Peace Now (2019). *The Human Costs and Gendered Impact of Sanctions on North Korea*. https://koreapeacenow.org/wp-content/uploads/2019/10/human-costs-and-gendered-impact-of-sanctions-on-north-korea.pdf. Accessed: 4 June 2021.

Lee, Michelle Ye Hee and Min Joo Kim (2022). As World Reopens, North Korea is One of Two Countries Without Vaccines. 24 April 2022, *The Washington Post*. https://www.washingtonpost.com/world/2022/04/24/north-korea-covid-vaccines-covax/. Accessed: 24 April 2022.

Lee, Seong Bong (2018). The Effect of South Korean Economic Sanctions on North Koreas Foreign Currency Acquisition. *21st Century Political Science Review*, 28(3): 119–137. [이성봉 (2018). 남한의 경제제재가 북한의 외화 획득에 미친 영향. 21세기정치학회보, 28(3): 119–137].

Lim, Sojin (2014). *Recipient Country Capacity Assessment for the Development Cooperation Project Feasibility Study*. Seongnam: Korea International Cooperation Agency [임소진 (2014). 개발협력 프로젝트 사전(타당성)조사 수원국 역량진단. 성남, 한국국제협력단].

Maass, Matthias (2011). Beyond Economic Sanctions: Rethinking the North Korean Sanctions Regime. *North Korean Review*, 7(2): 45–56.

OCHA (2022). *Global Humanitarian Overview 2022*. New York: United Nations Office for the Coordination of Humanitarian Affairs.

Park, Kyung-Ae (2009). Regime Change in North Korea?: Economic Reform and Political Opportunity Structures. *North Korea Review*, 5(1): 23–45.

Sen, Amartya (1999). *Development as Freedom*. New York: Anchor Books.

Smith, Hazel (2020). The Ethics of United Nations Sanctions on North Korea: Effectiveness, Necessity and Proportionality. *Critical Asian Studies*, 52(2): 182–203.

Stirling, John (2011). Trade Union in a Fragile State: The Case of Sierra Leone. *Industrial Relations Journal*, 42(3): 236–253.

Wertz, Daniel (2020). *Understanding US and International Sanctions on North Korea*.Washington, D.C.: The National Committee on North Korea.

Zadeh-Cummings, Nazanin and Lauren Harris (2020). The Impact of Sanctions Against North Korea on Humanitarian Aid. *Journal of Humanitarian Affairs*, 2(1): 44–52.

Index

Note: Page numbers in *italics* indicate figures, **bold** indicate tables in the text

For Product Safety Concerns and Information please contact our EU representative GPSR@taylorandfrancis.com
Taylor & Francis Verlag GmbH, Kaufingerstraße 24, 80331 München, Germany

www.ingramcontent.com/pod-product-compliance
Ingram Content Group UK Ltd.
Pitfield, Milton Keynes, MK11 3LW, UK
UKHW030809150425
457412UK00007B/83

9781032486901